MW00769729

Discover China

走遍中國

STUDENT'S BOOK TWO 学生用书2

macmillan education

FOREIGN LANGUAGE TEACHING AND RESEARCH PRESS 外研社

Introduction

Discover China is a four-level Mandarin Chinese course, specially designed for beginner to intermediate level students studying Chinese in English-speaking countries. It employs a communicative and integrated approach to language learning. Emphasis is placed on communication in real contexts through pair work, group work and a variety of independent and integrated activities to help students become confident Chinese language speakers.

Key features

Discover China's unique communicative course design includes a number of distinctive features:

- **Topic-driven content in real-life contexts** gets students engaged and motivated. The topics in each book are organized around the lives and travel experiences of five young students in China.
- **A truly communicative approach** lets students learn the language by using it in real-life situations, providing them with the tools they need to communicate in Chinese naturally.
- **Structured and effective learning design** based on the sequence "presentation, practice and production", with activities moving from controlled practice to personalized tasks, facilitates effective learning of the language.
- **Systematic vocabulary and grammar development** comes through topic-based practice and extension exercises. The lexical syllabus is based on levels 1-4 of the *Hanyu Shuiping Kaoshi* (HSK test) and the grammatical syllabus takes students up to the Vantage level (level B2) of the Common European Framework.
- **Student-centred grammar learning supplemented with detailed grammar reference** allows students to discover the rules for themselves through identifying patterns in the language samples. The grammar reference provides comprehensive and detailed explanations.
- **Meaningful and integrated character writing practice** through grouping characters with common radicals. These high-frequency characters are presented within the context of the unit theme.
- **Insights into Chinese culture**, through "Cultural Corner" sections linked to the unit topics, promoting a deeper cultural understanding. Fascinating full-colour photos, showing the real China, provide visual appeal and draw students into this diverse culture.
- **Simplified Chinese characters** are used to facilitate learning of the written language used by the majority of Chinese speakers.
- **Pinyin matched to the word level** instead of individual characters helps students understand how to write and space pinyin meaningfully. *Discover China* follows the official pinyin orthography of the mainland of China. All pinyin shows the character's original tone, except in those parts of the pronunciation and speaking section where special rules about tonal change are introduced.
- **Extra pair work activities** for each unit provide additional communicative speaking practice.
- **Supported by free online resources** including teacher's books, assessment tasks, unit quizzes, extra character writing sheets and more.

Workbook

The Workbook provides extensive consolidation of the language skills and knowledge taught in the Student's Book.

Each Workbook unit features clear language objectives which correspond with the Student's Book unit structure and activities. A wide variety of vocabulary and grammar exercises, as well as extra reading and listening activities, provide practice of the core language presented in the Student's Book. Writing practice sections give students the option to extend their Chinese character writing skills beyond the Student's Book requisites. A self-assessment at the end of each unit using "I can..." descriptors enables students to reflect on their individual progress.

Characteristics of each level

Books 1 and 2 cover basic language relating to everyday topics. The focus is on listening and speaking, although there is a writing activity at end of each lesson 2. Character writing practice is available in both the Student's Book and Workbook to help students learn how to write Chinese characters with the correct stroke order.

Book 1 is for beginners who have not studied any Chinese. To avoid overwhelming students with character reading at the very beginning, pinyin is placed above all Chinese words and characters to provide the necessary language support. However, to help students develop character recognition skills, pinyin does not appear for conversations and passages in the Workbook. Activities in the online unit quizzes, which simulate test questions from the HSK test, have no pinyin.

Book 2 follows on naturally from Book 1. Pinyin is used only in activities with new words and phrases, and the activities in the pronunciation and speaking section of each unit. Most other activities in the book do not carry pinyin. However, versions of all the main conversations and reading passages with pinyin are available for download from *Discover China's* free resources website.

Books 3 and 4 cover language from school life and the work environment. The focus is on the development of language skills, which is conducted through various approaches including guided writing. The lessons contain activities to further enhance students' language skills in all areas across different contexts and functions. A new guided writing section teaches students how to compose natural texts following authentic-like texts. The conversations and reading passages are longer, and pinyin only appears in each unit's vocabulary boxes.

Storylines

- **Book 1** presents the fundamentals of the Chinese language, following the characters' day-to-day lives in Beijing. From simple introductions to going shopping, eating out or playing sports, students encounter a broad range of situations and learn the basic language skills they require.

- **Book 2** includes "survival Chinese" for travel and living in China, as the characters hit the road on their winter holidays. They see the Terracotta Warriors in Xi'an and try authentic Sichuan food in Chengdu, make new friends and broaden their knowledge of Chinese to handle typical subjects such as food and drink, hotels, sightseeing and going to the doctor.

- **Book 3** takes a deeper look at China's diverse culture. Steve lands his dream job and is sent on assignment as a photojournalist to exciting places all over China. Amanda pursues her love of Chinese history and takes the Chinese history class. This provides students with rich exposure to the use of Chinese language across various cultural and social contexts.

- **Book 4** prepares students to use Chinese for work-related purposes. Mark takes up an internship at a Chinese company in Shenzhen, and Yeong-min volunteers at a summer camp for international students studying in China. Both gain valuable experience working with different people and dealing with different situations. Encouraged by Wang Yu, Steve showcases his talent in a photo competition themed around Yunnan. Wang Yu herself goes to study in the US, and finds that living abroad gives her a new perspective on the experiences of her overseas friends in China.

Unit structure

Student Book 2 | Unit 3 Happy New Year! 新年好！

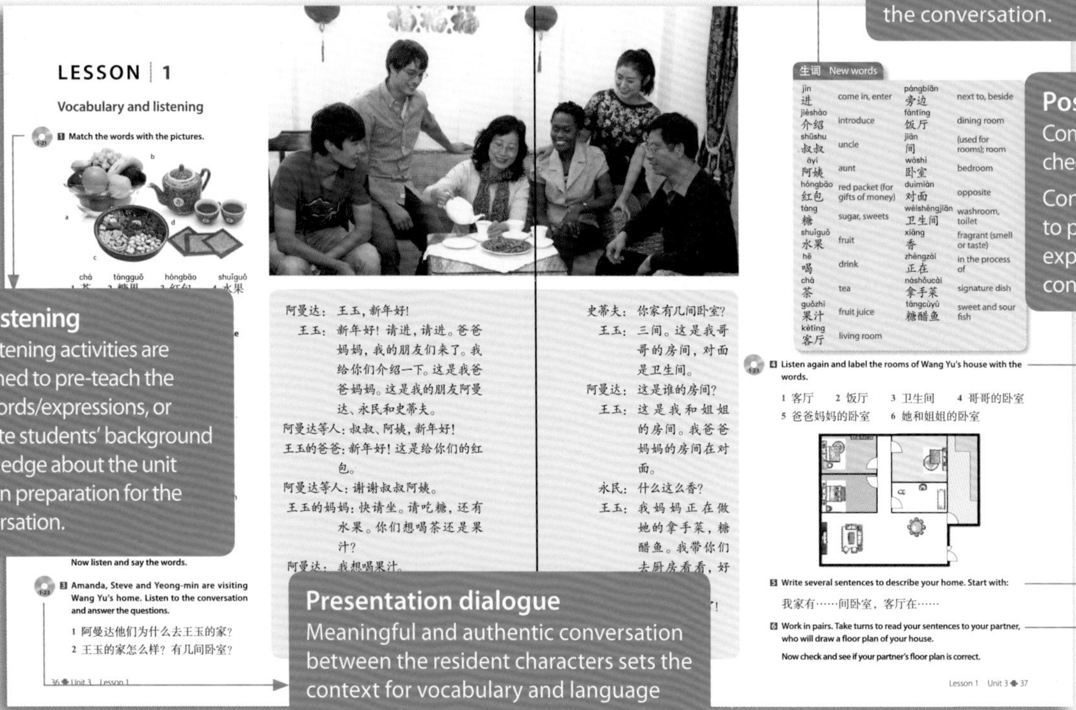

LESSON | 1

Vocabulary and listening

1 Match the words with the pictures.

Now listen and say the words.

3 Amanda, Steve and Yeong-min are visiting Wang Yu's home. Listen to the conversation and answer the questions.

1 阿曼达他们为什么去王玉的家？
2 王玉的家怎么样？有几间卧室？

阿曼达：王玉，新年好！
王玉：新年好！请进，请进。爸爸妈妈，我的朋友们来了。我给你们介绍一下。这是我爸爸妈妈。这是我的朋友阿曼达、永民和史蒂夫。
阿曼达等人：叔叔、阿姨，新年好！
王玉的爸爸：新年好！这是给你们的红包。
阿曼达等人：谢谢叔叔阿姨。
王玉的妈妈：快请坐。请吃糖，还有水果。你们想喝茶还是果汁？
阿曼达：我想喝果汁。

史蒂夫：你家有几间卧室？
王玉：三间。这是我哥哥的房间，对面是卫生间。
阿曼达：这是谁的房间？
王玉：这是我和姐姐的房间。我爸爸妈妈的房间在对面。
永民：什么这么香？
王玉：我妈妈正在做她的拿手菜，糖醋鱼。我带你们去厨房看看，好

生词 New words

jìn 进	come in, enter	pángbiān 旁边	next to, beside
jièshào 介绍	introduce	fàntīng 饭厅	dining room
shūshu 叔叔	uncle	jiān 间	(used for rooms); room
āyí 阿姨	aunt	wòshì 卧室	bedroom
hóngbāo 红包	red packet (for gifts of money)	duìmiàn 对面	opposite
táng 糖	sugar, sweets	wèishēngjiān 卫生间	washroom, toilet
shuǐguǒ 水果	fruit	xiāng 香	fragrant (smell or taste)
hē 喝	drink	zhèngzài 正在	in the process of
chá 茶	tea	náshǒucài 拿手菜	signature dish
guǒzhī 果汁	fruit juice	tángcùyú 糖醋鱼	sweet and sour fish
kètīng 客厅	living room		

4 Listen again and label the rooms of Wang Yu's house with the words.

1 客厅 2 饭厅 3 卫生间 4 哥哥的卧室
5 爸爸妈妈的卧室 6 她和姐姐的卧室

5 Write several sentences to describe your home. Start with:

我家有……间卧室，客厅在……

6 Work in pairs. Take turns to read your sentences to your partner, who will draw a floor plan of your house.

Now check and see if your partner's floor plan is correct.

36 Unit 3 Lesson 1

Lesson 1 Unit 3 37

New words list
Target words are set out in the order they appear in the conversation.

Post-listening
Comprehension questions are used to check understanding.
Controlled activities allow students to practise the target words/expressions, and role-play the conversation.

Pre-listening
Pre-listening activities are designed to pre-teach the key words/expressions, or activate students' background knowledge about the unit topic in preparation for the conversation.

Presentation dialogue
Meaningful and authentic conversation between the resident characters sets the context for vocabulary and language presentation.

Pronunciation
Difficult pronunciation points for English speakers are presented and practised in context to prepare students for communicative activities in the unit.

Chinese to go
Simple and useful colloquial expressions or language "chunks" of immediate use are provided to students.

Pre-reading
Pre-reading activities are designed to pre-teach the key words, or activate students' background knowledge about the unit topic in preparation for the reading passage.

Reading
Reading texts cover a wide range of text types relevant to students' everyday lives, such as diaries, articles, blogs and online posts.

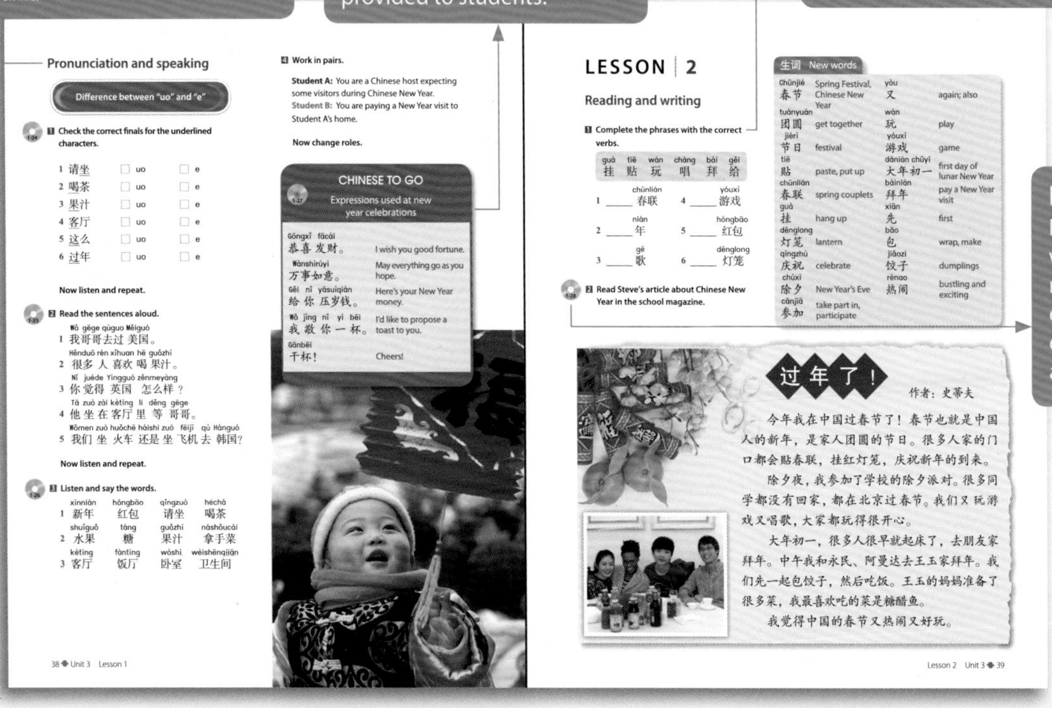

Pronunciation and speaking

Difference between "uo" and "e"

1 Check the correct finals for the underlined characters.

1 请坐 □ uo □ e
2 喝茶 □ uo □ e
3 果汁 □ uo □ e
4 客厅 □ uo □ e
5 这么 □ uo □ e
6 过年 □ uo □ e

Now listen and repeat.

2 Read the sentences aloud.

1 我哥哥去过美国。
2 很多人喜欢喝果汁。
3 你觉得英国怎么样？
4 他坐在客厅里等哥哥。
5 我们坐火车还是坐飞机去韩国？

Now listen and repeat.

3 Listen and say the words.

1 新年 红包 请坐 喝茶
2 水果 糖 果汁 拿手菜
3 客厅 饭厅 卧室 卫生间

4 Work in pairs.

Student A: You are a Chinese host expecting some visitors during Chinese New Year.
Student B: You are paying a New Year visit to Student A's home.

Now change roles.

CHINESE TO GO
Expressions used at new year celebrations

恭喜发财。	I wish you good fortune.
万事如意。	May everything go as you hope.
给你压岁钱。	Here's your New Year money.
我敬你一杯。	I'd like to propose a toast to you.
干杯！	Cheers!

LESSON | 2

Reading and writing

1 Complete the phrases with the correct verbs.

挂 贴 玩 唱 拜 给

1 ____ 春联 4 ____ 游戏
2 ____ 年 5 ____ 红包
3 ____ 歌 6 ____ 灯笼

2 Read Steve's article about Chinese New Year in the school magazine.

生词 New words

Chūnjié 春节	Spring Festival, Chinese New Year	yòu 又	again; also
tuányuán 团圆	get together	wán 玩	play
jiérì 节日	festival	yóuxì 游戏	game
tiē 贴	paste, put up	dànián chūyī 大年初一	first day of lunar New Year
chūnlián 春联	spring couplets	bàinián 拜年	pay a New Year visit
guà 挂	hang up	xiān 先	first
dēnglong 灯笼	lantern	bāo 包	wrap, make
qìngzhù 庆祝	celebrate	jiǎozi 饺子	dumplings
chúxī 除夕	New Year's Eve	rènao 热闹	bustling and exciting
cānjiā 参加	take part in, participate		

过年了！

作者：史蒂夫

今年我在中国过春节了！春节也就是中国人的新年，是家人团圆的节日。很多人家的门口都会贴春联，挂红灯笼，庆祝新年的到来。

除夕夜，我参加了学校的除夕派对。很多同学都没有回家，都在北京过春节。我们又玩游戏又唱歌，大家都玩得很开心。

大年初一，很多人很早就起床了，去朋友家拜年。中午我和永民、阿曼达去王玉家拜年。我们先一起包饺子，然后吃饭。王玉的妈妈准备了很多菜，我最喜欢吃的菜是糖醋鱼。

我觉得中国的春节又热闹又好玩。

38 Unit 3 Lesson 1

Lesson 2 Unit 3 39

Post-reading
Controlled, guided and freer activities allow students to practise the target language in a sequence that is most effective for learning.

Language in use
Grammar points are presented and practised through an inductive or "discovery" approach, drawing on students' existing knowledge.

Short, simple examples help students analyse and discover the grammar rules.

Grammar reference
Grammar reference at the back of the book provides detailed explanation of the grammar rules as a handy resource for both teachers and students.

Exercises allow students to practise and consolidate the rules.

Communication activity
Meaningful and realistic communication in relevant contexts is facilitated through role-plays and speaking tasks.

Character writing
Common radicals in characters from the unit are introduced and practised to build students' vocabulary.

Review and practice
Builds on language acquisition by recycling previously learnt target language, through which students can also assess their progress.

Additional speaking practice
Activities are function-oriented, requiring students to use relevant vocabulary and language points in realistic and contextualized ways.

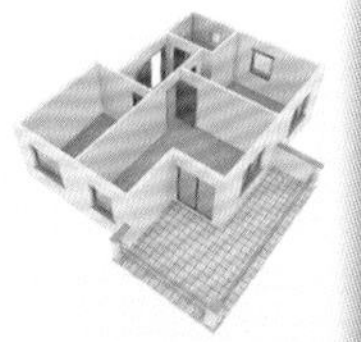

Vocabulary extension
More topic-related words are introduced for flexible learning.

Vocabulary review
Blanks created to distinguish between words to write and words to recognize help students further consolidate their vocabulary. All target words are presented in black and non-target words in colour for easy reference.

Cultural Corner
Cultural points linked to the unit topic enable a greater understanding and appreciation of Chinese life and culture.

Practice writing common characters following the correct stroke order prepares students for writing Chinese.

Contents

Grammar and Vocabulary	Pronunciation	Cultural Corner	Character Practice
• The auxiliary word 得 • Topic-comment sentences • 了 as a particle and an auxiliary word • Expressing succession using 一……就…… • Words for students' daily routines	Difference between "z" and "zh"	Planning ahead	Radicals 灬 and 心
• Expressing similarity using A和B + 差不多/一样 • Making comparisons using A比/没有B + adjective • Expressing future actions with 要/会 • Weather, seasons and clothes	Difference between "c" and "ch"	From freezing snow to tropical forest	Radicals 口 and 冫
• Expressing actions in progress using 正在 • Expressing "both... and..." with 又……又…… • Expressing sequences with 先……然后…… • Rooms in a house, Chinese New Year activities	Difference between "uo" and "e"	Being a guest in China	Radicals 艹 and 广
• Talking about distance using 离/多远 • Expressing distance using 从A到B • Using 以后 / ……的时候 • Words for transport, distance and directions	The initials: "zh" "ch" "sh"	The art of paper-cutting	Radicals 礻 and 纟
• Expressing possession, existence or location with 有 • Expressing adequacy with 够/不够 • Complements expressing result • Questions about size with (有) 多大/长/宽 • Words for hotel check-in, room facilities and everyday items	Tone sandhi: 3rd + 3rd tones	Family inns in the countryside	Radicals 方 and 八
• Expressing passive voice using 被 • Expressing a continuing action or state with 着 • 是……的 constructions • Rules and signs, history and cultural relics	Difference between "ü" and "üe"	Tang poetry	Radicals 彡 and 厂

Grammar and Vocabulary	Pronunciation	Cultural Corner	Character Practice
• Noun phrases with 的 • Giving instructions using imperatives • 把 sentences • Flavours, food and drink, ingredients and cooking instructions	Difference between "en" and "eng"	Eating out: ordering shared dishes	Radicals 米 and 犭
• Duplication of verbs • "The more … the more …" 越……越…… • Notional passive • Souvenirs, prices, package and travel experiences	The finals: "ian" and "üan"	Tea houses in Chengdu and *Longmen Zhen*	Radicals 走 and 刂
• Expressing result of an action with 到 • Expressing percentages using 百分之…… • 除了……以外，还…… • Words for natural scenery, landscape features and feelings	Difference between "j" and "z"	Famous mountains in China	Radicals 寸 and 阝 (left)
• Serial verb constructions • Affirmative-negative questions • Expressing immediate actions with (就) 要……了 • Appearance, features, sportswear and sizes	The neutral tone	Who is beautiful?	Radicals 目 and 子
• The auxiliary word 地 • 多 and 少 • Expressing the duration of action • Symptoms of illness, medical advice and instructions, health and activities	Tone sandhi: 不 and 一	Traditional Chinese medicine	Radicals 疒 and 火
• Wh-questions • Difference between 有一点 and 一点儿 • The auxiliary words 的/地/得 • Characteristics, personalities and hobbies	Difference between "s" and "sh"	The Confucian personality	Radicals 忄 and 马

Classroom expressions

1-2 Classroom expressions used by teachers

Qǐng gēn wǒ dú
请跟我读。 Please read after me.

Qǐng tīng lùyīn
请听录音。 Please listen to the recording.

Yuèdú duǎnwén
阅读短文。 Read the passage.

Qǐng huídá wèntí
请回答问题。 Please answer the questions.

Wánchéng jùzi
完成句子。 Complete the sentences.

Xuǎnzé zhèngquè dá' àn
选择正确答案。 Choose the correct answers.

Jīntiān wǒmen shàng dì-yī kè
今天我们上第一课。 Today we are going to study Lesson 1.

Qǐng dǎkāi shū fāndào dì-shí yè
请打开书翻到第十页。 Please open your books and turn to page 10.

Wǒmen xiān xuéxí yíxià shēngcí
我们先学习一下生词。 Let's study the new words first.

Nǎ wèi tóngxué zhīdào zhège cí de yìsi
哪位同学知道这个词的意思? Who knows the meaning of this word?

Nǐ kěyǐ dàshēng yìdiǎnr ma
你可以大声一点儿吗? Could you speak a bit louder?

Xiàmiàn wǒmen zuò duìhuà liànxí
下面我们做对话练习。 Next let's do speaking practice.

Liǎng rén yì zǔ zuò liànxí
两人一组做练习。 Work in pairs.

Bǎ jùzi fānyì chéng Zhōngwén Yīngwén
把句子翻译成中文/英文。 Translate the sentences into Chinese/English.

Zhǎochū yǔ túpiàn duìyìng de cíyǔ
找出与图片对应的词语。 Match the words with the pictures.

Gēnjù túpiàn zàojù
根据图片造句。 Write a sentence to describe the picture.

1-3

Classroom expressions used by students

Wǒ yǒu yí gè wèntí 我有一个问题。	I have a question.
Zhège zì dú dì jǐ shēng 这个字读第几声？	What tone is this character?
Zhège zì zěnme xiě 这个字怎么写？	How do you write this character?
Zhège cí shì shénme yìsi 这个词是什么意思？	What does this word mean?
Zhè jù huà yòng Yīngyǔ / Hànyǔ zěnme shuō 这句话用英语 / 汉语怎么说？	How do you say this sentence in English/Chinese?
Wǒ méiyǒu tīng qīngchu nín néng chóngfù yí biàn ma 我没有听清楚，您能重复一遍吗？	I didn't hear clearly. Could you repeat that?
Nín néng shuō màn yìdiǎnr ma 您能说慢一点儿吗？	Could you speak a bit more slowly?
Zhège cí kěyǐ zhèyàng yòng ma 这个词可以这样用吗？	Can I use the word this way?
Shénme shíhou jiāo zuòyè / kǎoshì 什么时候交作业 / 考试？	When are we going to hand in the homework/have the test?
Wǒ kěyǐ qù xǐshǒujiān ma 我可以去洗手间吗？	May I go to the toilet?

Places in *Discover China*

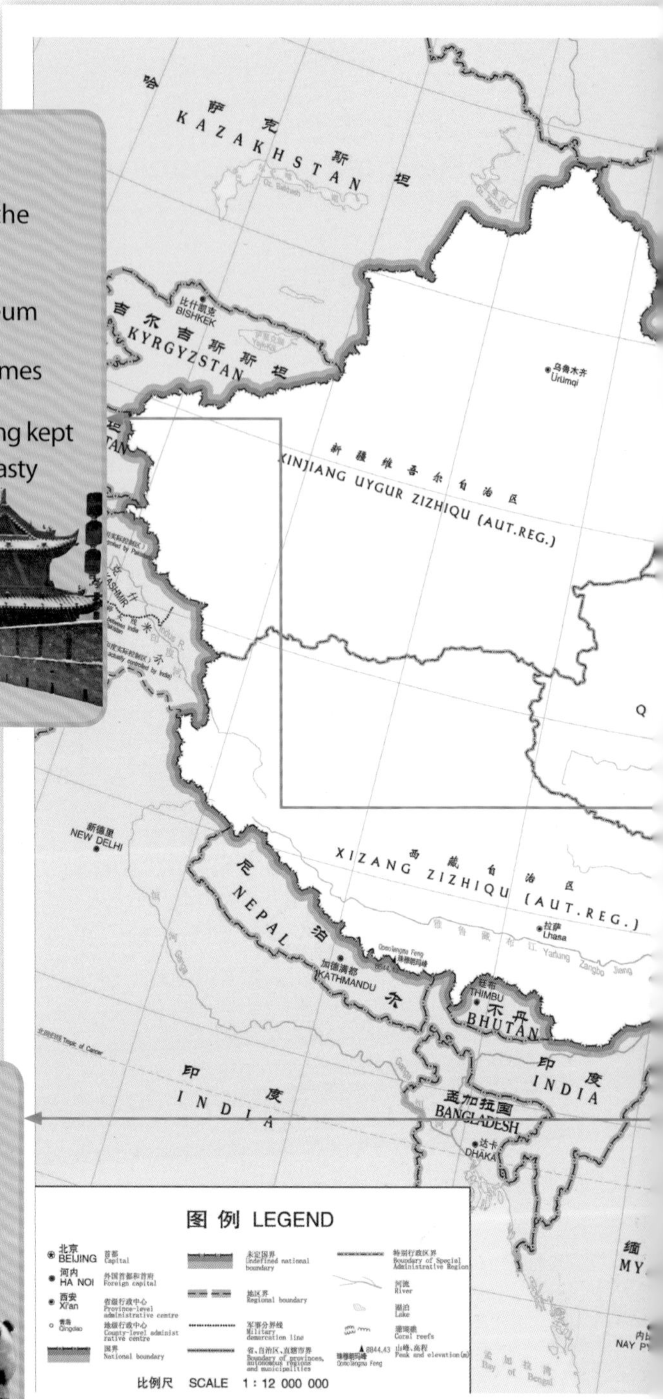

Xi'an

西安 (Xī' ān) capital city of Shaanxi Province, ancient capital of the Tang Dynasty, starting point of the Silk Road

陕西历史博物馆 (Shǎnxī Lìshǐ Bówùguǎn) the Shaanxi History Museum

钟楼 (Zhōnglóu) Bell Tower, used to announce the hours in ancient times

大雁塔 (Dàyàn Tǎ) Big Wild Goose Pagoda, where the monk Xuan Zang kept the Buddhist scrolls he brought back from India during the Tang Dynasty

古城墙 (Gǔchéngqiáng) Xi'an's ancient city walls, the best preserved fortification from the Ming Dynasty, built on the remains of the Tang capital, Chang'an

大清真寺 (Dàqīngzhēn Sì) the Great Mosque of Xi'an

Lintong

临潼 (Líntóng) a county 30 kilometres to the east of Xi'an, where the Terracotta Warriors were discovered

兵马俑 (Bīngmǎyǒng) the Terracotta Warriors, burial goods of the Emperor Qin Shihuang, the first emperor of China

Chengdu

成都 (Chéngdū) capital city of Sichuan Province

卧龙自然保护区 (Wòlóng Zìrán Bǎohùqū) Wolong Nature Reserve, also called "Panda Country"

九寨沟 (Jiǔzhàigōu) Jiuzhaigou Valley, a place of stunning natural beauty, which gets its name from the nine Tibetan villages in the mountains

Historical timeline

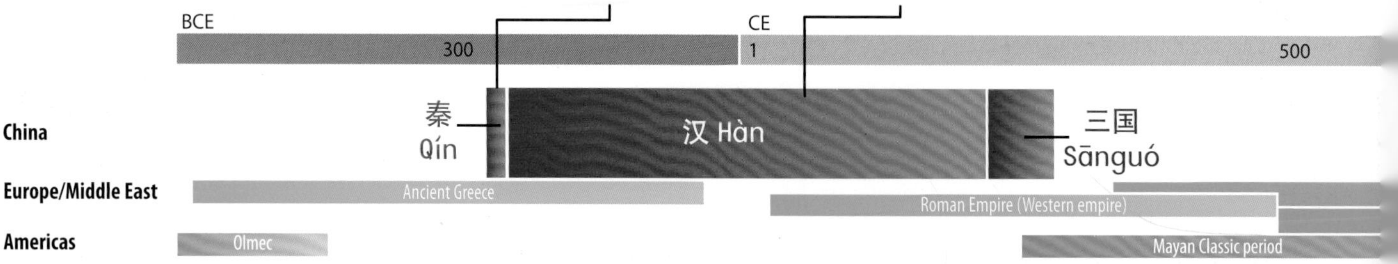

* This timeline does not include all dynasties and eras in China's history. The selected eras illustrate some notable contemporaneous periods in China and abroad.

Harbin

哈尔滨 (Hā' ěrbīn) capital city of Heilongjiang Province

冰雪节 (Bīngxuějié) the annual Snow & Ice Festival, featuring ice sculptures

Beijing

北京 (Běijīng) capital of China

故宫 (Gùgōng) the Forbidden City, royal residence of the Ming and Qing dynasties

长城 (Chángchéng) the Great Wall

Yunnan

云南 (Yúnnán) province in south-west China

泼水节 (Pōshuǐjié) Water-Splashing Festival, celebrated by the Dai people

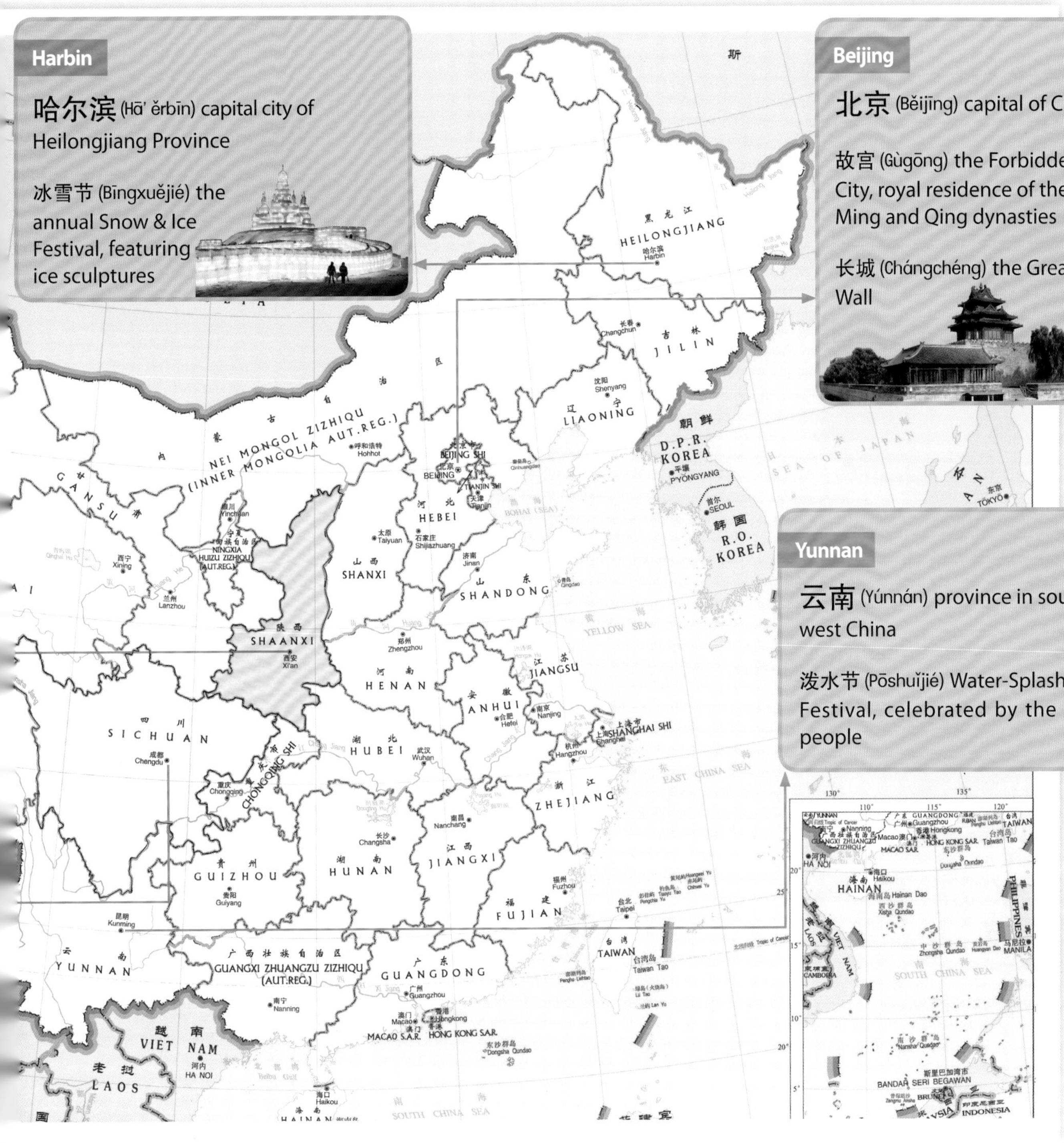

唐三彩
Tángsāncǎi

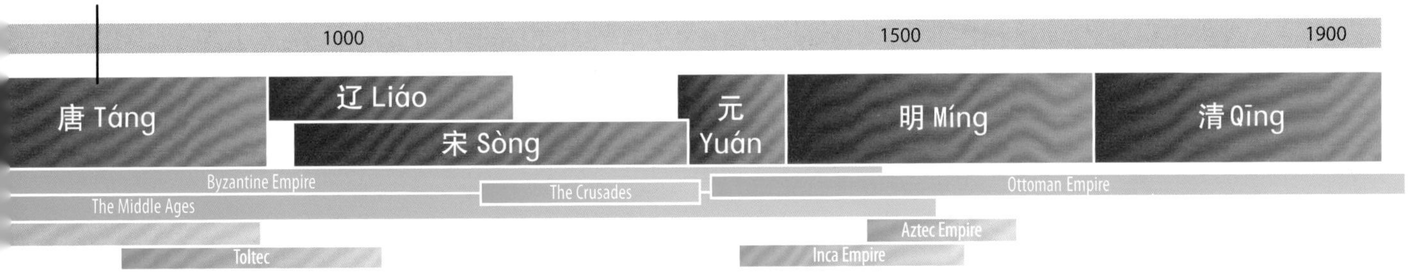

Meet the characters

Mǎkè
Mark Johnson (马克) comes from Brisbane. Mark went on holiday to China after completing high school, and decided to stay and learn Chinese at a university in Beijing. Mark enjoys the outdoors, and he likes surfing and sailing.

Āmàndá
Amanda da Silva (阿曼达) is Mark's classmate, from São Paulo. She loves travelling and has a keen interest in history. As well as Chinese language, Amanda is also taking classes in Chinese history at the university.

Shǐdìfū
Steve Brown (史蒂夫), another classmate of Mark and Amanda's, comes from London. He works part-time for a UK-based magazine and is a keen photographer. He enjoys exploring different cultures, and meeting different people.

Wáng Yù
Wang Yu (王 玉) was born in Beijing. She knows the others from university, where she studies music. She has played the piano since she was five. She likes cooking and sports including swimming and tennis.

Jīn Yǒngmín
Kim Yeong-min (金 永民) is also studying Chinese at the university. He comes from Seoul. Like Wang Yu, Yeong-min is a musician, and plays guitar in a local band. He plans to study Chinese medicine after he finishes his courses in Chinese. Yeong-min likes to spend his free time reading and listening to music.

UNIT 1

Jīntiān zhēn máng!
今天真忙!
What a busy day!

LESSON 1

Vocabulary and listening

1-4

1 Number the events of a student's day in the correct order.

a

shàngkè
☐ 上课

b

qǐchuáng
☐ 起床

c

shuìjiào
☐ 睡觉

d

zuò zuòyè
☐ 做 作业

e

zuò yùndòng
☐ 做 运动

f

chīfàn
☐ 吃饭

Now listen and say the phrases.

1-5

2 Steve invites Amanda and Yeong-min to have a meal together after class. Listen to the conversation and answer the questions.

1 阿曼达放学后要做什么？
2 中国的大学每天早上几点开始上课？
3 永民可以一起去吃饭吗？

史蒂夫：放学以后，我们一起去吃饭吧。东门附近有个上海饭馆很不错。

阿曼达：我去过那个饭馆，那里的菜很好吃！但是今天我不能去。

史蒂夫：为什么？

阿曼达：我要去打网球。

永民：真的吗？我不知道你会打网球。你跟谁打？

阿曼达：跟王玉。她打网球打得很好。你会打网球吗？

永民：不会。史蒂夫，你呢？

史蒂夫：我也不会。我觉得我应该多做运动。我住在伦敦的时候每天上课前都去跑步，但是在中国就不可能。

永民：为什么在中国不可能？

史蒂夫：因为中国大学的上课时间太早了，每天早上八点开始上课。我觉得这么早起床去教室很难。这么早去跑步当然不可能！

阿曼达：我觉得八点不那么早。我每天七点起床，吃早饭，然后去上课。

史蒂夫：永民，你和我去吃饭吗？

永民：对不起，我的中文作业还没做完，明天要交给老师。我还要复习，准备星期三的考试。

阿曼达：没关系，我们可以下次一起吃饭。

生词 New words

fàngxué 放学	school is over	chuáng 床	bed
néng 能	can	jiàoshì 教室	classroom
wèishénme 为什么	why	nán 难	difficult
de 得	(indicates result, degree or condition)	zuòyè 作业	homework
shàngkè 上课	have class	hái 还	still, yet; also
qián 前	before	wán 完	completed
jiù 就	exactly; as soon as	jiāo 交	hand in, submit
kěnéng 可能	possible	fùxí 复习	revise, review
yīnwèi 因为	because	zhǔnbèi 准备	prepare (for)
zǎo 早	early	kǎoshì 考试	exam, test
zhème 这么	so, such	méiguānxi 没关系	it doesn't matter
qǐchuáng 起床	get up	xiàcì 下次	next time

1-5

3 Listen again and check the correct answers.

1 史蒂夫想放学后去做什么？

☐ a 跑步 ☐ b 吃饭

2 阿曼达每天早上几点起床？

☐ a 七点 ☐ b 八点

3 永民打算做什么？

☐ a 做中文作业 ☐ b 复习准备考试

4 Work in pairs. Talk about your plans after class today and invite your partner to join you. Decline your partner's invitation and give reasons why you cannot join them.

Pronunciation and speaking

Difference between "z" and "zh"

1 Check the correct initials for the characters. (1-6)

1	做	☑ z	☐ zh
2	早	☑ z	☐ zh
3	中	☐ z	☑ zh
4	知	☐ z	☑ zh
5	住	☐ z	☑ zh
6	作	☑ z	☐ zh

Now listen and repeat.

2 Check the correct pinyin for the words. (1-7)

1	早起	☑ zǎoqǐ	☐ zhǎoqǐ
2	多做	☑ duōzuò	☐ duōzhuò
3	住在	☐ zùzhài	☑ zhùzài
4	作业	☑ zuòyè	☐ zhuòyè
5	知道	☐ zīdào	☑ zhīdào
6	中国	☐ Zōngguó	☑ Zhōngguó

Now listen and repeat.

3 Listen and say the words. (1-8)

1	shàngkè 上课	fàngxué 放学	chī zǎofàn 吃 早饭
	qǐchuáng 起床	pǎobù 跑步	zuò yùndòng 做 运动
	kǎoshì 考试	fùxí 复习	jiāo zuòyè 交 作业

4 Work in pairs. Ask each other what you usually do at the following times.

6:00 – 8:00 a.m.	8:00 – 12:00 a.m.
12:00 – 3:00 p.m.	3:00 – 7:00 p.m.
7:00 – 12:00 p.m.	0:00 – 6:00 a.m.

Now work with another pair. Tell them about your partner's daily routine.

CHINESE TO GO

(1-9)

Being late

Jǐ diǎn le 几点了?	What time is it?! (Don't you know the time?!)
Nǐ zěnme cái lái 你怎么才来?	Why are you so late?
Lùshang dǔchē 路上堵车。	There was a traffic jam on the way.
Wǒ qǐchuáng wǎn le 我起床晚了。	I got up late.
Wǒ de biǎo màn le 我的表慢了。	My watch is slow.

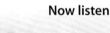

LESSON 2

Reading and writing

1 Work in pairs. Check the activities that you do every day.

- ☐ a 吃早饭 (chī zǎofàn)
- ☐ b 看报纸 (kàn bàozhǐ)
- ☐ c 上课 (shàngkè)
- ☐ d 写日记 (xiě rìjì)
- ☐ e 拍照 (pāizhào)
- ☐ f 读故事 (dú gùshi)

1-10

2 Read Mark's diary and answer the questions.

1 马克喜欢上中文课吗？为什么？

2 马克和朋友一起吃饭觉得怎么样？

3 为什么马克觉得很累？

生词 New words

máng	忙	busy
chídào	迟到	be late
cái	才	not until
yǐjīng	已经	already
bù hǎoyìsi	不好意思	embarrassed
ràng	让	let, allow
dú	读	read
gùshi	故事	story
tóngxué	同学	classmate
yòng	用	use
bàozhǐ	报纸	newspaper
yǒuqù	有趣	interesting
túshūguǎn	图书馆	library
jiè	借	borrow; lend
běn	本	(used for books)
tiānqì	天气	weather
kāixīn	开心	happy
yìbiān	一边	while, at the same time
shuōhuà	说话	speak
lèi	累	tired
rìjì	日记	diary
shàngchuáng	上床	get in bed, go to bed
shuìjiào	睡觉	sleep

一月十二日　星期三

今天真忙！我七点半起床，没吃早饭就出去了。路上人很多，我迟到了，八点五分才到教室。老师已经在上课了，我觉得很不好意思。上课的时候，老师让我们读一些中文故事。有些同学觉得读故事没有用，他们喜欢看中文报纸。但是我觉得这些故事很有趣。有时间我要去图书馆借几本中文故事书。

放学以后，我去了公园跟我的朋友李明见面。今天天气很好，我们在公园拍了一些很漂亮的照片。我觉得很开心。

晚上八点我跟王玉和永民一起吃晚饭。我们一边吃饭一边说话，大家都很高兴。晚上十一点我才回到宿舍。我觉得很累，一写完日记就上床睡觉。

3 Read the diary again and check the true statements.

- ☐ 1 马克到教室的时候，老师还没有来。
- ☐ 2 一些同学觉得读故事没有用。
- ☐ 3 马克在公园拍的照片很漂亮。
- ☐ 4 晚上八点马克和朋友们一起吃了饭。
- ☐ 5 马克一回宿舍就上床睡觉了。

4 Make a list of the things you did yesterday.

时间	上午	下午	晚上
做什么			
和谁一起			
觉得怎么样			

Now use the list to write a diary entry. Use Mark's diary to help you.

Language in use

The auxiliary word 得

1 Look at the sentences.

Subject	Verb phrase	Verb	得	Complement
她	打网球	打	得	很好。
马克		来	得	很早。
他	（吃饭）	吃	得	很多。
小王		跑	得	不快。
你		做	得	不好。

Now check the two correct explanations.

- ☐ 1 得 is used between a verb and its complement to indicate the result, degree or condition of an action.
- ☐ 2 There can be two verbs in the sentence, with the second verb being the same as the verb in the first verb phrase.
- ☐ 3 得 can be put between the subject and the verb to indicate result, degree or condition.

2 Write three sentences about yourself, using 得 to indicate result or degree.

Topic-comment sentences

1 Look at the sentences.

Topic	Comment
这么早起床去教室	很难。
这么早去跑步	当然不可能。
我的中文作业	明天要交给老师。
电影院离这里	远不远？

Now check the two correct explanations.

- ☐ 1 Topic-comment sentences are used to provide comments or more information about certain things.
- ☐ 2 The topic must always be put at the beginning, and consist of a verb phrase or a noun phrase.
- ☐ 3 A verb is always necessary in the comment in a topic-comment sentence.

2 Write the sentences in Chinese.

1 It takes ten minutes to get there by taxi.
2 The supermarket is very close to the school.
3 It's not possible to go to bed and sleep before 10 p.m.

了 as a particle and an auxiliary word

1 Look at the sentences.

Subject	Predicate
王玉	买了那条裙子。
他	吃了午饭。
我	迟到了。
老师	已经在上课了。

Now check the two correct explanations.

- ☐ 1 了 can be used after a verb as an auxiliary word to indicate that an action has taken place.
- ☐ 2 了 can also be used at the end of a statement as a particle to indicate a change of situation or state.
- ☐ 3 The meaning of the sentence will not be affected no matter where 了 is placed.

2 Put 了 in the correct places in the sentences.

1 上个星期我爸爸去北京。
2 他在伦敦住三年。
3 下个月我就十八岁。

Expressing succession using 一……就……

1 Look at the sentences.

Subject 1	一	Verb phrase 1	Subject 2	就	Verb phrase 2
我	一	写完日记		就	上床睡觉。
我	一	吃完饭		就	出来了。
他	一	回来，	我	就	出去。
老师	一	来，	我们	就	开始上课。

Now check the two correct explanations.

- ☐ 1 一……就…… is used to connect two events or actions that happen one after the other.
- ☐ 2 一……就…… is used to connect two events or actions that happen at the same time.
- ☐ 3 The subjects of the verb phrases connected by 一……就…… can be different.

2 Join the two sentences together, using 一……就…….

1 他回家。他做作业。
2 永民到电影院。电影开始了。
3 她开始工作。她买了一个新手机。

Turn to page 160 for grammar reference.

LESSON | 3

Communication activity

1 **Work in groups of three. Interview each other about your lifestyles, using the questionnaire below.**

生活方式问卷

1 你每天早上几点起床?

☐ 6–7点 ☐ 7–9点 ☐ 9–11点

2 你每星期做几个小时作业?

☐ 1小时以下 ☐ 1–3小时 ☐ 3小时以上

3 你每星期做几个小时运动?

☐ 2小时以下 ☐ 2–5小时 ☐ 5小时以上

4 你喜欢什么运动? ____________

5 你在哪里复习准备考试?

☐ 图书馆 ☐ 宿舍/家里 ☐ 公园

6 你晚上通常做什么? ____________

7 你周末喜欢做什么? ____________

2 **Report to the class, describing people who have similar lifestyles to yours and people who have different lifestyles.**

Turn to pages 148 and 154 for more speaking practice.

Cultural corner

Planning ahead

Chinese culture has traditionally valued being well-prepared for the future. Chinese people like to make long-term plans for their lives and to be financially secure. Wary of spending too much, they like to save money for housing, children's education, and medical emergencies. Many parents also help their children, especially sons, with mortgages and wedding expenses. They often begin to put aside money when the child is just a baby.

Unlike western people, who usually book flights and hotels several months ahead, Chinese people often only book a month or so ahead at best. Most hotels accept on-the-spot bookings. Trains are still the most popular means of transport in China, and people often book train tickets just a few days before their trip.

Character writing

These are two common radicals in Chinese. Do you know any other characters with the same radicals?

Radicals	Meaning	Examples
灬	fire	点、照
心	heart	您、想

1 Look at the characters and identify the radicals.

然　熊　怎　意

2 Match the words with the meanings.

1 不好意思　　a photo
2 开心　　b 7 o'clock
3 七点　　c happy
4 照片　　d embarrassed

3 Trace the characters in the boxes.

心

意

点

照

Review and practice

1 Match the words with the meanings.

1 起床　　a do homework
2 吃饭　　b write a diary
3 上课　　c sleep
4 做作业　　d have a meal
5 写日记　　e get up
6 睡觉　　f have class

2 Write four sentences about what you did yesterday, using the words from Activity 1.

3 Answer the questions using your own information.

1 明年你多大？
2 你的中文作业什么时候要交给老师？
3 你打网球打得怎么样？
4 你打算去中国旅行吗？为什么？

4 Write two sentences to describe each picture, using the words below.

一边……一边……　　才
一……就……　　已经

a

b

Vocabulary extension

Match the words with the pictures.

1 伤心 shāngxīn	2 生气 shēngqì	3 快乐 kuàilè
4 吵架 chǎojià	5 笑 xiào	6 哭 kū

a

b

c

Now work in pairs. Ask and answer questions about what happened to you yesterday and your feelings.

Vocabulary review

Fill in the blanks.

报纸	bàozhǐ	*n.*	newspaper
本	běn	*measure word*	(used for books)
不好意思	bù hǎoyìsi		embarrassed
才	cái	*adv.*	not until
迟到	chídào	*v.*	be late
床	chuáng	*n./measure word*	bed
得	de	*auxiliary word*	(to indicate result, degree or condition)
读	dú	*v.*	read
放学	fàngxué	*v.*	school is over
复习	fùxí	*v.*	revise, review
故事	gùshi	*n.*	story
还	hái	*adv.*	still, yet; also
交	jiāo	*v.*	hand in; submit
教室	jiàoshì	*n.*	classroom
借	jiè	*v.*	borrow; lend
就	jiù	*adv./ conj.*	exactly; as soon as
开心	kāixīn	*adj.*	happy
考试	kǎoshì	*n.*	exam, test
______	kěnéng	*adj.*	possible
累	lèi	*adj.*	tired
忙	máng	*adj.*	busy
没关系	méiguānxi		it doesn't matter
难	nán	*adj.*	difficult
能	néng	*modal v.*	can
起床	qǐchuáng	*v.*	get up
前	qián	*n.*	before
让	ràng	*v.*	let, allow

日记	rìjì	*n.*	diary
上床	shàngchuáng	*v.*	go to bed
上课	shàngkè	*v.*	have class
睡觉	shuìjiào	*v.*	sleep
说话	shuōhuà	*v.*	speak
天气	tiānqì	*n.*	weather
同学	tóngxué	*n.*	classmate
图书馆	túshūguǎn	*n.*	library
完	wán	*v.*	complete
为什么	wèishénme	*adv.*	why
下次	xiàcì	*n.*	next time
一边	yìbiān	*adv.*	while; same time
已经	yǐjīng	*adv.*	already
因为	yīnwèi	*conj.*	because
用	yòng	*n./v.*	use
有趣	yǒuqù	*adj.*	interesting
早	zǎo	*adj.*	early
这么	zhème	*pron.*	so, such
准备	zhǔnbèi	*v.*	prepare (for)
作业	zuòyè	*n.*	homework
吵架	chǎojià	*v.*	argue
哭	kū	*v.*	cry
快乐	kuàilè	*adj.*	happy
伤心	shāngxīn	*adj.*	sad
生气	shēngqì	*adj.*	angry
笑	xiào	*v.*	laugh, smile

* The words in colour are not target words for the unit.

UNIT

2

Wǒ xǐhuan xià xuě tiān!

我喜欢下雪天!

I love the snow!

LESSON | 1

Vocabulary and listening

1-11

1 Work in pairs. Talk about what you can see in the picture. Use the words below to help you.

	chūntiān	xiàtiān	qiūtiān	dōngtiān
1	春天	夏天	秋天	冬天
	màozi	wéijīn	shǒutào	duǎnkù
2	帽子	围巾	手套	短裤

Now listen and say the words.

1-12

2 Work in pairs. Talk about which of the words below can be used to describe the weather in the picture from Activity 1.

lěng	nuǎnhuo	xiàxuě
☑ 冷	☐ 暖和	☑ 下雪
rè	liángshuǎng	xiàyǔ
☐ 热	☐ 凉爽	☐ 下雨

Now listen and say the words.

1-13

3 Mark, Amanda and Yeong-min talk about what to wear while travelling. Listen to the conversation and answer the questions.

1 他们要去什么地方玩？西安

2 那里的天气怎么样？很冷，风很大，还会下雪。

阿曼达：马克，你为什么穿这么多衣服？今天的天气很好，气温二十度。

马克：这里的天气比布里斯班的冷，我当然要多穿一些。

永民：那去西安旅行，你会穿什么衣服呢？听说西安冬天很冷，风很大，还会下雪。

阿曼达：我喜欢下雪天！

马克：下雪？！我会多穿几件毛衣，戴围巾和手套，再带件大衣。

永民：穿这么多衣服，你还能走路吗？西安冬天的气温和首尔的差不多，我不打算带太多衣服。

阿曼达：成都的天气怎么样？和西安一样冷吗？

永民：成都没有西安那么冷。成都在南方，那里比北方暖和。

阿曼达：那么我可以穿我最喜欢的T恤和短裤，戴太阳镜了！

马克：我可以穿冲浪短裤！

永民：不行，不行！虽然成都没有西安那么冷，但是冬天的气温也在十度以下，你不能穿T恤和短裤。当然，如果你想看起来很酷，你可以戴墨镜。

生词 New words

chuān 穿	wear (clothes)	shǒutào 手套	gloves
qìwēn 气温	air temperature	zài 再	then; again
dù 度	degree	dài 带	bring, take
bǐ 比	compare, contrast	chàbuduō 差不多	almost
lěng 冷	cold	yíyàng 一样	same
tīngshuō 听说	it is said that, I hear that	nuǎnhuo 暖和	warm
dōngtiān 冬天	winter	tàiyáng 太阳	sun
fēng 风	wind	duǎnkù 短裤	shorts
dà 大	big, large	xíng 行	OK, right
xiàxuě 下雪	snow	suīrán 虽然	although
máoyī 毛衣	sweater, jumper	rúguǒ 如果	if
dài 戴	wear (clothing accessories like hat, scarf, etc.)	mòjìng 墨镜	sunglasses
wéijīn 围巾	scarf		

1-13

4 **Listen again and check the clothes they can wear on their trip.**

☐ a 毛衣　　☐ d 围巾

☐ b 手套　　☐ e 大衣

☐ c T恤　　☐ f 短裤

5 **Work in groups of three. Look at the photo and talk about the weather and clothes you could wear.**

Pronunciation and speaking

Difference between "c" and "ch"

1-14

1 Check the correct initials for the underlined characters.

1 成都 ☐ c ☑ ch

2 冲浪 ☐ c ☑ ch

3 下次 ☑ c ☐ ch

4 吃饭 ☐ c ☑ ch

Now listen and repeat.

1-15

2 Say the sentences aloud.

1 Wǒmen kěyǐ xiàcì yìqǐ chī Hánguó cài
我们 可以 下次 一起 吃 韩国 菜。

2 Chéngdū de Chuāncài hěn hǎochī
成都 的 川菜 很 好吃。

3 Wǒ shíyī diǎn cái shàngchuáng shuìjiào
我 十一 点 才 上床 睡觉。

4 Dōngtiān qù Sìchuān bù néng chuān duǎnkù
冬天 去 四川 不 能 穿 短裤。

5 Wǒmen kěyǐ zuò chuán cānguān jǐngdiǎn
我们 可以 坐 船 参观 景点。

Now listen and repeat.

1-16

3 Listen and say the words.

1	tiānqì 天气	lěng 冷	nuǎnhuo 暖和	dōngtiān 冬天
2	duǎnkù 短裤	máoyī 毛衣	wéijīn 围巾	shǒutào 手套
3	qìwēn 气温	chuān 穿	dài 戴	mòjìng 墨镜

4 Write down information about your most recent leisure travel, including time, place, season, weather and the clothes you wore.

Now work in pairs. Ask and answer questions about each other's travel experiences.

CHINESE TO GO

1-17

Talking about the weather

Dòng sǐ le 冻死了！	It's freezing!
Yǔ zhēn dà 雨真大！	It's pouring with rain!
Bié wàngle dài sǎn 别忘了带伞。	Don't forget to bring an umbrella.
Guāfēng le 刮风了。	It's windy.
Shénme guǐ tiānqì 什么鬼天气！	What nasty weather!

LESSON | 2

Reading and writing

1 Match the weather words with their symbols.

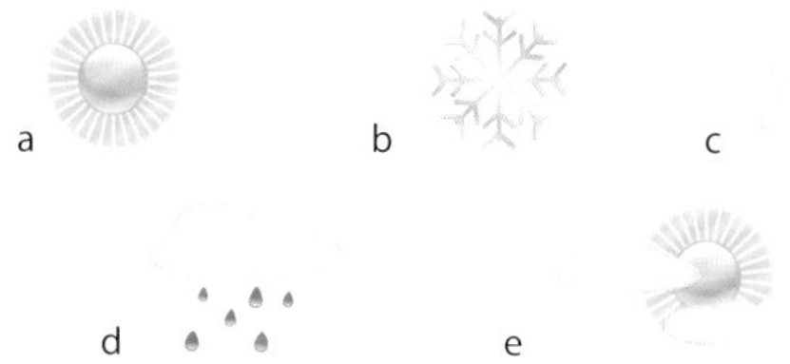

qíng	yīn	duōyún	yǔ	xuě
1 晴 a	2 阴	3 多云 c	4 雨 d	5 雪 b

2 Read the online weather report for Xi'an and Chengdu, and check the true statements.

☐ 1 冷空气下个星期只会影响北方地区。

☑ 2 白天和夜间的气温都会下降10℃。

☐ 3 西北和西南一些地方降温更多。

生词 New words

yùbào 预报	forecast	chābié 差别	difference
qǐ 起	since, starting from	dádào 达到	reach, get up to
kōngqì 空气	air	yǐshàng 以上	above
jiāng 将	(for future tense, written)	shàng 上	above, on top of
yǐngxiǎng 影响	influence; affect	duōyún 多云	cloudy
bùfen 部分	part	zhuǎn 转	change
dìqū 地区	area	qíng 晴	sunny
shòu 受	suffer, receive, be subjected to	yīn 阴	overcast
xiàjiàng 下降	decrease	língxià 零下	below zero
báitiān 白天	daytime	xiǎo 小	small
yèjiān 夜间	nighttime	yǔ 雨	rain

天气预报

从下个星期起，冷空气将影响我国大部分地区。受冷空气的影响，北方的气温将下降4-8℃，很多地方白天和夜间的气温差别将达到10℃，西北和西南一些地方的温差将在15℃以上。

西安

日期	二月七日 星期一	二月八日 星期二	二月九日 星期三
天气	多云转晴	多云转阴	大雪
气温	−4℃ / 1℃	−5℃ / 2℃	−6℃ / 1℃

成都

日期	二月七日 星期一	二月八日 星期二	二月九日 星期三
天气	晴	多云转阴	小雨
气温	1℃ / 7℃	0℃ / 6℃	−2℃ / 6℃

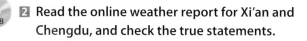

3 Read again and check the correct words to complete the sentences.

1 西安二月八日的气温是 ______。

☐ a 0℃/6℃ ☑ b -5℃/2℃

2 成都星期一的气温是 ______。

☐ a -4℃/1℃ ☑ b 1℃/7℃

3 下个星期三西安会 ______。

☑ a 下大雪 ☐ b 下小雨

4 二月七日成都的天气是 ______。

☑ a 晴 ☐ b 多云转晴

1-19

4 Listen and match the letters of the cities to the correct places on the map.

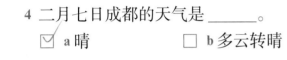

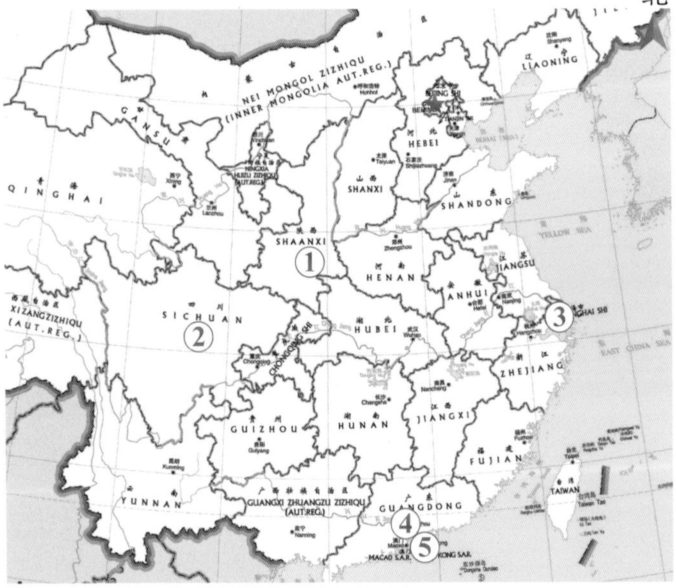

a 北京 Běijīng ☆ c 西安 Xī' ān 1 e 广州 Guǎngzhōu 4

b 上海 Shànghǎi 3 d 成都 Chéngdū 2 f 香港 Xiānggǎng 5

1-20

Now listen and put the weather symbols from Activity 1 in the correct places on the map.

5 Think of a destination you would like to travel to. Describe what the weather would be like and the clothes and other items you would need to bring.

Language in use

Expressing similarity using A 和 B + 差不多/一样

1 Look at the sentences.

A	和	B	Adjective	Complement
西安冬天的气温	和	首尔的（气温）	差不多。	
他的工作	和	我的（工作）	差不多。	
我的看法	和	你的（看法）	一样。	
王玉	和	阿曼达	一样	高。

Now check the two correct explanations.

☑ 1 和 is used to connect A and B to express similarity.

☐ 2 差不多 means "the same", while 一样 means "almost the same".

☑ 3 A complement can be used after 一样 while 差不多 often stands alone.

2 Write the sentences in Chinese.

1 The weather next week will be similar to the weather this week.

2 The length of the journey by bus is similar to the length of the journey by train.

3 Is the winter in London as cold as the winter in Beijing?

4 Are you as tall as her?

Making comparisons using A 比/没有 B + adjective

1 Look at the sentences.

A	比/没有	B	Adjective
这里的天气	比	布里斯班的（天气）	冷。
布里斯班的天气	没有	这里的（天气）	冷。
南方	比	北方	暖和。
北方	没有	南方	暖和。
你	比	她	高。
她	没有	你	高。

Now check the two correct explanations.

- ☑ 1 比 is used to show that A is higher in degree than B in terms of the adjective used.
- ☐ 2 没有 is used to show that A is higher in degree than B.
- ☑ 3 When the same head noun exists in both A and B, the second head noun can be omitted.

2 Rewrite the sentences using 没有.

1 西安的冬天比成都冷。
2 北方的温差比南方大。
3 今天比昨天暖和。
4 这件大衣比那件大衣漂亮。

Expressing future actions with 要/会

1 Look at the sentences.

Adverbial of time	Subject	Modal verb	Verb	Complement
晚上	我	要	复习	星期三的考试。
明天	我	要	交	作业。
	你	会	穿	什么衣服呢？
周末	我	不会	去	公园。

Now check the two correct explanations.

- ☑ 1 要 is used to express future action indicating the need or intention of the subject or doer.
- ☑ 2 会 is used to express future action showing a high probability.
- ☐ 3 要 and 会 can be used after the verb when expressing future actions.

2 Complete the sentences using 要 or 会.

1 今年冬天你 ______ 去韩国旅行吗？
2 这个周末我 ______ 去看爷爷奶奶。
3 今天晚上王玉 ______ 上课，所以她不 ______ 和我们一起去看电影。

Turn to page 161 for grammar reference.

LESSON | 3

Communication activity

1 **Write two true statements about yourself and the weather, and one false statement. For example,**

我每年冬天都去韩国玩。
我喜欢滑雪。
我去韩国的时候穿T恤和短裤。

Now work in pairs. Listen to your partner's statements, and guess which statement is false.

2 **Explain the reasons for your guess. Use the following expressions where appropriate.**

我觉得……，因为……，……的时候，可能/不可能

Turn to pages 148 and 154 for more speaking practice.

Cultural corner

From freezing snow to tropical forest

As one of the largest countries in the world, China covers a vast territory, and different parts of the country have very different weather conditions, from the frozen winters of the north-east, to the tropical climate of Hainan in the south, and the arid deserts to the west.

Such differences in the weather naturally affect the lifestyles of people in the different regions, affecting the food that grows locally and so appears in local cuisine, and shaping regional customs. Even a stranger can be sure of a warm welcome and a hot drink in Harbin, where exposure to the cold can have serious consequences. In tropical parts of Yunnan, the annual water-splashing festival lets you celebrate the new year and keep cool at the same time.

Character writing

These are two common radicals in Chinese. Do you know any other characters with the same radicals?

Radicals	Meaning	Examples
囗	enclosure	国、园
冫	ice	冲、冰

1 Look at the characters and identify the radicals.

围　冷　回　次

2 Match the words with the meanings.

1 围巾 c　　a next time
2 回家 d　　b very cold
3 很冷 b　　c scarf
4 下次 a　　d go home

3 Trace the characters in the boxes.

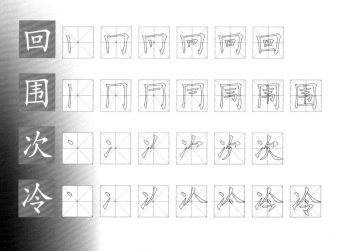

回
围
次
冷

Review and practice

1 Match the words with the meanings.

1 天气 c　　a air temperature
2 暖和 e　　b air
3 温差 d　　c weather
4 气温 a　　d temperature difference
5 空气 b　　e warm

2 Write three sentences about the weather in your area. Compare it with another place you know, using "A 比/没有 B + adjective".

3 Write three sentences about a friend, explaining your similarities, using "A 和 B + 差不多/一样".

4 Write two sentences to describe each picture.

a

b

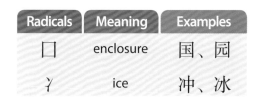

Vocabulary extension

Match the words with the pictures.

1 雨伞 yǔsǎn	2 雨鞋 yǔxié	3 羽绒服 yǔróngfú
4 风衣 fēngyī	5 夹克 jiákè	6 牛仔裤 niúzǎikù

Now work in pairs. Discuss in what season or weather you would wear or use these things.

a

b

Vocabulary review

Fill in the blanks.

白天	báitiān	n.	daytime
比	bǐ	v.	compare, contrast
部分	bùfen	n.	part
差别	chābié	n.	difference
差不多	chàbuduō	adj.	almost
穿	chuān	v.	wear (clothes)
达到	dádào	v.	reach; get up to
大	dà	adj.	big, large
带	dài	v.	bring, take
戴	dài	v.	wear (clothing accessories like hat, scarf, etc.)
地区	dìqū	n.	area
冬天	dōngtiān	n.	winter
度	dù	n.	degree
短裤	duǎnkù	n.	shorts
多云	duōyún	n.	cloudy
风	fēng	n.	wind
将	jiāng	adv.	(for future tense, written)
空气	kōngqì	n.	air
冷	lěng	adj.	cold
零下	língxià	n.	below zero
毛衣	máoyī	n.	sweater, jumper
墨镜	mòjìng	n.	sunglasses
暖和	nuǎnhuo	adj.	warm
起	qǐ	v.	since, starting from
气温	qìwēn	n.	temperature
晴	qíng	adj.	sunny
如果	rúguǒ	conj.	if
上	shàng	n./v.	above, on top of; begin to do
手套	shǒutào	n.	gloves

受	shòu	v.	suffer, receive, be subjected to
虽然	suīrán	conj.	although
太阳	tàiyáng	n.	sun
听说	tīngshuō	v.	it's said, I heard that
围巾	wéijīn	n.	scarf
下降	xiàjiàng	v.	decrease
小	xiǎo	adj.	small
下雪	xiàxuě	v.	snow
行	xíng	v.	OK, right
夜间	yèjiān	n.	night
一样	yíyàng	adj.	same
以上	yǐshàng	n.	above
阴	yīn	adj.	overcast
影响	yǐngxiǎng	v./n.	influence; affect
雨	yǔ	n.	rain
预报	yùbào	n./v.	forecast
再	zài	adv.	then; again
转	zhuǎn	v.	change
春天	chūntiān	n.	spring
风衣	fēngyī	n.	windcheater
夹克	jiákè	n.	jacket
凉爽	liángshuǎng	adj.	cool
帽子	màozi	n.	hat
牛仔裤	niúzǎikù	n.	jeans
秋天	qiūtiān	n.	autumn
热	rè	adj.	hot
夏天	xiàtiān	n.	summer
羽绒服	yǔróngfú	n.	down jacket
雨伞	yǔsǎn	n.	umbrella
雨鞋	yǔxié	n.	rain boots

UNIT 3

xīnnián hǎo
新年 好！

Happy New Year!

LESSON 1

Vocabulary and listening

1-21 **1 Match the words with the pictures.**

chá 1 茶	tángguǒ 2 糖果	hóngbāo 3 红包	shuǐguǒ 4 水果

Now listen and say the words.

1-22 **2 Work in pairs. Label the rooms of the house with the words.**

kètīng 1 客厅	chúfáng 2 厨房	wèishēngjiān 3 卫生间
fàntīng 4 饭厅	wòshì 5 卧室	

Now listen and say the words.

1-23 **3 Amanda, Steve and Yeong-min are visiting Wang Yu's home. Listen to the conversation and answer the questions.**

1 阿曼达他们为什么去王玉的家？
2 王玉的家怎么样？有几间卧室？

阿曼达：王玉，新年好！

王玉：新年好！请进，请进。爸爸妈妈，我的朋友们来了。我给你们介绍一下。这是我爸爸妈妈。这是我的朋友阿曼达、永民和史蒂夫。

阿曼达等人：叔叔、阿姨，新年好！

王玉的爸爸：新年好！这是给你们的红包。

阿曼达等人：谢谢叔叔阿姨。

王玉的妈妈：快请坐。请吃糖，还有水果。你们想喝茶还是果汁？

阿曼达：我想喝果汁。

史蒂夫和永民：我喝茶。

永民：你家地方很大，也很漂亮。

王玉：我带你们参观一下我家。这是客厅，旁边是饭厅。

史蒂夫：你家有几间卧室？
王玉：三间。这是我哥哥的房间，对面是卫生间。
阿曼达：这是谁的房间？
王玉：这是我和姐姐的房间。我爸爸妈妈的房间在对面。
永民：什么这么香？
王玉：我妈妈正在做她的拿手菜，糖醋鱼。我带你们去厨房看看，好吗？
阿曼达和史蒂夫：太好了！

生词 New words

jìn	进	come in, enter	pángbiān	旁边	next to, beside
jièshào	介绍	introduce	fàntīng	饭厅	dining room
shūshu	叔叔	uncle	jiān	间	(used for rooms); room
āyí	阿姨	aunt	wòshì	卧室	bedroom
hóngbāo	红包	red packet (for gifts of money)	duìmiàn	对面	opposite
táng	糖	sugar, sweets	wèishēngjiān	卫生间	washroom, toilet
shuǐguǒ	水果	fruit	xiāng	香	fragrant (smell or taste)
hē	喝	drink	zhèngzài	正在	in the process of
chá	茶	tea	náshǒucài	拿手菜	signature dish
guǒzhī	果汁	fruit juice	tángcùyú	糖醋鱼	sweet and sour fish
kètīng	客厅	living room			

1-23

4 Listen again and label the rooms of Wang Yu's house with the words.

1 客厅　2 饭厅　3 卫生间　4 哥哥的卧室
5 爸爸妈妈的卧室　6 她和姐姐的卧室

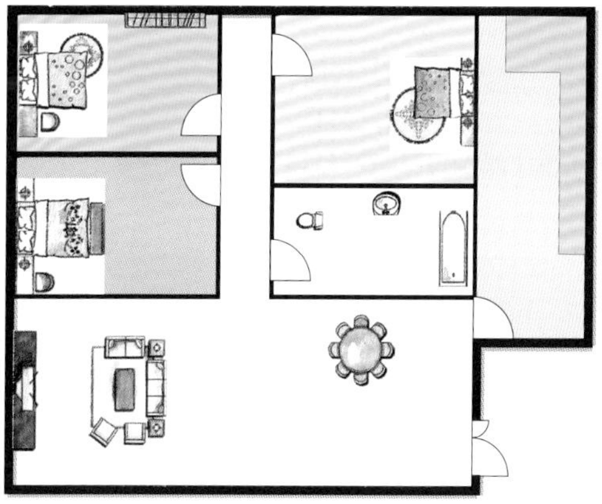

5 Write several sentences to describe your home. Start with:

我家有……间卧室，客厅在……

6 Work in pairs. Take turns to read your sentences to your partner, who will draw a floor plan of your house.

Now check and see if your partner's floor plan is correct.

Pronunciation and speaking

Difference between "uo" and "e"

1-24

1 Check the correct finals for the underlined characters.

1 请坐 ☐ uo ☐ e
2 喝茶 ☐ uo ☐ e
3 果汁 ☐ uo ☐ e
4 客厅 ☐ uo ☐ e
5 这么 ☐ uo ☐ e
6 过年 ☐ uo ☐ e

Now listen and repeat.

1-25

2 Read the sentences aloud.

Wǒ gēge qùguo Měiguó
1 我哥哥去过 美国。

Hěnduō rén xǐhuan hē guǒzhī
2 很多 人 喜欢 喝 果汁。

Nǐ juéde Yīngguó zěnmeyàng
3 你 觉得 英国 怎么样？

Tā zuò zài kètīng li děng gēge
4 他 坐 在 客厅 里 等 哥哥。

Wǒmen zuò huǒchē háishi zuò fēijī qù Hánguó
5 我们 坐 火车 还是 坐 飞机 去 韩国？

Now listen and repeat.

1-26

3 Listen and say the words.

1	xīnnián 新年	hóngbāo 红包	qǐngzuò 请坐	hēchá 喝茶
2	shuǐguǒ 水果	táng 糖	guǒzhī 果汁	náshǒucài 拿手菜
3	kètīng 客厅	fàntīng 饭厅	wòshì 卧室	wèishēngjiān 卫生间

4 Work in pairs.

Student A: You are a Chinese host expecting some visitors during Chinese New Year.
Student B: You are paying a New Year visit to Student A's home.

Now change roles.

CHINESE TO GO

1-27

Expressions used at new year celebrations

Gōngxǐ fācái 恭喜 发财。	I wish you good fortune.
Wànshìrúyì 万事如意。	May everything go as you hope.
Gěi nǐ yāsuìqián 给 你 压岁钱。	Here's your New Year money.
Wǒ jìng nǐ yì bēi 我 敬 你 一 杯。	I'd like to propose a toast to you.
Gānbēi 干杯！	Cheers!

LESSON | 2

Reading and writing

1 Complete the phrases with the correct verbs.

guà	tiē	wán	chàng	bài	gěi
挂	贴	玩	唱	拜	给

1 _____ chūnlián 春联
2 _____ nián 年
3 _____ gē 歌
4 _____ yóuxì 游戏
5 _____ hóngbāo 红包
6 _____ dēnglong 灯笼

2 Read Steve's article about Chinese New Year in the school magazine.

生词 New words

Chūnjié 春节	Spring Festival, Chinese New Year	yòu 又	again; also
tuányuán 团圆	get together	wán 玩	play
jiérì 节日	festival	yóuxì 游戏	game
tiē 贴	paste, put up	dànián chūyī 大年初一	first day of lunar New Year
chūnlián 春联	spring couplets	bàinián 拜年	pay a New Year visit
guà 挂	hang up	xiān 先	first
dēnglong 灯笼	lantern	bāo 包	wrap, make
qìngzhù 庆祝	celebrate	jiǎozi 饺子	dumplings
chúxī 除夕	New Year's Eve	rènao 热闹	bustling and exciting
cānjiā 参加	take part in, participate		

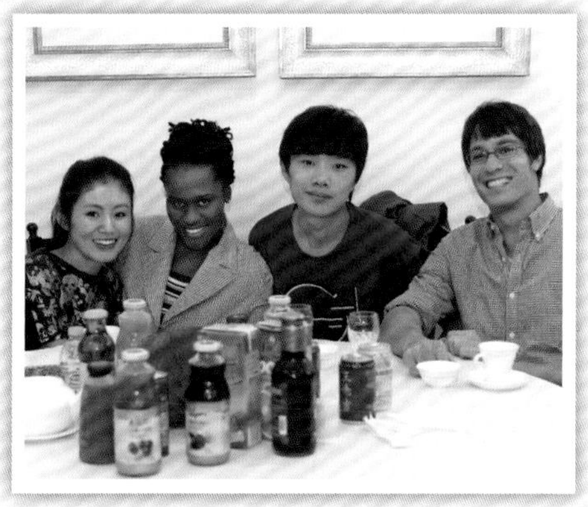

过年了！

作者：史蒂夫

今年我在中国过春节了！春节也就是中国人的新年，是家人团圆的节日。很多人家的门口都会贴春联，挂红灯笼，庆祝新年的到来。

除夕夜，我参加了学校的除夕派对。很多同学都没有回家，都在北京过春节。我们又玩游戏又唱歌，大家都玩得很开心。

大年初一，很多人很早就起床了，去朋友家拜年。中午我和永民、阿曼达去王玉家拜年。我们先一起包饺子，然后吃饭。王玉的妈妈准备了很多菜，我最喜欢吃的菜是糖醋鱼。

我觉得中国的春节又热闹又好玩。

3 Choose the correct answers to the questions.

1 What is the first paragraph mainly about?

☐ a 红灯笼　☐ b 春节　☐ c 春联

2 What is the second paragraph mainly about?

☐ a 除夕派对　☐ b 同学　☐ c 玩游戏

3 What is the main subject of the third paragraph?

☐ a 包饺子　☐ b 吃饭　☐ c 拜年

4 Read again and answer the questions.

1 除夕夜史蒂夫去了哪里？做了什么？
2 中国人在哪里贴春联和挂红灯笼？
3 史蒂夫他们为什么大年初一去王玉家？
4 他们在王玉家做了什么？
5 史蒂夫最喜欢吃什么菜？
6 史蒂夫觉得中国的春节怎么样？

5 Complete the description of a major festival in your country.

在我的国家，最 重要 (zhòngyào) (important) 的节日是 ______。这个节日是 _____ 月 _____ 日。

这一天，我们会 ________。我们先 ____________，然后 ______________。我最喜欢 __________。

我觉得这个节日又 __________ 又 ____________。

Language in use

Expressing actions in progress using 正在

1 Look at the sentences.

Adverbial	Subject	正在	Verb phrase
	我妈妈	正在	做她的拿手菜。
老师进来的时候，	同学们	正在	看书。
你打电话的时候，	王玉	正（在）	包饺子。
昨天下午三点，	他们	（正）在	玩游戏。

Now check the two correct explanations.

☐ 1 正在 is used to indicate an action in progress at a specific time or during a certain period of time.

☐ 2 正在 is only used for actions happening in the present.

☐ 3 Either 正 or 在 can be omitted if the emphasis is not on the action happening at a specific time.

2 Write the sentences in Chinese.

1 They are playing football at the sports ground.
2 I was watching TV at 8 o'clock yesterday evening.
3 She was attending class when you called.
4 At 4 o'clock every afternoon, Mark is jogging.

Expressing "both… and…" with 又……又……

1 Look at the sentences.

First condition/quality	Second condition/quality
我们玩游戏。	我们唱歌。
我们又玩游戏又唱歌。	
他们贴春联。	他们挂红灯笼。
他们又贴春联又挂红灯笼。	
中国的春节很热闹。	中国的春节很好玩。
中国的春节又热闹又好玩。	
他很高。	他很帅。
他又高又帅。	
王玉的家很大。	王玉的家很漂亮。
王玉的家又大又漂亮。	

Now check the two correct explanations.

☐ 1 又……又…… is used to express conditions or qualities that occur one after the other.

☐ 2 又……又…… is used to connect two verb phrases or adjectives as the predicate.

☐ 3 The phrases connected by 又……又…… must be of the same structures or parts of speech.

2 Join the two sentences together, using 又……又…….

1 他们唱歌。他们跳舞。
2 中国菜很好吃。中国菜很便宜。
3 坐火车很快。坐火车很方便。

Expressing sequences with 先……然后……

1 Look at the sentences.

First event/action	Second event/action
我们先一起包饺子，	（我们）然后吃饭。
我们先去西安，	然后（我们）去成都。
他们先喝茶，	然后参观王玉的家。
王玉先吃晚饭，	然后看电影。

Now check the two correct explanations.

☐ 1 先……然后…… is used to connect two actions or events that happen at the same time.

☐ 2 先 must be placed between the subject and the verb of the first event, while 然后 is usually put at the beginning of the clause stating the second event.

☐ 3 If the subjects of the verb phrases connected by 先……然后…… are the same, the second subject is usually omitted.

2 Join the two sentences together, using 先……然后…….

1 安娜看书。安娜打篮球。
2 永民跟老师见面。永民吃饭。
3 马克看电影。马克去同学的生日派对。

Turn to page 162 for grammar reference.

LESSON | 3

Communication activity

1 **Work in groups of four. You are planning a New Year party. The theme is "China". Create a party plan. Think about:**

Theme	中国!
Time and place	
Decorations	
Costumes	
Games and activities	
Food and drink	

2 **Share your party plan with another group.**

Turn to pages 149 and 155 for more speaking practice.

Cultural corner

Being a guest in China

When invited to a Chinese household, a guest can typically expect a sumptuous meal prepared by the host. Although the meal will be carefully prepared and the quantity more than enough, the host will constantly say "I'm afraid it's not much, I hope you don't mind." During the meal, the host will serve food and drink all the time. They want to make sure the guests always have some food on their plates. Some guests will leave some food uneaten to suggest that they are so full they cannot eat any more.

Good gifts to bring to a Chinese household include fruit, wine, and tea. The choice of gifts one should bring depends on the relationship between the guest and host. If they are friends, fruit makes a good gift. If the host is older than the guest, the guest may bring wine or tea, or a small present which comes from your country as a token to express thanks for being invited.

Character writing

These are two common radicals in Chinese. Do you know any other characters with the same radicals?

Radicals	Meaning	Examples
艹	grass / plants	菜、英
广	big room / space	床、应

1 **Look at the characters and identify the radicals.**

茶　节　店　庆

2 **Match the words with the meanings.**

1 庆祝　　a Spring Festival
2 喝茶　　b get up
3 起床　　c celebrate
4 春节　　d drink tea

3 **Trace the characters in the boxes.**

节

茶

庆

床

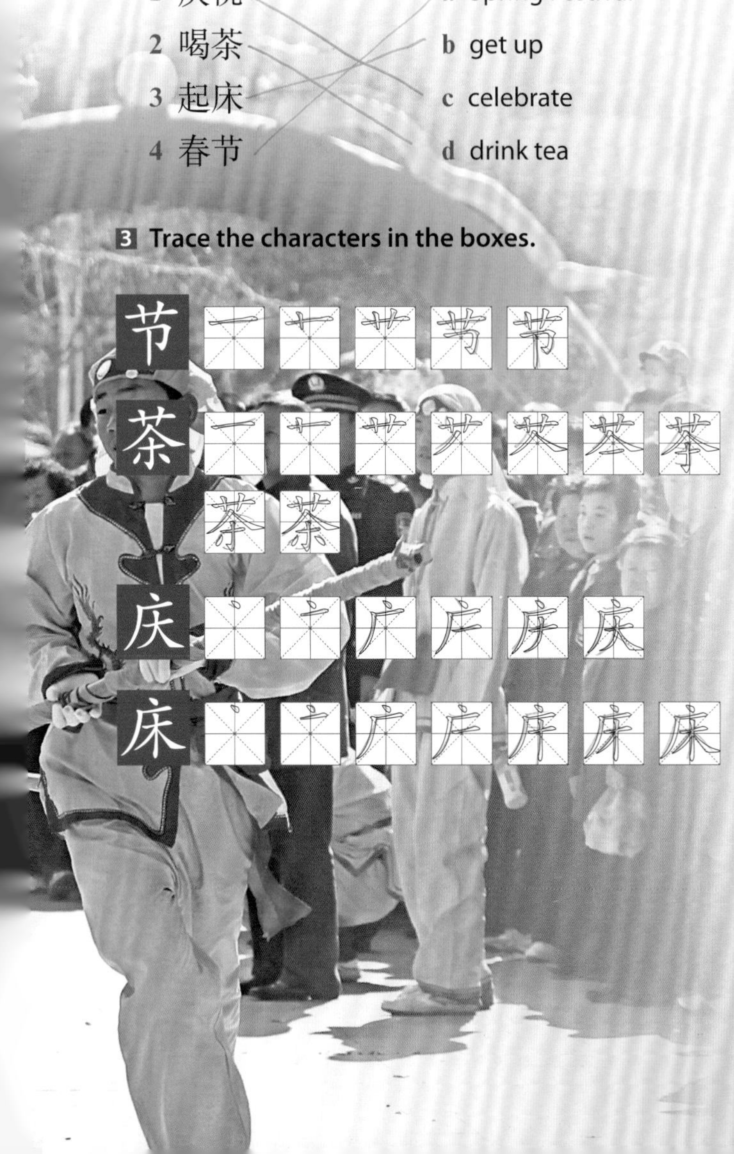

Review and practice

1 **Circle the odd words out.**

1 饺子　糖醋鱼　拿手菜
2 对面　节日　旁边
3 拜年　春联　灯笼
4 热闹　团圆　参加
5 挂　贴　游戏

2 **Answer the questions using 正在.**

1 昨天下午四点你在做什么？
2 今天早上八点你在做什么？
3 你上课的时候，你的家人正在做什么？

3 **Complete the paragraph using appropriate words.**

今天是安娜的生日。早上七点，安娜 已经 起床了。她 先 学中文，然后 去打篮球。晚上六点是安娜的生日派对。朋友们 又 跳舞 又 唱歌。大家 都 很高兴。

4 **Write two sentences to describe the picture, using 又……又…… and 正在.**

她又坐又看书.

Vocabulary extension

Match the words with the different fruits in the picture.

chéngzi 1 橙子	lí 2 梨	xiāngjiāo 3 香蕉
píngguǒ 4 苹果	pútao 5 葡萄	xīguā 6 西瓜

Now work in pairs. Ask and answer questions about what fruit you like.

A: 你喜欢吃水果吗？你最喜欢什么水果？

B: 我喜欢吃水果，我最喜欢……

Vocabulary review

Fill in the blanks.

阿姨	āyí	*n.*	aunt
拜年	bàinián	*v.*	________
____	bāo	*v.*	wrap, make
参加	cānjiā	*v.*	________
____	chá	*n.*	tea
除夕	chúxī	*n.*	New Year's Eve
春节	Chūnjié	*n.*	________
春联	chūnlián	*n.*	spring couplets
大年初一	dànián chūyī		first day of lunar New Year
灯笼	dēnglong	*n.*	lantern
____	duìmiàn	*n.*	opposite
饭厅	fàntīng	*n.*	dining room
挂	guà	*v.*	________
果汁	guǒzhī	*n.*	fruit juice
____	hē	*v.*	drink
红包	hóngbāo	*n.*	red packet (for gifts of money)
间	jiān	*measure word / n.*	(used for rooms); room
饺子	jiǎozi	*n.*	dumplings
节日	jiérì	*n.*	________
____	jièshào	*v.*	introduce
____	jìn	*v.*	come in, enter
客厅	kètīng	*n.*	living room
拿手菜	náshǒucài	*n.*	________
____	pángbiān	*n.*	next to, beside
庆祝	qìngzhù	*v.*	________
____	rènao	*adj.*	bustling and exciting
叔叔	shūshu	*n.*	________
____	shuǐguǒ	*n.*	fruit
糖	táng	*n.*	________
糖醋鱼	tángcùyú	*n.*	sweet and sour fish
贴	tiē	*v.*	________
团圆	tuányuán	*v.*	get together
____	wán	*v.*	play
卫生间	wèishēngjiān	*n.*	________
卧室	wòshì	*n.*	bedroom
____	xiān	*adv.*	first
香	xiāng	*adj.*	fragrant (smell or taste)
游戏	yóuxì	*n.*	________
又	yòu	*adv.*	again; also
____	zhèngzài	*adv.*	in the process of
橙子	chéngzi	*n.*	orange
梨	lí	*n.*	pear
苹果	píngguǒ	*n.*	apple
葡萄	pútao	*n.*	grape
西瓜	xīguā	*n.*	watermelon
香蕉	xiāngjiāo	*n.*	banana

UNIT 4

Wǒmen zěnme qù ne

我们怎么去呢？

How do we get there?

LESSON 1

Vocabulary and listening

1-29

1 Match the words with the signs.

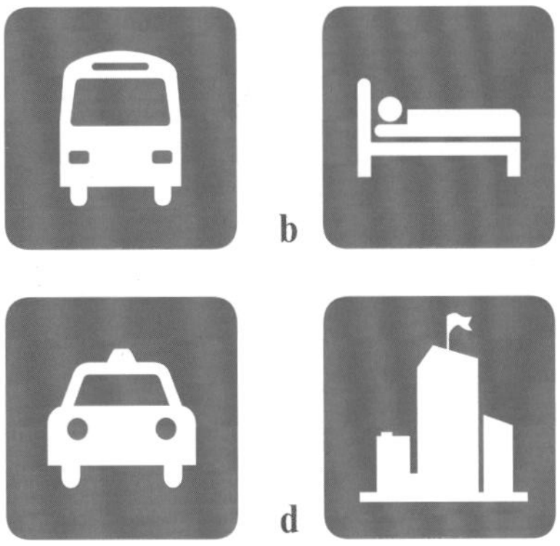

a b c d

1	shìzhōngxīn 市中心	2	chūzūchē zhàn 出租车 站
3	bīnguǎn 宾馆	4	gōnggòng qìchē zhàn 公共 汽车 站

Now listen and say the words.

1-30

2 Listen and complete the signs.

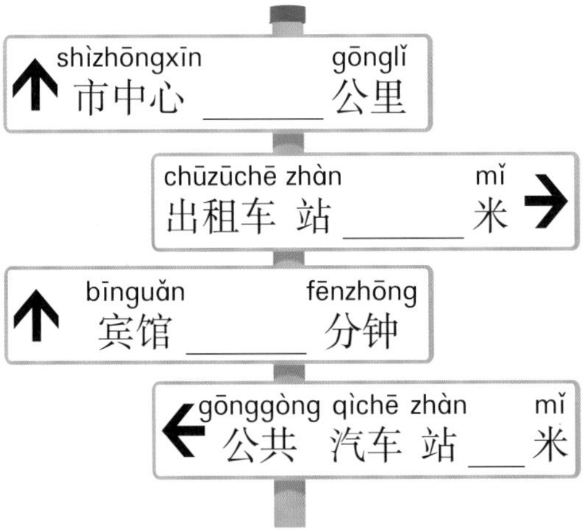

1-31

3 Mark, Amanda and Yeong-min have arrived in Xi'an. Listen to the conversation and answer the questions.

1 他们为什么要问路？
2 他们想去哪些地方？
3 西安有什么好玩的地方？

永民：坐了十几个小时的火车，终于到西安了。对了，怎么去古城宾馆呢？

马克：古城宾馆应该在钟楼附近，咱们到外面问问人吧。……请问，从这里到钟楼怎么走？有多远？

路人：钟楼在市中心，离这里很近，差不多五公里，坐出租车十分钟就到。

马克：请问出租车站在哪里？

路人：往前走五十米，再向右拐，你就可以看到出租车站。

阿曼达：谢谢您。那您知道从市中心怎么去古城墙和兵马俑吗？

路人：古城墙在市中心南边，走路就可以到。兵马俑很远，在西安市东边三十公里，你们可以坐出租车或者公共汽车去。

永民：西安还有什么好玩的地方吗？

路人：你们应该去大雁塔，它在西安市的南边。

马克：大雁塔看起来像大雁吗？哈哈……

永民：马克，别开玩笑了。

阿曼达：大清真寺呢？

路人：那里也应该去。大清真寺在钟楼附近，很容易找！

阿曼达：我知道了。太谢谢您了。

路人：不客气。祝你们在西安玩得开心！再见。

生词 New words

zhōngyú 终于	at last, finally	qiáng 墙	wall
gǔ 古	old, ancient	zǒulù 走路	walk
bīnguǎn 宾馆	hotel	xiàng 像	look like
zánmen 咱们	we, us	kāi wánxiào 开 玩笑	make a joke
wàimiàn 外面	outside	róngyì 容易	easy
gōnglǐ 公里	kilometre	zhǎo 找	look for, find
xiàng 向	to	bú kèqi 不客气	You're welcome.
yòu 右	right side, right	zhù 祝	wish
guǎi 拐	turn	zàijiàn 再见	goodbye
nín 您	you (respectful form)		

1-31

4 Listen again and mark the correct locations of the following places on the map.

1 Zhōnglóu 钟楼　2 Gǔchéngqiáng 古城墙　3 Dàyàntǎ 大雁塔

4 Qīngzhēnsì 清真寺　5 Bīngmǎyǒng 兵马俑

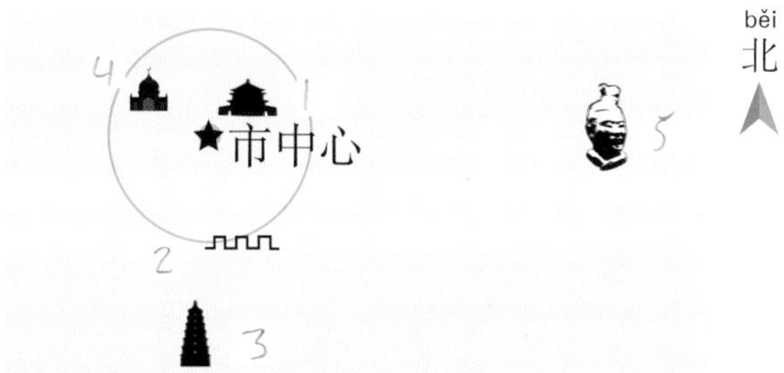

5 Work in pairs. Ask and answer questions about

- how far away the following places are;
- how to get to these places from where you are now.

Use the conversation in Activity 3 to help you.

洗手间　地铁站

图书馆　公共汽车站

Pronunciation and speaking

The initials: "zh" "ch" "sh"

1-32

1 Check the correct initials for the underlined characters.

1	城市	☐ zh	☐ ch	☑ sh
2	中心	☑ zh	☐ ch	☐ sh
3	这里	☑ zh	☐ ch	☐ sh
4	差不多	☐ zh	☑ ch	☐ sh
5	出租车	☐ zh	☑ ch	☐ sh
6	十分钟	☐ zh	☐ ch	☑ sh

Now listen and repeat.

1-33

2 Say the sentences aloud.

Wǒ zài zhège shāngdiàn mǎile yí gè shǒujī
1 我在这个 商店 买了一个手机。

Shūdiàn de shòuhuòyuán wèn wǒ de shēngrì
2 书店 的 售货员 问我的生日。

Zhège shǔjià wǒ qù Zhōngguó zuò zhìyuànzhě
3 这个暑假我去 中国 做 志愿者。

Nǐ rènshi zài chāoshì shàngbān de rén ma
4 你认识在超市 上班 的人吗？

Now listen and repeat.

1-34

3 Listen and say the words.

airport

	fēijīchǎng	huǒchēzhàn	shìzhōngxīn
1	飞机场	火车站	市中心
	zěnme zǒu	wǎng qián zǒu	xiàng yòu guǎi
2	怎么走	往前走	向右拐
	duō yuǎn	fùjìn	róngyì
3	多远	附近	容易
	wǔshí mǐ	zuǒyòu	chàbuduō
4	五十米	左右	差不多

4 Write down information about how to get to the following places from your current location, including the means of transport, the time required and the cost.

huǒchēzhàn 火车站　　fēijīchǎng 飞机场

shìzhōngxīn 市中心　　zuì jìn de shūdiàn 最近的 书店

Now work in pairs. Ask and answer questions about how to get to these places.

CHINESE TO GO

1-35

Asking for repetition and clarification

Wǒ méi tīng qīngchu 我没听清楚。	I didn't catch that.
Qǐng zài shuō yí biàn 请再说一遍。	Please say that again.
Nǐ míngbai ma 你明白吗？	Do you understand?
Wǒ bù míngbai 我不明白。	I don't understand.
Nín shì shuō 您是说……？	Do you mean ...?

LESSON 2

Reading and writing

1 Work in pairs. Talk about your journey to class every day, using the words in the box. Say

- how far away your home is
- how long the journey takes
- how you travel
- what time you leave and arrive.

kāi chē 开车 drive a car	jìnrù 进入 enter
líkāi 离开 leave	dàodá 到达 arrive
shàng xiàchē 上/下车 get on/off (a vehicle)	

1-36

2 Read the travel guide about Xi'an and answer the questions.

1 从市中心去兵马俑可以坐什么车？

2 坐什么车又快又方便？

3 坐什么车最不方便？为什么？

西安 旅游指南

怎么去兵马俑博物馆？

从市中心去兵马俑博物馆可以坐出租车，也可以坐公共汽车或者火车。

出租车/开车

坐出租车或者开车又快又方便，出租车车费大约一百八十元。从市中心到高速公路只要十五分钟左右。在高速公路上开三十公里以后，进入临潼。离开高速公路以后，再开大约十分钟，就到兵马俑博物馆。

公共汽车

坐公共汽车比较慢，要一小时十五分钟左右。西安火车站有去兵马俑的公共汽车，车票每张七元。

火车

坐火车没有坐出租车或者公共汽车那么方便。从西安坐火车到临潼火车站以后，还要坐出租车才能到兵马俑博物馆。车费不太贵——火车票六元，出租车费三十元左右。高速公路堵车的时候，坐火车比较快。但是，火车有时候会晚点。

生词 New words

bówùguǎn 博物馆 museum	gāosù gōnglù 高速公路 motorway, freeway	piào 票 ticket
kāi 开 drive (a car); open; prescribe	jìnrù 进入 enter	zhāng 张 (for thin, flat things); open
kuài 快 fast	líkāi 离开 leave	dǔchē 堵车 traffic jam
chēfèi 车费 (bus/train/taxi) fare	bǐjiào 比较 comparatively, in comparison	yǒushí hou 有时（候） sometimes
dàyuē 大约 approximately	màn 慢 slow	wǎndiǎn 晚点 be delayed
yuán 元 *yuan*, Chinese currency unit		

3 Read again and complete the table.

	时间	价钱
出租车	最短	180元
公共汽车	比较长	7元
火车	最长	36元

Now work in pairs. Say which way you would prefer to travel, and why.

4 A friend is travelling by train to visit you. Write him/her an email explaining how to get to your home from the railway station.

Language in use

Talking about distance using 离/多远

1 Look at the sentences.

Topic			Comment
A	离	B	
伦敦	离	香港	多远?
伦敦	离	香港	有 9000 公里。
钟楼	离	这里	多远?
钟楼	离	这里	很近。
火车站	(离)	(这里)	(有)多远?
			不远。

Now check the two correct explanations.

- ☐ 1 离 is used to introduce the starting point of a distance between two places.
- ☑ 2 多远 is used to ask about how far away one place is from another.
- ☑ 3 离 and 这里 can be left out if the starting point is obviously known in the context.

2 Write questions about the underlined parts of the sentences.

1 北京离成都<u>不远</u>。
2 北京离纽约有 <u>6000 多公里</u>。
3 图书馆离这里 <u>很近</u>。

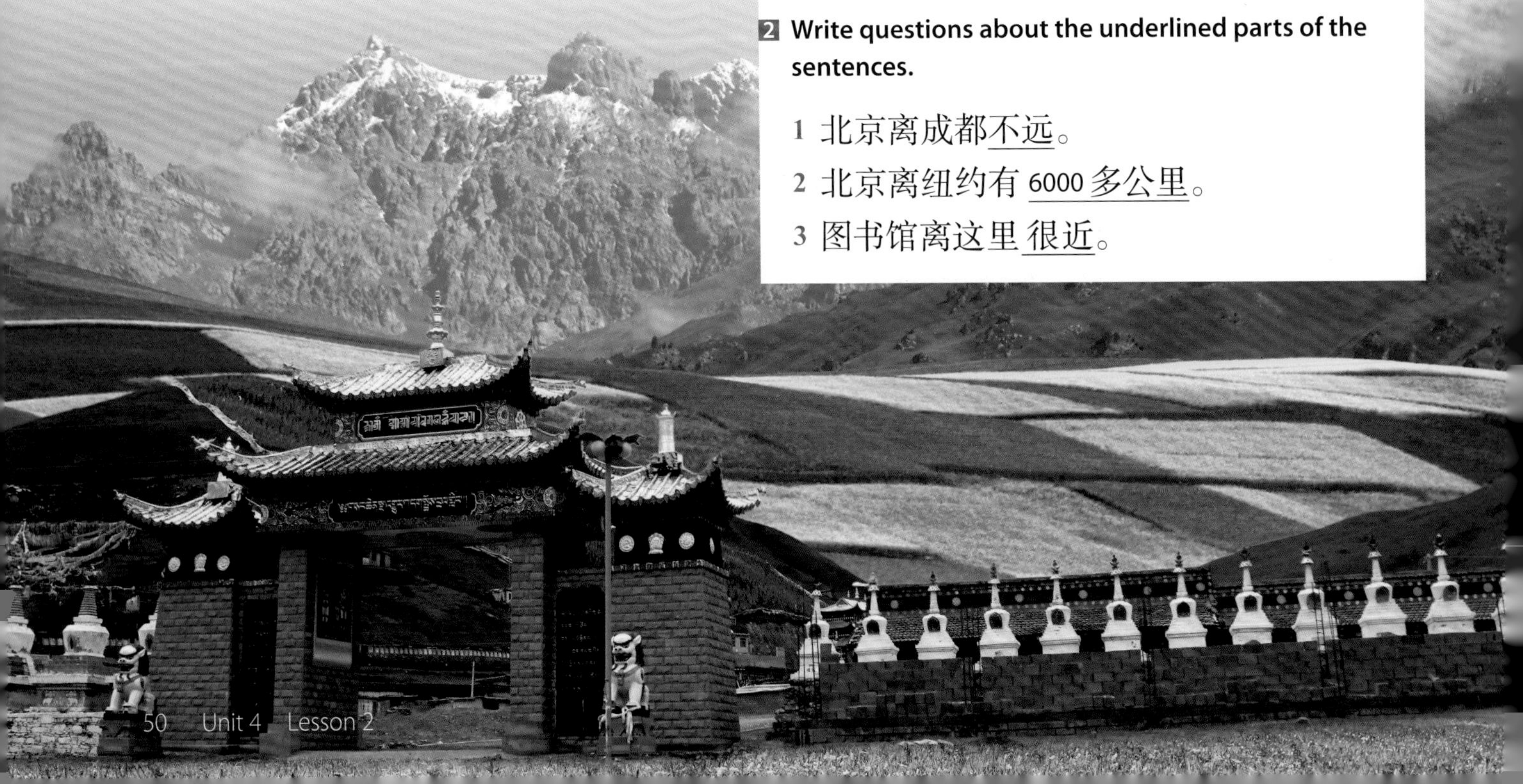

Expressing distance using 从A到B

1 Look at the sentences.

Topic				Comment	
从	A	到	B	Verb phrase	Duration
从	这里	到	钟楼，	坐出租车，	十分钟就到。
从	市中心	到	兵马俑，	坐公共汽车	要一个小时。
从	市中心	到	高速公路，	开车	要十五分钟左右。
从	宿舍 sù shè dorm	到	超市，	走路	大约五分钟。

Now check the two correct explanations.

☑ 1 从 is used before A to indicate the starting point, while 到 is used before B, indicating the end point.

☐ 2 The verb phrase for means of transport can be used after the duration.

☑ 3 The verb phrase for means of transport must be used before the duration.

2 Complete the sentences.

1 从我家到 Rik Aid 走路 10分钟。

2 从市中心到 我家 开车 40分钟。

3 从伦敦到 北京 坐飞机 12小时。

Using 以后/…… 的时候

1 Look at the sentences.

Adverbial clause		Main sentence/Action 2
Action 1	以后	
离开高速公路	以后，	再开大约十分钟。
After leaving the motorway, drive on for about ten minutes.		
回北京	以后，	我们可以看京剧。
After going back to Beijing, we can watch Beijing opera.		

Adverbial clause		Main sentence/Action 2
Action 1	的时候	
我到教室	的时候，	老师已经在上课了。
When I got to the classroom, the teacher was already giving the class.		
去西安旅行	的时候，	你会穿什么衣服？
What will you wear when you go travelling to Xi'an?		

Now check the two correct explanations.

☐ 1 以后 and ……的时候 are used at the beginning of an adverbial clause, meaning "after" and "when" respectively.

☑ 2 The positions of 以后 and ……的时候 in Chinese sentences are different from where "after" and "when" are placed in English sentences.

☑ 3 以后 and ……的时候 can not be used to express the same concept of time.

2 Write the sentences in Chinese.

1 I called my mother after I arrived in Beijing.

2 She was sleeping when I left home.

3 I do my homework after I get back home every day.

Turn to page 163 for grammar reference.

LESSON | 3

Communication activity

1. Your class are going on a weekend trip together. As a class, discuss and agree on a destination.

2. Work in groups of four. Plan the trip, including means of transport, the best route to get there, and things to see and do on the trip.

3. Present your plan to the class.

4. Work with the whole class. Decide on the best plan.

Turn to pages 149 and 155 for more speaking practice.

Cultural corner

The art of paper-cutting

Paper-cuttings, a common souvenir often found in markets and temple fairs around China, are a traditional form of folk art. Paper was a precious commodity in very ancient times, and before the 6th century (the date of the oldest surviving paper-cut) none but the very wealthiest could have afforded to use it for artwork. But as paper became more widely available, paper-cutting became a popular artform, allowing everyone to express their creativity with just a pair of scissors and a few sheets of paper, from high-born courtiers to lowly artisans.

In rural China, paper-cutting is a traditional activity for women, and skill at paper-cutting used to be considered a great advantage in a prospective bride.

Paper-cuttings were traditionally used for religious rites, ornamentation and portraits. Nowadays, they are most commonly used for decoration on walls, windows, mirrors and lanterns. They also make good gifts for friends, and are a popular choice as souvenirs.

Character writing

These are two common radicals in Chinese. Do you know any other characters with the same radicals?

Radicals	Meaning	Examples
礻	spirit	礼、福
纟	silk	丝、绿

1 Look at the characters and identify the radicals.

祝　给　级　视

2 Match the words with the meanings.

1 终于　　a TV
2 祝　　b at last
3 电视　　c approximately
4 大约　　d wish

3 Trace the characters in the boxes.

视

祝

约

终

Review and practice

1 Match the words with the meanings.

1 堵车　　a arrive
2 晚点　　b traffic jam
3 进入　　c leave
4 到达　　d enter, come into
5 离开　　e delayed

2 Write four sentences about your daily activities using 以后 and ……的时候.

3 Work in pairs. Ask and answer questions about how far away the following places are from your home, and how to get to them.

1 学校　　4 北京
2 地铁站　　5 香港
3 飞机场　　6 伦敦

4 Write two sentences to describe each picture, including the means of transport.

a

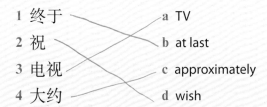

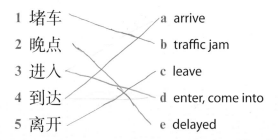

b

Vocabulary extension

Look at Mark's train ticket and complete the text message.

cì	次	service number of a train
chē	车	carriage of a train
yìngzuò	硬座	hard seat
dàngrì	当日	on the date stated
yǒuxiào	有效	valid

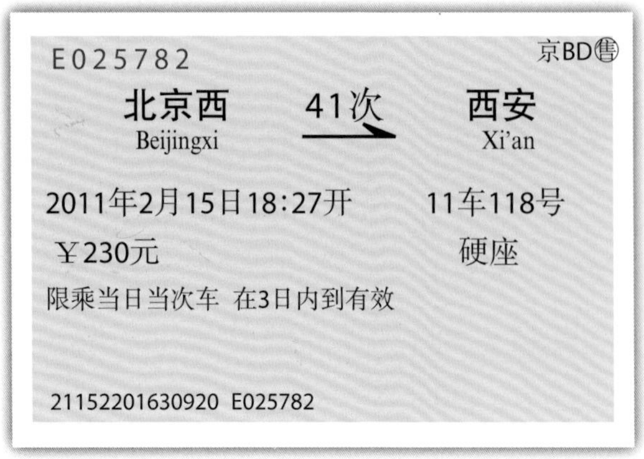

E025782
京BD售
北京西
Beijingxi
41次
西安
Xi'an
2011年2月15日18:27开
11车118号
¥230元
硬座
限乘当日当次车 在3日内到有效
21152201630920 E025782

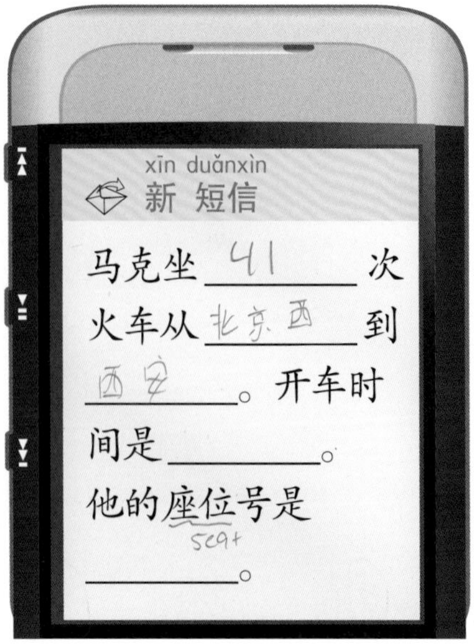

xīn duǎnxìn
新 短信
马克坐 41 次火车从 北京西 到 西安。开车时间是______。
他的座位号是 seat ______。

Vocabulary review

Fill in the blanks.

比较	bǐjiào	*adv.*	comparatively, in comparison
宾馆	bīnguǎn	*n.*	hotel
博物馆	bówùguǎn	*n.*	museum
不客气	bú kèqi		You're welcome.
车费	chēfèi	*n.*	(bus/train/taxi) fare
大约	dàyuē	*adv.*	approx.
堵车	dǔchē	*v.*	traffic jam
高速公路	gāosù gōnglù	*n.*	motorway, freeway
公里	gōnglǐ	*n.*	kilometre
古	gǔ	*adj.*	old; ancient
拐	guǎi	*v.*	turn
进入	jìnrù	*v.*	enter
开	kāi	*v.*	drive (a car); open; prescribe
开玩笑	kāi wánxiào		make joke
快	kuài	*adj.*	fast
离开	líkāi	*v.*	exit, leave
慢	màn	*adj.*	slow
您	nín	*pron.*	you (respectful form)
票	piào	*n.*	ticket
墙	qiáng	*n.*	wall
容易	róngyì	*adj.*	easy

外面	wàimiàn	*n.*	outside
晚点	wǎndiǎn	*adj.*	delay
向	xiàng	*prep.*	to
像	xiàng	*v.*	such as
有时(候)	yǒushí hou	*adv.*	sometimes
右	yòu	*n.*	right side, right
元	yuán	*n.*	*yuan*, Chinese currency unit
再见	zàijiàn	*v.*	bye
咱们	zánmen	*pron.*	we, us
张	zhāng	*measure word/v.*	(for thin, flat things); open
找	zhǎo	*v.*	look for, find
终于	zhōngyú	*adv.*	finally
祝	zhù	*v.*	wish
走路	zǒulù	*v.*	walk
车	chē	*n.*	carriage of a train
次	cì	*n.*	service number of a train
当日	dàngrì	*n.*	on the date stated
到达	dàodá	*v.*	arrive
上/下车	shàng xià chē	*v.*	get on/off (a vehicle)
硬座	yìngzuò	*n.*	hard seat
有效	yǒuxiào	*v.*	valid

Review 1

Vocabulary

1 Match the verbs with the nouns to make phrases.

1 交 a 故事
2 准备 b 报纸
3 读 c 毛衣
4 看 d 考试
5 戴 e 作业
6 穿 f 手套

2 Make words using the characters in the box.

响 和 降 云 报 别 温 气

1 气 温
2 差 别
3 暖 和
4 影 响
5 空 气
6 下 降
7 多 云
8 预 报

Now make sentences using the words given.

9 空气 / 影响 冷空气影响北西地区。

10 预报 / 下降

3 Complete the sentences with the words in the box.

参加 拜年 喝 庆祝 介绍 贴

1 你能给我们 介绍 一下吗？

2 过年的时候很多人家的门口都会 贴 春联。

3 你想 喝 什么？果汁还是茶？

4 大年初一我去朋友家 拜年 。

5 很多人 参加 了学校的除夕派对。

6 你想怎样 庆祝 生日？

4 Put the words in the correct categories.

a 走路 e 下雪 i 气温
b 拜年 f 开车 j 红灯笼
c 堵车 g 晴 k 晚点
d 红包 h 春联 l 阴

天气	春节	交通
e g i l	b j d h	a k c f

Now write five sentences about what Chinese people do at the Spring Festival.

Grammar

1 Match the parts to complete the sentences.

1 周末前做完作业 c

2 公园离我家不远，b

3 我一回家，e

4 我们先吃饭，f

5 你去看电影的时候，a

6 从这里到市中心，d

a 王玉正在学校上课。

b 坐公共汽车要半个小时。

c 当然不可能。

d 走路只要10分钟。

e 就给她打电话。

f 然后去看电影。

as soon as　　not until

2 Complete the sentences using 就 and 才.

1 电影开始以后马克 __就__ 来。

2 早上六点半王玉 __才__ 起床了。

3 他今天很累，晚上八点 __就__ 上床睡觉了。

4 做完作业以后你 __才__ 可以出去。

3 Complete the sentences using 要 and 会.

1 今天晚上我 __要__ 复习准备考试。

2 下个月气温 __会__ 下降很多。

3 我爸爸明天 __要__ 去伦敦。

4 Make sentences using 又……又…… and the words given.

1 便宜 / 漂亮

2 读故事 / 看报纸

3 唱歌 / 玩游戏

5 Write a sentence to describe each picture, using 得 to indicate result or degree.

a

b

6 Write three sentences about what you did yesterday, using 得 to indicate result or degree.

7 **Write three sentences about things you often do at the same time, using 一边……一边…….**

8 **Complete the sentences using 以后 and …… 的时候.**

1 起床 以后，我洗脸刷牙。

2 马克来我家 的时候，我正在贴春联。

3 放学 以后，他们去打篮球。

4 暑假 ______，我们要去上海旅行。

9 **Write four sentences to describe your city or town, using "A 比/没有 B + adjective" and "A 和 B + 差不多/一样".**

Integrated skills

1-37

1 **Listen and choose the correct answers to the questions.**

1 他住在伦敦的时候每天上课前都做什么?

a 打网球　　b 跑步

2 他在这里每天上课前都去跑步吗?

a 去　　b 不去

3 哪里的天气比较冷?

a 成都　　b 首尔

4 去成都需要带很多衣服吗?

a 需要　　b 不需要

5 人们怎样庆祝新年?

a 贴春联　　b 挂红灯笼

6 春联贴在哪里?

a 门口　　b 卧室

7 怎么去邮局?

a 往前走三十米，再向左拐。

b 往前走三十米，再向右拐。

1-38

2 **Listen and choose the most appropriate responses.**

1 a 对不起，我要复习准备明天的考试。

b 我们可以下次一起吃饭。

2 a 下雪？！没问题，我可以多穿一些衣服。

b 太好了！那我可以穿我最喜欢的T恤和短裤了！

3 a 新年好！谢谢阿姨。

b 太好了。

4 a 我给你们介绍一下。

b 我带你们参观一下我家。

5 a 火车站离市中心不远，坐出租车十分钟就到。

b 火车站离这里很近，走路就可以到。

6 a 兵马俑很远，你们可以坐旅游车去。

b 兵马俑在西安市东边三十公里。

3 **Complete the passage using the words in the box.**

方便	冷	暖和	穿
天气	景点 "place"	历史 history	戴

西安在中国的西北部。这里四个季节的 _天气_ 都不一样：春天 _暖和_，夏天很热，秋天凉爽，冬天很 _冷_。夏天可以 _穿_ 裙子、T恤和短裤；冬天要 _穿_ 毛衣和大衣，_戴_ 围巾和手套。

西安有几千年的 _历史_，有很多有名的 _景点_。最有名的是兵马俑博物馆。西安的交通很 _方便_，你可以坐火车或者飞机去西安。

Now read again and check the true statements.

☐ 1 西安四个季节的天气都差不多。

☑ 2 冬天去西安不能穿短裤。

☐ 3 西安的景点不太有名。

☑ 4 你只能坐飞机去西安。

4 **Write about your travel plans for the winter holidays, including time, place, weather, what to wear, transport and highlights of the place. Make comparisons between the places you have considered and state reasons for your choice. Use 先……然后……, A 比 B + adjective, 又……又…….**

Enjoy Chinese

打

The character 打 is formed by the radical 扌 and the signific 丁. In ancient Chinese, the radical 扌 was 手 and the signific 丁 was 个. In modern Chinese, 打 is a common verb and can form a wide range of verb phrases indicating different activities. Here are some examples.

打网球	play tennis
打电话	make a phone call
打车	take a taxi

Now match the phrases with the meanings.

1 打井	a do a temporary job
2 打工	b hit someone
3 打人	c dig a well

UNIT
5
Qǐngwèn nín yùdìng
请问 您 预订
fángjiān le ma
房间 了吗？
Do you have a reservation?

LESSON | 1

Vocabulary and listening

1-39

1 Check the furniture that you can find in the picture.

☐ yīguì 衣柜	☐ shāfā 沙发
☐ chuáng 床	☐ shūguì 书柜
☐ zhuōzi 桌子	☐ yǐzi 椅子

Now listen and say the words.

1-40

2 Match the phrases with the meanings.

1 yùdìng fángjiān 预订 房间	a fill in a registration card
2 bànlǐ rùzhù 办理 入住	b take a room card
3 tián dēngjìkǎ 填 登记卡	c make a reservation
4 ná fángkǎ 拿 房卡	d check in

Now listen and say the phrases.

1-41

3 Mark, Amanda and Yeong-min check in at their hotel in Xi'an. Listen to the conversation and answer the questions.

1 马克有没有预订房间?
2 服务员为什么要问马克的手机号码?
3 阿曼达为什么打电话给服务员?

服务员：您好！欢迎光临古城宾馆。
马克：你好。我们想办理入住。
服务员：请问您预订房间了吗?
马克：预订了。我叫Mark Johnson。
服务员：请给我看一下你们的护照。
阿曼达和永民：给你。
服务员：你们订了一个标准间和一个单人间，一共四天，对吗?
马克：对。
服务员：请填一下入住登记卡。
马克：好的。…… 填完了，给你。
服务员：谢谢。…… 请问您的手机号码是16628958963吗?
马克：不是，我的手机号是16628958763。这是7，不是9。
服务员：好的，你们的房间号是826和832。这是房卡。

阿曼达：请问房间里可以上网吗？
服务员：可以。

［在房间里］

服务员：喂，您好！请问有什么可以帮助您的吗？

阿曼达：你好！我想上网，但是找不到互联网接口。

服务员：接口就在桌子的下面。

阿曼达：能不能再给我一床被子，这里很冷。

服务员：您房间的洗手间对面有一个衣柜，衣柜的最上面有一床被子，您可以拿出来用。

阿曼达：谢谢你，再见。

生词 New words

fúwùyuán	服务员	attendant, waiter, waitress	shàngwǎng	上网	go online
huānyíng	欢迎	welcome	lǐ	里	in, inside
guānglín	光临	come, be present	wéi	喂	hello, hey
bànlǐ	办理	handle, process	bāngzhù	帮助	help
rùzhù	入住	check in	hùliánwǎng	互联网	the Internet
yùdìng	预订	reserve; reservation	jiēkǒu	接口	connection, interface
hùzhào	护照	passport	zhuōzi	桌子	desk, table
biāozhǔn	标准	standard	xiàmian	下面	under, beneath
dānrén	单人	single (person)	bèizi	被子	quilt
yígòng	一共	altogether, in total	yīguì	衣柜	wardrobe
tián	填	fill in	ná	拿	take, get
dēngjì	登记	register	chū	出	go/come out

1-41

4 **Listen again and check the correct words or phrases to complete the sentences.**

1 服务员要看他们的 ________。
☐ a 护照　☐ b 登记卡

2 互联网接口在 ________。
☐ a 衣柜的上面　☐ b 桌子的下面

5 **Work in pairs. Look at the booking information and act out a conversation between the receptionist at a hotel and a tourist checking into the hotel.**

华伟酒店

姓名	马大伟	天数	两天
房间	一个单人间	房价	¥500/天

Pronunciation and speaking

Tone sandhi: 3rd + 3rd tones

1-42

1 Look at the tone marks for the first character of each word. How does the tone change?

1 你好 ní hǎo
2 洗手间 xíshǒujiān
3 给你 géi nǐ
4 可以 kéyǐ

Now listen and repeat.

1-43

2 Listen and check the tones you hear.

1 我想	☐ wó xiǎng	☑ wǒ xiǎng
2 很冷	☐ hén lěng	☑ hěn lěng
3 景点	☑ jíngdiǎn	☐ jǐngdiǎn
4 很好	☐ hén hǎo	☑ hěn hǎo

Now listen again and repeat.

1-44

3 Say the sentences aloud.

Kéyǐ géi wǒ kàn yíxià nín de hùzhào ma
1 可以给我看一下您的护照吗？

Wó xiǎng qù hěn duō hǎowán de jíngdiǎn
2 我想去很多好玩的景点。

Wǒ kéyǐ géi nǐ zhǎo yíxià
3 我可以给你找一下。

Now listen and repeat.

1-45

4 Listen and say the words.

1	yīguì 衣柜	zhuōzi 桌子	yǐzi 椅子	xíshǒujiān 洗手间
2	hùzhào 护照	bèizi 被子	jiēkǒu 接口	dēngjìkǎ 登记卡
3	duìmiàn 对面	xiàmian 下面	pángbiān 旁边	shàngmian 上面

5 Write down what things would be in your dream hotel room and their locations.

6 Work in pairs.

Student A: Describe your hotel room to Student B using the information in Activity 5.
Student B: Draw a picture of Student A's room.

Now change roles.

7 Check each other's pictures to see if they match the description in Activity 5.

CHINESE TO GO

1-46

Accommodation expressions

Yǒu kòngfáng ma 有空房吗？	Do you have any vacancies?
Bāo zǎocān ma 包早餐吗？	Is breakfast included?
Wó xiǎng dìng fáng 我想订房。	I'd like to book a room.
Wǒ yào tuì fáng 我要退房。	I'd like to check out.
Kéyǐ shuākǎ ma 可以刷卡吗？	Can I pay by credit card?

LESSON 2

Reading and writing

1 Match the words with the things in the picture.

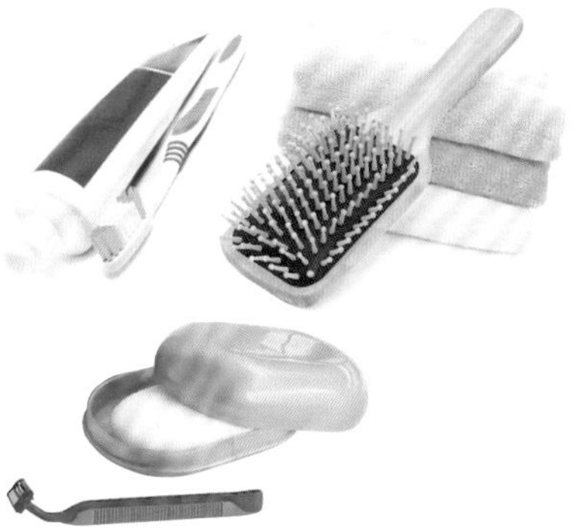

- ☐ a 毛巾 (máojīn)
- ☐ b 牙刷 (yáshuā)
- ☐ c 牙膏 (yágāo)
- ☐ d 肥皂 (féizào)
- ☐ e 剃须刀 (tìxūdāo)
- ☐ f 梳子 (shūzi)

Now check the things you use every day.

生词 New words

jiē	街	street	féizào	肥皂	soap	lìngwài	另外	in addition, besides
chuángdān	床单	bed sheet	shūzi	梳子	comb	zìjǐ	自己	oneself
máojīn	毛巾	towel	miǎnfèi	免费	free of charge	diànnǎo	电脑	computer
gānjìng	干净	clean	xǐyī	洗衣	wash clothes	cháng	长	long; length
rìyòngpǐn	日用品	daily necessities	xǐ	洗	wash	kuān	宽	wide; width
yágāo	牙膏	toothpaste	zhènghǎo	正好	just right	gòu	够	adequate, enough
yáshuā	牙刷	toothbrush	shūfu	舒服	comfortable	gèzi	个子	height, stature

1-47 **2 Read the website comments from Amanda and another hotel guest about the hotel in Xi'an, and answer the questions.**

1 阿曼达觉得古城宾馆怎么样？

2 王伟觉得这个宾馆怎么样？

爱旅游　爱生活　请选择　搜索

旅游宝典　景区大全 | 景区美图 | 旅游线路 | 火车票交易 | 逛社区 | 写博客 | 旅游投诉 | 旅

搜虎旅游 | 景点大全>陕西>西安

用户评级
208人推荐
45人不推荐

古城宾馆
星级：★★★
地区：西安市中心
地址：西安市西大街18号

推荐　阿曼达　发表于：2011-2-7

这个宾馆在市中心，交通很方便。这里的房间很不错，床单和毛巾都很干净。房间里的日用品，比如牙膏、牙刷、肥皂和梳子等，都是免费的。宾馆的洗衣服务又快又好，我下午拿大衣去洗，晚上就洗好了。有些人觉得房间太小了，但是我觉得房间的大小正好，很舒服。另外，房间里有互联网接口，我可以用自己的电脑上网，很方便。

不推荐　王伟　发表于：2011-2-5

宾馆的交通很方便，服务也很好，但是房间太小了。我住的房间长3米，宽2.5米，比其他宾馆的房间小多了。房间里的床也不够大，单人床长1.8米，宽1.2米，个子高的人就不够用。

3 Check the true statements.

- [✗] 1 房间里的毛巾和床单不太干净。
- [✓] 2 房间里的日用品都是免费的。
- [✗] 3 阿曼达觉得房间太小了。
- [✗] 4 王伟觉得房间和床的大小正好。

4 Read again and list the positive and negative things Amanda and Wang Wei said about the hotel.

5 Write some comments about a hotel you know, including transportation, room facilities and service. Describe both the good and bad points. Use the descriptions in Activity 2 to help you.

Language in use

> Expressing possession, existence or location with **有**

1 Look at the sentences.

Subject	Verb	Noun phrase
我	有	中文报纸。
她	有	一件大衣。
学校	有	很多教室。

Now check the two correct explanations.

- [✓] 1 有 is used to say that someone possesses something.
- [] 2 The subject of a possessive sentence with 有 must be a person.
- [✓] 3 有 means "have", "own" or "possess".

2 Look at the sentences.

Subject		Verb	Noun phrase
Attribute	Location		
洗手间的	对面	有	一个衣柜。
衣柜的	最上面	有	一床被子。
学校	附近	没有	超市。

supermarket

Now check the two correct explanations.

- [] 1 有 is used to express the existence or location of a place or something in relation to another.
- [✓] 2 The location phrase often contains a place or object that is smaller in size than what is contained in the noun phrase.
- [✓] 3 有 means "exist" or "there is/are".

3 Answer the questions using 有.

1 学校附近有什么？

2 教室里有什么？ *classroom*

3 你有哥哥或者姐姐吗？你家有几个人？

huò zhě – maybe

Expressing adequacy with 够/不够

1 Look at the sentences.

Adjective phrase	Subject	Verb	Complement
这个	房子	够	大。
我的	时间	不够	用。
	饭菜	不够	吃。

Now check the two correct explanations.

☐ 1 够 and 不够 are used to express whether something is sufficient for a particular purpose.

☐ 2 The complement of the verb 够 can be an adjective or a verb.

☐ 3 够 and 不够 can be put after the complement to express adequacy.

2 Write the sentences in Chinese.

1 This dress is not long enough.
2 There is enough time to finish the homework.
3 There are enough people to complete the work.

Complements expressing result

1 Look at the sentences.

Subject	Verb	Complement
我	填	完了。
衣服	洗	好了。
我	找	不到接口。

Now check the two correct explanations.

☐ 1 Only an adjective can be used after a verb to indicate the result of an action.

☐ 2 After a verb, another verb or verb phrase can be used to indicate the result of an action.

☐ 3 The subject of the verb can be a person or a thing.

2 Write the sentences in Chinese.

1 I have finished doing my homework.
2 Did you see her?
3 Dinner is ready.

Questions about size with (有) 多大/长/宽

1 Look at the sentences.

Subject	Predicate	
	Verb	Question word
房间	（有）	多大/长/宽？
单人床	（有）	多大/长/宽？

Subject	Measurement	Size	Measurement
房间	长	3米。	
房间	宽	2.5米。	
房子	（有）	3米	高。
单人床	长	1.8米。	
单人床	宽	1.2米。	
桌子	（有）	1米	宽。

Now check the two correct explanations.

☐ 1 多 is used before words expressing measurements to form question words about size.

☐ 2 The words expressing measurements can be put before or after the words for size.

☐ 3 A verb is required in sentences stating sizes.

2 Answer the questions with your own information.

1 你多高？
2 你家的房子多大？
3 你的房间多大？

Turn to page 164 for grammar reference.

LESSON | 3

Communication activity

1 Work in groups of four. You are going on a trip to Beijing and need to find a hotel. Compare the hotel listings below and choose the one you like best.

旅游宝典 | 景区大全 | 景区美图 | 旅游线路

搜虎旅游 | 景点大全>北京

华伟酒店

★★★★ ☺☺

- 房间又大又舒服：标准间长10米，宽5米
- 免费洗衣、日用品
- 房价比较贵，1300元/天
- 到机场坐出租车大约5分钟，到市中心坐出租车要30分钟左右。

朝阳宾馆

★★★ ☺☺☺

- 房间不大不小：标准间长8米，宽4米
- 免费日用品，可以上网
- 房价不贵，800元/天
- 离朝阳公园很近，到天安门坐出租车只要15分钟。

前门宾馆

★ ☺☺

- 房间比较小：标准间长4米，宽3米
- 单人床不够大，公用洗手间，免费旅游指南
- 房价很便宜，400元/天，但是服务不太好。
- 在市中心，离天安门200米，交通很方便。

2 Make a list of the reasons for your choice.

3 Present your choice and reasons to another group.

▶ Turn to pages 150 and 156 for more speaking practice.

Cultural corner

Family inns in the countryside

Chinese people are well known for their hospitality. Hosts are expected to serve their guests with the best they have to make them feel at home. This is generally true in the country, where farmers or peasants provide free shelter and food even to strangers.

Due to the hustle and bustle of city life, the countryside is becoming a popular holiday destination for China's urban residents. Family inns in the countryside developed from traditional hospitality and are run by local villagers who open up their own houses to accommodate travellers.

At family inns, guests are served home-made meals prepared by their hosts using local ingredients. They participate in farm work, experience the quiet and relaxing pace of life in the country, and enjoy the beautiful country scenery. Family inns are becoming more and more popular because of their modest cost, the hospitality of local people, and the simple, relaxing environment.

Character writing

These are two common radicals in Chinese. Do you know any other characters with the same radicals?

Radicals	Meaning	Examples
方	square, side	旅、旁
八	eight	分、公

1 Look at the characters and identify the radicals.

只　房　兵　方

2 Match the words with the meanings.

1 一共　　a convenient
2 房间　　b kilometre
3 方便　　c in total
4 公里　　d room

3 Trace the characters in the boxes.

方

房

公

共

Review and practice

1 Put the sentences in the correct order.

a 请您填一下入住登记卡。
b 再见！
c 可以给我看一下您的护照吗？
d 您的房间号是826。
e 欢迎光临！
f 您需要什么帮助？
g 希望您住得开心。
h 请问您预订房间了吗？

Now work in pairs. Act out the conversation between a hotel receptionist and a hotel guest.

2 Write three sentences about the position of three objects you can see in the picture, using 有.

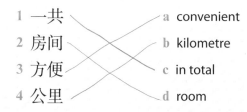

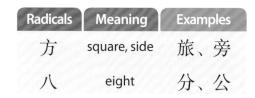

3 Answer the questions, using 够.

1 你每天睡几个小时？你觉得睡觉的时间够吗？
2 今天的天气怎么样？你穿的衣服够暖和吗？

4 Work in pairs. Ask and answer questions about the size of three objects you can see in the classroom.

Vocabulary extension

1 Look at the buttons on a hotel telephone.

zǒngjī 总机	sòngcān fúwù 送餐 服务
qiántái 前台	kèfángbù 客房部

Now match the words with the meanings.

a room service
b housekeeping
c front desk/reception
d operator

2 Work in pairs. Talk about your most recent stay at a hotel. Try to use the words from Activity 1.

Vocabulary review

Fill in the blanks.

办理	bànlǐ	v.	handle, process
______	bāngzhù	v./n.	help
被子	bèizi	n.	______
标准	biāozhǔn	n.	standard
______	cháng	adj./n.	long; length
______	chū	v.	go/come out
床单	chuángdān	n.	______
单人	dānrén	n.	single (person)
登记	dēngjì	v.	______
______	diànnǎo	n.	computer
肥皂	féizào	n.	______
服务员	fúwùyuán	n.	attendant, waiter, waitress
干净	gānjìng	adj.	clean
______	gèzi	n.	height, stature
够	gòu	v.	______
光临	guānglín	v.	come, be present
互联网	hùliánwǎng	n.	______
护照	hùzhào	n.	______
______	huānyíng	v.	welcome
接口	jiēkǒu	n.	connection, interface
街	jiē	n.	street
宽	kuān	adj./n.	______
______	lǐ	n.	in, inside
另外	lìngwài	conj.	in addition, besides
毛巾	máojīn	n.	towel
免费	miǎnfèi	adj.	______

拿	ná	v.	______
日用品	rìyòngpǐn	n.	______
______	rùzhù	v.	check in
上网	shàngwǎng	v.	go online
梳子	shūzi	n.	______
舒服	shūfu	adj.	comfortable
填	tián	v.	fill in
______	wéi	interj.	hello, hey
洗	xǐ	v.	wash
______	xǐyī	v.	wash clothes
下面	xiàmian	n.	______
牙膏	yágāo	n.	toothpaste
牙刷	yáshuā	n.	toothbrush
______	yígòng	adv.	altogether, in total
衣柜	yīguì	n.	wardrobe
预订	yùdìng	v.	______
正好	zhènghǎo	adj.	just right
______	zhuōzi	n.	desk, table
自己	zìjǐ	pron.	oneself
客房部	kèfángbù	n.	housekeeping
前台	qiántái	n.	front desk/reception
沙发	shāfā	n.	sofa
送餐服务	sòngcān fúwù	n.	room service
剃须刀	tìxūdāo	n.	razor
椅子	yǐzi	n.	chair
总机	zǒngjī	n.	operator

UNIT 6

Jìnzhǐ pāizhào
禁止拍照！

No photos!

LESSON 1

Vocabulary and listening

1-48

1 Match the signs with the meanings.

a

b

c

d

1 禁止 拍照 (jìnzhǐ pāizhào)　　2 不得 入内 (bùdé rùnèi)

3 安静 (ānjìng)　　4 严禁 饮食 (yánjìn yǐnshí)

Now listen and say the phrases.

1-49

2 Mark, Amanda and Yeong-min go to see the Terracotta Warriors. Listen to the conversation and answer the questions.

1 学生票多少钱一张？
2 兵马俑是谁发现的？
3 永民觉得那个兵俑像谁？
4 他们看到了什么告示牌？

售票员：您好。
马克：你好。请给我三张学生票。
售票员：可以给我看看学生证吗？
马克：给你。
售票员：谢谢。这是三张票，一共是135元。你们的导游会在入口处等你们。

[在博物馆里]
永民：请问兵马俑是怎么被发现的？
导游：1974年，当地的农民在打井的时候发现了兵马俑。这个兵俑高1.83米，和真人差不多高。
阿曼达：当时的中国人真的有1.83米高吗？现在大部分人都没有那么高。
导游：它可能比当时的人高一点儿。
永民：这个兵俑看起来很像我们的汉语老师——丁老师，你们觉得呢？

阿曼达：是啊，他看起来很像我们没交作业时的丁老师，哈哈……

导游：嘘…… 请安静，这里不能大声说话。

马克：我们应该拍张照片送给丁老师。

永民：等一下，那个告示牌上写着"禁止拍照"。

马克：对不起，我没有看到。

阿曼达：我想过去看看那个兵马俑有多高。

马克：不要过去，这个告示牌上写着"不得入内"。

阿曼达：啊？什么都不可以……

生词 New words

shòupiàoyuán 售票员	ticket seller	Hànyǔ 汉语	Chinese language
zhèng 证	certificate	xū 嘘	shh
dǎoyóu 导游	tour guide	ānjìng 安静	silent
rùkǒuchù 入口处	entrance	shēng 声	voice, sound
děng 等	wait (for)	sòng 送	give (as a gift); send
bèi 被	(for passive voice)	gàoshìpái 告示牌	sign, noticeboard
fāxiàn 发现	discover	zhe 着	(used to indicate continuation of action or state)
dāngdì 当地	local		
nóngmín 农民	farmer; rural people	jìnzhǐ 禁止	forbid
dǎ jǐng 打 井	dig a well		
dāngshí 当时	at that time		

1-49

3 Listen again and check the true statements.

☐ 1 他们的导游会在售票处等他们。

☐ 2 那个兵俑和当时的中国人一样高。

☐ 3 博物馆里不能拍照。

4 Work in pairs. Look at the signs and guess the meanings.

a

b

5 Make some signs showing rules for visitors to your home. Do not use any words on your signs.

Now work in pairs. Guess the meanings of your partner's signs.

Pronunciation and speaking

Difference between "ü" and "üe"

1-50 **1 Check the correct finals for the underlined characters.**

1 学生	☐ ü	☐ üe
2 汉语	☐ ü	☐ üe
3 觉得	☐ ü	☐ üe
4 大约	☐ ü	☐ üe
5 京剧	☐ ü	☐ üe
6 音乐	☐ ü	☐ üe

Now listen and repeat.

1-51 **2 Read the sentences aloud.**

Míngtiān huì xià dà yǔ
1 明天 会 下 大 雨。

Wǒ juéde jīngjù hěn hǎotīng
2 我 觉得 京剧 很 好听 。

Jīnnián liùyuè wǒ yào qù Guìlín lǚyóu
3 今年 六月 我 要 去 桂林 旅游。

Wáng Yù hé Mǎkè yào qù tīng yīnyuèhuì
4 王 玉 和 马克 要 去 听 音乐会。

Xīn tóngxué de jiā zǒulù dàyuē shí fēnzhōng
5 新 同学 的 家 走路 大约 十 分钟 。

Now listen and repeat.

1-52 **3 Listen and say the words.**

	gàoshìpái	jìnzhǐ	bùdé	ānjìng
1	告示牌	禁止	不得	安静
	shòupiàoyuán	dǎoyóu	nóngmín	rùkǒuchù
2	售票员	导游	农民	入口处
	kàn qilai	dāngshí	fāxiàn	dǎ jǐng
3	看起来	当时	发现	打井

4 Write down information about a famous historical site that you are familiar with, including its location, size, how old it is, what it is for and why it is significant.

Now work in pairs. Ask and answer questions about each other's sites. Try to work out what your partner's site is.

CHINESE TO GO

1-53 Expressions for visiting tourist attractions

Jǐ diǎn kāimén 几 点 开门？	What time do you open?
Ménpiào duōshao qián yì zhāng 门票 多少 钱 一 张？	How much is one ticket?
Chūkǒu zài nǎr 出口 在 哪儿？	Where is the exit?
Jiǎnjiè yǒu Yīngwén de ma 简介 有 英文 的 吗？	Do you have an English brochure?

LESSON 2

Reading and writing

1 Work in pairs. Discuss what you know about these words.

1	2	3
Hàncháo 汉朝	tángrén 唐人	Hànzì 汉字

1-54

2 Read Mark's online post about his trip to the Shaanxi History Museum and answer the questions.

1 什么是"汉语"？它是怎样得名的？
2 为什么中国城被称为"唐人街"？

生词 New words

wàn 万	ten thousand	yú 于	at, in
wénwù 文物	cultural relic, artefact	wénzì 文字	writing, script
liǎojiě 了解	get to know, understand	qiángshèng 强盛	powerful, prosperous
shù 数	number, figure	cháodài 朝代	dynasty
mínzú 民族	ethnic group	zhīyī 之一	one of
Hànzú 汉族	Han ethnicity	hǎiwài 海外	overseas
démíng 得名	get one's name	chēng 称	call; weigh
		suǒyǐ 所以	therefore, so

博客首页 | 微博：最火交流工具 看明星动态 | 登录 | 注册 | 发博文 | 博文 | 搜索

首页 | 博文 | 图片 | 关于我

马克的资料

播客 | 微博
进入我的空间
加好友 | 发纸条
写留言 | 加关注

博客等级：22
博客积分：806
博客访问：5,631,496

我的博文

陕西历史博物馆

来西安的第三天，我们参观了陕西历史博物馆。博物馆里有37万件文物，是了解中国历史的好地方。

博物馆里有很多汉朝的文物。中国人数最多的民族是汉族，得名于汉朝（公元前206年—公元220年）。汉族人说的话叫汉语，他们用的文字叫汉字。当然现在大部分中国人都会说汉语，写汉字。

这是唐朝的文物，叫唐三彩。唐朝（公元618年—907年）是中国历史上最强盛的朝代之一。最早去海外的中国人称他们自己为唐人，所以中国城也叫唐人街。

3 Read again and check the true statements.

☐ 1 陕西历史博物馆有370,000件文物。

☐ 2 汉族是中国人数最少的民族。

☐ 3 唐三彩是汉朝的文物。

☐ 4 唐人街是中国人住的地方。

4 Complete the timeline using the information in Mark's online post.

5 Write about a historical period that you are familiar with, including its timeframe, notable people and what it is famous for.

Language in use

Expressing passive voice using 被

1 Look at the sentences.

Subject	Adverb	Verb	Object	Complement
当地的农民		发现了	兵马俑。	
南方人		称	他们自己	为"唐人"。
马克		拿走了	永民的护照。	
弟弟	没	吃	你的饺子。	

Subject	Adverb	Adverbial		Verb	Complement
		被	Doer		
兵马俑		被	当地的农民	发现	了。
南方人		被	(他们自己)	称	为"唐人"。
永民的护照		被	(马克)	拿	走了。
你的饺子	没	被	(弟弟)	吃	了。

Now check the two correct explanations.

☐ 1 被 is used to make a passive sentence, emphasizing the subject being acted upon.

☐ 2 被 can be placed after the verb in the passive voice.

☐ 3 The doer of the action can be omitted in the passive voice.

2 Rewrite the sentences using 被.

1 她吃了我的晚饭。

2 他拿走了我的书。

3 人们称她为"马大姐"。

4 人们称海外中国人住的地方为唐人街。

Expressing a continuing action or state with 着

1 Look at the sentences.

Subject	Verb	Auxiliary word	Complement
这个告示牌上	写	着	“禁止拍照”。
那个告示牌上	写	着	“不得入内”。
桌子上	放	着	两张电影票。
王玉家门口	贴	着	春联。
她	穿	着	一件大衣。

Now check the two correct explanations.

☐ 1 着 is used after a verb to indicate the continuation of an action or a state.

☐ 2 着 is used after a verb only to indicate an ongoing action in the present.

☐ 3 着 is used before the complement of the verb.

2 Write the sentences in Chinese using 着.

1 A book is on the table.
2 I'm wearing a green T-shirt.
3 Two red lanterns are hanging on the gate.

是……的 constructions

1 Look at the sentences.

Subject	是	Time / Place / Manner	Predicate	的
兵马俑	是	什么时候	发现	的？
兵马俑	是	1974 年	发现	的。
这些照片	是	在桂林	拍	的。
你	（是）	怎么	去	的？
我	（是）	坐火车	去	的。
我	不是	坐火车	去	的。

Now check the two correct explanations.

☐ 1 是……的 is used to talk about a certain aspect of a past action or event, such as when, where or how.

☐ 2 是 is usually placed right after the subject and cannot be omitted.

☐ 3 的 is put at the end of the sentence and cannot be omitted.

2 Write questions about the underlined parts of the sentences using 是……的.

1 马克<u>去年</u>去桂林旅行。
2 我在<u>北京</u>认识王玉。
3 安娜<u>坐飞机</u>去新加坡。

Turn to page 165 for grammar reference.

LESSON | 3

Communication activity

1 Work in groups of three. Choose a dynasty from page 74. Find out more about this dynasty and complete the table.

Dynasty	
Time period	
Notable people	
Most important city	
Why it is famous	
Museum(s) to recommend	

Now prepare a presentation about the dynasty. Find pictures to make your presentation interesting.

2 Work with two other groups who chose different dynasties. Give your presentation.

Turn to pages 150 and 156 for more speaking practice.

Cultural corner

Tang poetry

The Tang dynasty represented a golden age for Chinese poetry. Over 40,000 poems by more than 2,000 poets survive from the period, and doubtless many more poems were written at the time. Although centuries old, many Tang poems are still widely read in China today.

Tang poets worked in the ancient style, but also developed new forms requiring great technical skill. The poems of the Tang dynasty have a wide range of subjects, from social concerns to patriotic fervour, encompassing realism, romanticism, natural beauty and personal feelings.

The Tang era saw the birth of some of China's most famous poets, including Li Bai, Du Fu, Wang Wei and Bai Juyi. Poems by these poets and others became the prototypes for centuries of Chinese poetry that followed, and many people in China today can still recite one or two from memory.

Jìng yè sī
静夜思
李白

In the Still of the Night
by Li Bai

Chuáng qián míngyuè guāng 床 前 明月 光，	Bright moonlight at the foot of my bed–
Yí shì dìshàng shuāng 疑是 地上 霜。	Could there have been a frost already?
Jǔtóu wàng míngyuè 举头 望 明月，	Lifting my head, I look to the bright moon.
Dītóu sī gùxiāng 低头思 故乡。	Sinking back again, I think of home.

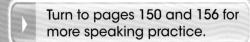

Character writing

These are two common radicals in Chinese. Do you know any other characters with the same radicals?

Radicals	Meaning	Examples
彡	bristle	影、彩
厂	cliff	厅、厨

1 Look at the characters and identify the radicals.

雁　衫　参　厕

2 Match the words with the meanings.

1 参观　　a history
2 历史　　b living room
3 唐三彩　　c visit
4 客厅　　d three-colour glazed pottery of the Tang dynasty

3 Trace the characters in the boxes.

参

彩

历

厅

Review and practice

1 Circle the odd words out.

1 民族	农民	导游	售票员
2 文字	朝代	强盛	海外
3 参观	发现	禁止	安静
4 送	所以	了解	得名

2 Write the sentences in Chinese.

1 My ticket was taken by him.
2 Xi'an is known as an ancient city of history.
3 This story book has been borrowed by Mark.

3 Write two sentences about what you did yesterday.

Now write questions about your sentences using 是……的.

4 Work in pairs. Talk about what you see in the classroom, using 着.

5 Match the meanings with the signs.

1 售票处/在这里买票　2 禁止使用手机
3 安全出口/从这里离开　4 严禁饮食

a

b

c

d

Vocabulary extension

Match the words with the signs.

1 失物 招领 (shīwù zhāolǐng)
2 禁止 饮酒 (jìnzhǐ yǐnjiǔ)
3 禁止 宠物 入内 (jìnzhǐ chǒngwù rù nèi)
4 禁止 吸烟 (jìnzhǐ xīyān)

a

b

c

d

Now work in pairs. Write complete sentences to explain these signs.

Vocabulary review

Fill in the blanks.

安静	ānjìng	*adj.*	silent
被	bèi	*auxiliary word*	(for passive voice)
朝代	cháodài	*n.*	dynasty
称	chēng	*v.*	call; weigh
打井	dǎ jǐng	*v.*	dig a well
当地	dāngdì	*n.*	______
______	dāngshí	*n.*	at that time
导游	dǎoyóu	*n.*	______
得名	démíng	*v.*	get one's name
______	děng	*v.*	wait (for)
发现	fāxiàn	*v.*	______
告示牌	gàoshìpái	*n.*	sign, noticeboard
海外	hǎiwài	*n.*	overseas
______	Hànyǔ	*n.*	Chinese language
汉族	Hànzú	*n.*	Han ethnicity
禁止	jìnzhǐ	*v.*	______
了解	liǎojiě	*v.*	______
民族	mínzú	*n.*	ethnic group
______	nóngmín	*n.*	farmer; rural people
强盛	qiángshèng	*adj.*	______
入口处	rùkǒuchù	*n.*	entrance
声	shēng	*n.*	voice, sound

售票员	shòupiàoyuán	*n.*	______
数	shù	*n.*	______
______	sòng	*v.*	give (as a gift); send
所以	suǒyǐ	*conj.*	______
______	wàn	*num.*	ten thousand
文物	wénwù	*n.*	cultural relic, artefact
______	wénzì	*n.*	writing, script
嘘	xū	*interj.*	shh
于	yú	*prep.*	at, in
______	zhe	*auxiliary word*	(used to indicate continuation of action or state)
证	zhèng	*n.*	certificate
之一	zhīyī	*n.*	______
宠物	chǒngwù	*n.*	pet
入内	rùnèi	*v.*	enter
失物招领	shīwù zhāolǐng		lost and found
吸烟	xīyān	*v.*	smoke tobacco
饮酒	yǐnjiǔ	*v.*	drink alcohol
饮食	yǐnshí	*n./v.*	food and drink; eat and drink

UNIT 7

Sìchuan cài yòu má yòu là

四川菜又麻又辣!

Sichuan food is really spicy!

LESSON | 1

Vocabulary and listening

2-2

1 **Work in pairs. Guess the flavour of each dish using the words in the box.**

má 麻	suān 酸	xián 咸
là 辣	tián 甜	xiāng 香

tángcùyú
a 糖醋鱼

gōngbǎo jīdīng
b 宫保 鸡丁

Now listen and say the words.

2-3

2 **Mark, Yeong-min and Amanda are going out for lunch in Chengdu. Listen to the conversation and answer the questions.**

1 阿曼达喜欢吃什么？
2 为什么马克说他们应该吃川菜？
3 饭馆的拿手菜是什么？

[在出租车上]

马克：你们喜欢吃四川菜吗？
永民：我喜欢。四川菜又麻又辣，很好吃。
阿曼达：你是韩国人，当然喜欢吃辣的。我喜欢吃广东菜，不咸不辣，比较清淡。
马克：上海菜也很好吃，又甜又香。
阿曼达：你不是只爱吃麦当劳和肯德基吗？
马克：虽然我爱吃快餐，但是到了四川，我们就应该吃川菜。
永民：饭馆就要到了。……麻烦你在左边停车。

[在饭馆]

服务员：请问你们几位？
永民：三位。

服务员：这边请。请问三位想喝什么？
马克：先给我来一瓶汽水。
阿曼达：我要一杯苹果汁。
永民：我要一杯水。
服务员：这是菜单。
永民：你们的拿手菜是什么？
服务员：麻婆豆腐、宫保鸡丁，还有水煮鱼。
永民：就要这三个菜吧。
服务员：还要其他菜吗？
阿曼达：炒鸡蛋吧，不辣。再要三碗米饭。麻烦你再给我们三双筷子和三个勺子。
服务员：好的。请稍等，饭菜很快就好。

生词 New words

má 麻	numb, numbing	píng 瓶	bottle
là 辣	spicy, hot	qìshuǐ 汽水	soft drink
Hánguó 韩国	Republic of Korea	bēi 杯	cup, glass
xián 咸	salty	píngguǒ 苹果	apple
qīngdàn 清淡	lightly flavoured	shuǐ 水	water
tián 甜	sweet	càidān 菜单	menu
ài 爱	love, like	chǎo 炒	stir-fry
Màidāngláo 麦当劳	McDonald's	jīdàn 鸡蛋	(chicken) egg
Kěndéjī 肯德基	KFC	wǎn 碗	bowl
máfan 麻烦	bother, trouble	mǐfàn 米饭	rice
zuǒ 左	left side, left	kuàizi 筷子	chopsticks
tíng 停	stop	sháozi 勺子	spoon
wèi 位	(for a person, respectful)	shāo 稍	a little, slightly

2-3

3 Listen again and check the food they ordered.

☐ a tángcùyú 糖醋鱼
☐ b gōngbǎo jīdīng 宫保 鸡丁
☐ c mápódòufu 麻婆豆腐
☐ d shuǐzhǔyú 水煮鱼
☐ e chǎo jīdàn 炒 鸡蛋
☐ f mǐfàn 米饭

4 Match the cuisines with the flavours.

1 四川菜
2 广东菜
3 上海菜

a 又甜又香
b 又麻又辣
c 比较清淡

5 Work in pairs. Ask and answer questions about the kinds of food you like, including the flavours.

Pronunciation and speaking

Difference between "en" and "eng"

2-4

1 Check the correct finals for the underlined characters.

1 很好吃	☐ en	☐ eng
2 肯德基	☐ en	☐ eng
3 请问	☐ en	☐ eng
4 什么	☐ en	☐ eng
5 稍等	☐ en	☐ eng
6 门口	☐ en	☐ eng

Now listen and repeat.

2-5

2 Say the sentences aloud.

Nǐ xǐhuan nǎge chéngshì
1 你 喜欢 哪个 城市 ？

Chéngdū de Chuāncài hěn hǎochī
2 成都 的 川菜 很 好吃。

Qǐng wèn fùjìn yǒu Kěndéjī ma
3 请 问 附近 有肯德基 吗?

Tā zài xuéxiào ménkǒu děng nǐ
4 他 在 学校 门口 等 你。

Qǐng shāo děng yīshēng mǎshàng jiù lái le
5 请 稍 等， 医生 马上 就 来 了。

Now listen and repeat.

2-6

3 Listen and say the words.

1	má 麻	là 辣	qīngdàn 清淡	tián 甜	xián 咸
2	shuǐ 水	chá 茶	qìshuǐ 汽水	guǒzhī 果汁	
3	jiǎozi 饺子	mǐfàn 米饭	jīdàn 鸡蛋	Chuāncài 川菜	

4 Work in groups of three. List some typical Chinese dishes and common drinks you know. Think about their flavour.

Now use your list to create a menu.

5 Act out a conversation at a Chinese restaurant, using your menu from Activity 4.

Student A: You are the waiter. Ask your customers what they would like to eat and drink.
Students B and C: You are the customers. Ask about the flavour of the different dishes and tell the waiter what you would like to eat and drink.

2-7

CHINESE TO GO

Useful expressions in a restaurant

Fúwùyuán 服务员！	Waiter! / Waitress!
Mǎidān Jiézhàng 买单。/ 结帐。	The bill, please.
Dǎbāo 打包。	Pack up this dish to take away.
Wǒ jiào wàimài 我 叫 外卖。	I'd like to order a delivery/takeaway.
Wǒ chī sù 我 吃 素。	I'm a vegetarian.

LESSON | 2

Reading and writing

1 Work in pairs. Tell each other which of the following ingredients your family often use when cooking.

a cōng 葱
b jiāng 姜
c jīròu 鸡肉
d niúròu 牛肉
e zhūròu 猪肉
f suàn 蒜

2-8

2 Read the recipe for mapo tofu and answer the questions.

1 做麻婆豆腐需要哪些原料？

2 应该先炒肉还是先炒豆腐？

学做中国菜——《麻婆豆腐》

[原料]

豆腐300克，牛肉末100克（猪肉或者鸡肉也可以）

油少量，豆瓣酱两勺，花椒粉少量，葱、姜、蒜少量，鸡汤半碗

[时间]

10–15分钟

[做法]

① 把豆腐切成小块，把葱、姜、蒜切成末。

② 把油放在锅里，加热；先放姜，然后放肉，把肉炒熟以后放在碗里。

③ 把油放在锅里，加热；先放葱、姜、蒜和豆瓣酱，炒香；然后放豆腐和肉，炒两分钟；再加入鸡汤，煮五分钟，最后加花椒粉。

麻婆豆腐

生词 New words

yuánliào 原料	ingredient	dòubànjiàng 豆瓣酱	spicy soybean paste	bǎ 把	(used to put the object of a verb before it)	jiārè 加热	heat up
kè 克	gram	huājiāofěn 花椒粉	pepper powder	qiē 切	cut	shú 熟	well done
niúròumò 牛肉末	minced beef	cōng 葱	spring onion	chéng 成	became, turn/change into	jiā 加	add
zhūròu 猪肉	pork	jiāng 姜	ginger	kuài 块	piece	zhǔ 煮	boil
jī 鸡	chicken	suàn 蒜	garlic	fàng 放	put, place	zuìhòu 最后	finally
yóu 油	oil	tāng 汤	soup	guō 锅	wok, pan		
shǎoliàng 少量	small quantity	zuòfǎ 做法	method, cooking steps

qíncài chǎo niúròu
芹菜 炒 牛肉

gōngbǎo jīdīng
宫保 鸡丁

gānbiān dòujiǎo
干煸 豆角

3 Read the recipe again and put the ingredients in the order in which they are used.

- ☐ a 鸡汤
- ☐ b 姜末
- ☐ c 葱、姜、蒜和豆瓣酱
- ☐ d 豆腐和炒熟的肉
- ☐ e 油
- ☐ f 肉末

4 Choose a dish from the pictures on page 84 or 85. Guess the main ingredients and how to make it.

Now write the recipe.

5 Work in pairs. Describe how to make your dish to each other without saying the name of the dish. Guess the name of the dish that is being described.

jiācháng dòufu
家常 豆腐

shuǐzhǔyú
水煮鱼

Language in use

Noun phrases with 的

1 Look at the sentences.

Subject	Verb phrase	Object / Noun phrase		
		Modifier		Head noun
永民	喜欢吃	辣	的	东西。
永民	喜欢吃	辣的。		
我	喜欢	黑色	的	裙子。
她	喜欢	白色的。		
这	不是	你	的	书。
这	不是	我的。		

Now check the two correct explanations.

- ☐ 1 的 is used after a modifier, which is usually a noun, pronoun or an adjective, to form a noun phrase.
- ☐ 2 A noun phrase with 的 should always contain a head noun.
- ☐ 3 The head noun can be left out to avoid repetition if it is known in the context.

2 Write the sentences in Chinese.

1 I don't like red. Do you have black ones?
2 She likes to eat sweet food.
3 I didn't bring my book. Can I borrow yours?

Giving instructions using imperatives

1 Look at the sentences.

Adverbial	Verb	Object/Complement
先	放	姜。
再	加	鸡汤。
	煮	五分钟。
给我	打	电话。

Now check the two correct explanations.

☐ 1 Imperatives are used to give instructions, make requests or raise enquiries.

☐ 2 Subjects are usually omitted from imperatives.

☐ 3 There should always be a verb in an imperative, expressing the action needed.

2 Work in pairs.

Student A: Give two of the following instructions in Chinese.
Student B: Follow Student A's instructions.

1 Go to the front of the room and say your name.
2 Put your Chinese book under your desk.
3 Put your Chinese book on my desk.
4 Open your book and read two sentences aloud.

Now change roles.

把 sentences

1 Look at the sentences.

Subject	把	Object	Verb	Complement
	把	豆腐	切	成小块。
	把	油	放	在锅里。
她	把	被子	拿	出来了。
我	把	书	放	在桌子上。

Now check the two correct explanations.

☐ 1 把 sentences are used to express the result of an action on an object.

☐ 2 The action verb is always put before the object that it acts upon.

☐ 3 A complement should always be used after the action verb.

2 Make sentences, using 把 and the given words.

1 鸡肉 / 切
2 葱 / 放
3 牛肉 / 切
4 中文书 / 放

Turn to page 166 for grammar reference.

LESSON | 3

Communication activity

Work in pairs.

Student A: You want to order a delivery from 辣婆婆 restaurant. Read the menu and decide which dishes you would like.

Student B: You are a new waiter at the restaurant. Familiarize yourself with the menu. Remember to ask the customer for their name, phone number and address when taking the order.

Là pópo
辣婆婆

liángcài
凉菜 Cold dishes

kǒushuǐjī
口水鸡 *** .... yuán 28元
steamed chicken in red chilli oil

fūqī fèipiàn
夫妻肺片 ***sliced beef in chilli sauce .... yuán 25元

wǔxiāng huāshēng
五香 花生 five-spice peanuts .... yuán 8元

Sìchuān pàocài
四川 泡菜 **Sichuan pickled cabbage .... yuán 8 元

rè cài
热菜 Hot dishes

shuǐzhǔ niúròu
水煮 牛肉 ***beef in hot chilli oil .... yuán 48元

gōngbǎo jīdīng
宫保 鸡丁 **Kung Pao chicken .... yuán 22元

mápó dòufu
麻婆 豆腐 ***tofu in spicy sauce .... yuán 12元

chǎo jīdàn
炒 鸡蛋 scrambled eggs .... yuán 8元

suānlàtāng
酸辣汤 **hot-and-sour soup .... yuán 6元

Yángzhōu chǎofàn
扬州 炒饭 Yangzhou fried rice .... yuán 10元

mǐfàn
米饭 rice .... yuán 3元

hěn là
***很辣 very spicy

zhōng là
**中 辣 moderately spicy

wēi là
*微辣 a little spicy

yǐnliào
饮料 Drinks

kělè
可乐 cola .... yuán tīng 5元/ 听

guǒzhī
果汁 fruit juice........................ yuán bēi 8元/杯

píjiǔ
啤酒 beer........................ yuán píng 8元/ 瓶

Now act out a phone conversation making the delivery order.

Turn to pages 151 and 157 for more speaking practice.

Cultural corner

Eating out: ordering shared dishes

Traditionally, Chinese diners choose a collection of dishes to share for the table, rather than ordering individually. Sharing food is not only a great way to try out different dishes, but is also good for balancing the flavours and nutrition of the overall meal. A hot, spicy dish can be balanced by a sweet or a mild one.

Nowadays, communal serving spoons or chopsticks are often used for the shared dishes for reasons of hygiene, rather than picking up the food directly with one's own utensils. While western hosts often let guests serve themselves, Chinese hosts consider it imperative that they urge their guests to eat more, and will even insist on putting food on their guests' plates. "Fighting for the bill" is another act of politeness in Chinese culture that is often performed at the end of a restaurant meal. It is not considered essential to have dessert at the end of a meal, and Chinese menus usually don't have many varieties of dessert.

Character writing

These are two common radicals in Chinese. Do you know any other characters with the same radicals?

Radicals	Meaning	Examples
米	rice	粘、糖
犭	dog, animal	狗、狮

1 Look at the characters and identify the radicals.

料　粉　猪　猫

2 Match the words with the meanings.

1 原料　　a pork
2 花椒粉　b ingredient
3 熊猫　　c pepper powder
4 猪肉　　d panda

3 Trace the characters in the boxes.

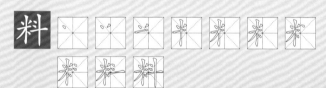

料

粉

猫

猪

Review and practice

1 Complete the conversations.

1 A: 您好! ___________?
B: 三位。
A: ___________。

2 A: 请问，_______________?
B: 我要一瓶汽水。

3 B: _______________?
A: 我们的拿手菜是水煮鱼。

2 Number the steps for cooking spaghetti in the correct order.

☐ a 加肉酱。
☐ b 把煮熟的面拿出来，放在碗里。
☐ c 把意大利面放在开水里，煮15分钟。
☐ d 把水放在锅里，煮开。

3 Work in pairs. Write instructions for how to boil an egg, using 把 sentences when appropriate.

Vocabulary extension

Look at the words for some common drinks.

kāfēi 咖啡	coffee	hóngjiǔ 红酒	red wine
niúnǎi 牛奶	milk	báijiǔ 白酒	rice wine
kělè 可乐	cola	hóngchá 红茶	black tea

Now work in pairs. Ask and answer questions about your favourite drinks for breakfast, lunch and dinner.

Vocabulary review

Fill in the blanks.

_____	ài	*v.*	love, like
把	bǎ	*prep.*	(used to put the object of a verb before it)
_____	bēi	*n.*	cup, glass
菜单	càidān	*n.*	_____
炒	chǎo	*v.*	_____
成	chéng	*v.*	become, turn/ change into
葱	cōng	*n.*	spring onion
豆瓣酱	dòubànjiàng	*n.*	spicy soybean paste
_____	fàng	*v.*	put, place
锅	guō	*n.*	wok, pan
韩国	Hánguó	*n.*	Republic of Korea
花椒粉	huājiāofěn	*n.*	pepper powder
鸡	jī	*n.*	chicken
_____	jīdàn	*n.*	(chicken) egg
_____	jiā	*v.*	add
加热	jiārè	*v.*	_____
姜	jiāng	*n.*	ginger
克	kè	*measure word*	_____
肯德基	Kěndéjī	*n.*	KFC
_____	kuài	*n.*	piece
筷子	kuàizi	*n.*	chopsticks
辣	là	*adj.*	_____
麻	má	*adj.*	numb, numbing
麻烦	máfan	*v.*	_____
麦当劳	Màidāngláo	*n.*	McDonald's
_____	mǐfàn	*n.*	rice
牛肉末	niúròumò	*n.*	_____
_____	píngguǒ	*n.*	apple
瓶	píng	*n.*	bottle

汽水	qìshuǐ	*n.*	_____
切	qiē	*v.*	cut
清淡	qīngdàn	*adj.*	_____
稍	shāo	*adv.*	a little, slightly
_____	sháozi	*n.*	spoon
少量	shǎoliàng	*adj.*	small quantity
熟	shú	*adj.*	_____
_____	shuǐ	*n.*	water
蒜	suàn	*n.*	garlic
_____	tāng	*n.*	soup
甜	tián	*adj.*	_____
_____	tíng	*v.*	stop
碗	wǎn	*n.*	bowl
_____	wèi	*measure word*	(for a person, respectful)
咸	xián	*adj.*	_____
_____	yóu	*n.*	oil
原料	yuánliào	*n.*	ingredients
猪肉	zhūròu	*n.*	pork
煮	zhǔ	*v.*	_____
_____	zuìhòu	*n.*	finally
_____	zuǒ	*n.*	left side, left
做法	zuòfǎ	*n.*	method, cooking steps
白酒	báijiǔ	*n.*	rice wine
红茶	hóngchá	*n.*	black tea
红酒	hóngjiǔ	*n.*	red wine
咖啡	kāfēi	*n.*	coffee
可乐	kělè	*n.*	cola
牛奶	niúnǎi	*n.*	milk
酸	suān	*adj.*	sour

UNIT 8

Kěyǐ piányi yìdiǎnr ma
可以便宜一点儿吗？
Could it be a little cheaper?

LESSON 1

Vocabulary and listening

2-9

1 Check the souvenirs you would like to buy in China.

wánjù ☐ 玩具	tángzhuāng ☐ 唐装
chájù ☐ 茶具	máobǐ ☐ 毛笔

Now listen and say the words.

2-10

2 Mark, Amanda and Yeong-min are at a market in Chengdu. Listen to the conversation and answer the questions.

1 马克为什么要买玩具熊猫？
2 为什么他说售货员的普通话很好？
3 阿曼达跟马克他们一起回宾馆吗？

售货员：你们好！ 进来看一看吧。
马克：小姐，这个熊猫多少钱？
售货员：很便宜，七十块。
马克：太贵了，可以便宜一点儿吗？
售货员：好吧，那就便宜一点儿。五十块怎么样？
阿曼达：我们是学生，钱不多。再便宜一点儿吧。三十块好不好？
售货员：你们真会讲价。三十块卖给你吧。
马克：谢谢。永民，你觉得王玉会喜欢这个熊猫吗？
永民：她一定喜欢！但是你怎么带回去呢？我们的行李已经太多了。
阿曼达：还是邮寄吧。宾馆附近有邮局。我还想给家人寄明信片呢。
售货员：你们是第一次来成都吗？普通话说得不错啊。
马克：你的普通话也很好啊！你说我们的韩国朋友应该买什么纪念品？

售货员：这件唐装怎么样？颜色很好看，很有中国味道。
永民：我可以试一试吗？
售货员：没问题。这件唐装是真丝的，穿着很舒服。
阿曼达：很帅啊！马克、永民，我想去那边看看，我们一会儿在宾馆见。
马克和永民：好，一会儿见！

［在邮局］
马克：麻烦您，我想寄这个包裹到北京。
工作人员：你需要填这张表。你看得懂吗？
马克：没问题。……填完了，给你。
工作人员：先称一下重量。……一点二公斤，平邮七块三毛，空邮十二块八毛。
马克：平邮多长时间？空邮多长时间？
工作人员：平邮两个星期左右，空邮五天就到。
马克：我寄空邮，给你钱。
工作人员：十三块，找你两毛。
马克：谢谢，再见。

2-10

3 Listen again and complete the sentences.

1 售货员说他们很会 ________。
2 马克买的熊猫便宜了 _____ 元。
3 邮局在宾馆的 ________。
4 永民试穿的唐装是 _______ 的。
5 空邮比平邮快 ________ 天。

4 Work in pairs. Act out the conversation.

Student A: You work at a post office.
Student B: You want to send one of the following items from the post office.

1 唐装：寄去日本，0.5公斤，平邮50元，空邮80元
2 茶具：寄去澳大利亚，1公斤，平邮90元，空邮120元

Now change roles.

生词 New words

jiǎngjià 讲价	bargain	jìniànpǐn 纪念品	souvenir	dǒng 懂	understand
mài 卖	sell	tángzhuāng 唐装	traditional Chinese clothes	chēng 称	weigh
yídìng 一定	definitely, for sure	wèidào 味道	taste, feel	zhòngliàng 重量	weight
xíngli 行李	luggage	zhēnsī 真丝	real silk, 100% silk	gōngjīn 公斤	kilogram
yóujì 邮寄	post, send by post	yíhuìr 一会儿	a little while	píngyóu 平邮	ordinary postage, surface mail
míngxìnpiàn 明信片	postcard	bāoguǒ 包裹	parcel, package	máo 毛	Chinese currency unit; *jiao* (coll.)
Pǔtōnghuà 普通话	Mandarin Chinese	biǎo gé 表(格)	form, table	kōngyóu 空邮	air mail

Pronunciation and speaking

The finals: "ian" and "üan"

1 Check the correct finals for the characters.

1 便	☐ ian	☐ üan
2 园	☐ ian	☐ üan
3 点	☐ ian	☐ üan
4 钱	☐ ian	☐ üan

Now listen and repeat.

2 Check the correct finals for the underlined characters.

1 便宜	☐ ian	☐ üan
2 一点儿	☐ ian	☐ üan
3 明信片	☐ ian	☐ üan
4 问卷	☐ ian	☐ üan
5 纪念品	☐ ian	☐ üan
6 医院	☐ ian	☐ üan

Now listen and repeat.

3 Say the sentences aloud.

Túshūguǎn de qiánbian yǒu jǐ gè yǎnyuán
1 图书馆 的 前边 有 几个 演员。

Wǒ xiǎng zuò zhìyuànzhě huòzhě yùndòngyuán
2 我 想 做 志愿者 或者 运动员。

Wáng Yù zài gōngyuán mén kǒu tián wènjuàn
3 王 玉 在 公园 门 口 填 问卷。

Mǎ Yuán mǎi de jìniànpǐn hěn piányi
4 马 园 买 的 纪念品 很 便宜。

Now listen and repeat.

4 Listen and say the words and expressions.

1 jìniànpǐn 纪念品 wánjù 玩具 míngxìnpiàn 明信片

2 wèidào 味道 zhēnsī 真丝 shūfu 舒服 hǎokàn 好看

3 Tài guì le 太贵了！ Piányi yìdiǎnr ba 便宜一点儿吧。

5 Work in pairs.

Student A: Find five items in your bag that you would like to sell, and decide the price of each item.
Student B: Choose three items you would like to buy from Student A, and bargain for the lowest possible price for each one.

Now change roles.

CHINESE TO GO

Shopping expressions

Zhège zěnme mài 这个 怎么 卖？	How much is this?
Shí kuài qián yì jīn 十 块 钱 一 斤。	Ten yuan per 500 grams.
Kěyǐ dǎzhé ma 可以 打折 吗？	Can you give any discount?
Dǎ qī zhé 打 七 折。	30% off.
Yǒu yōuhuì ma 有 优惠 吗？	Is there a special offer?
Mǎi yī sòng yī 买 一 送 一。	Buy one, get one free.

LESSON 2

Reading and writing

1 Match the nouns with the appropriate descriptions.

1	gǎnjué 感觉	a	hěn dìdao 很 地道
2	yàngzi 样子	b	hěn piàoliang 很 漂亮
3	chájù 茶具	c	shūfu 舒服
4	Chuāncài 川菜	d	hěn shuài 很 帅

2-16

2 Read Amanda's email to Wang Yu about her visit to Chengdu.

生词 New words

zuótiān	昨天	yesterday
jiā	家	(used for families or companies)
lǎo	老	old
dìdao	地道	typical, authentic
diǎn	点	order
yuè	越	more
bùdébù	不得不	have no choice, have to
gǎnjué	感觉	feel; feelings
búguò	不过	however, but
pà	怕	be afraid, fear
suǒyǒu	所有	all
guāng	光	used up, all gone
yàngzi	样子	appearance, look
tào	套	set
chájù	茶具	tea set
qízhōng	其中	among
gàosu	告诉	tell
Zhù hǎo	祝 好!	Best wishes.

邮件转移至　　确认　删除

邮箱 | 通讯录 | 相册 | 　　| 邮箱设置 | 帮助 |

王玉:

你好!

我和马克、永民已经到了成都。成都有很多好玩的景点,我们都玩得很开心。昨天晚上我们去了市中心附近的一家饭馆吃饭,饭馆的名字叫"老成都",听说那里的川菜很地道。我们点了麻婆豆腐、宫保鸡丁,还有水煮鱼。开始吃的时候觉得味道很好,但是越吃越辣,最后我不得不喝了一大杯水,才感觉好一些。不过,马克和永民不怕辣,所有的菜很快就吃光了。

今天下午我们去市场买东西,那里的东西又多又便宜。永民买了一件唐装,他穿唐装的样子很帅。我看到这套茶具和这条围巾,很漂亮,我想买其中的一件送给你妈妈。你能告诉我你妈妈喜欢茶具还是围巾吗?

祝好!

阿曼达

发送

3 Choose the correct answers to the questions.

1 What is the first paragraph mainly about?

☐ a 吃川菜
☐ b 喝水
☐ c 到成都

2 What is the main idea of the second paragraph?

☐ a 市场的东西又多又便宜
☐ b 永民穿唐装的样子
☐ c 买茶具还是围巾

4 Read again and check the true statements.

☐ 1 "老成都" 离市中心很近。
☐ 2 阿曼达不怕辣。
☐ 3 她不喜欢永民穿唐装的样子。
☐ 4 她想买东西送给王玉的妈妈。

5 Write an email to a friend about a recent shopping experience. Make sure you mention

- the time and place
- what happened
- your feelings about it.

Use Amanda's email in Activity 2 to help you.

Language in use

Duplication of verbs

1 Look at the sentences.

Subject	Modal verb	Verb phrase	Object
		听听	音乐吧。
		看一看吧。	
我	可以	试一试吗?	

Now check the two correct explanations.

☐ 1 The duplication of verbs is used to soften your tone when making suggestions or requests.
☐ 2 The duplication of verbs creates a more forceful tone in suggestions or requests.
☐ 3 一 can be added between the duplicated verbs to express a mild tone.

2 Write the sentences in Chinese, using duplicated verbs.

1 Can you talk a bit about the history of Sydney?
2 I would like to have a walk in the park.
3 You should take a look at this book.

"The more… the more…" 越……越……

1 Look at the sentences.

Subject	越	Verb / Adjective	越	Verb phrase / Adjective phrase
我	越	吃	越	想吃。
马克	越	走	越	快。
她	越	想	越	不开心。
钱	越	多	越	好。

Now check the two correct explanations.

☐ 1 越……越…… is used to indicate that one thing increases as something else continues or increases.

☐ 2 越 can be followed by a verb or an adjective.

☐ 3 Words linked by 越……越…… must be of the same part of speech.

2 Write sentences using 越……越…… and the given words.

1 他 / 长 / 高

2 我 / 说 / 高兴

3 她 / 跑 / 热

Notional passive

1 Look at the sentences.

Topic	Comment		
	Adverbial	Verb	Complement
表		填	完了。
所有的菜	很快就	吃	光了。
他的作业	还没有	写。	
钱	没	用	光。
书		放	在家里了。

Now check the two correct explanations.

☐ 1 In a notional passive, no passive marker such as 被 is used, even though the doer of the action is not stated.

☐ 2 Notional passive is only used when the doer of the action is not known in the context.

☐ 3 The particle 了 is used in a positive sentence, but not in a negative sentence with 没.

2 Write the sentences in Chinese, using notional passive.

1 My homework is finished.

2 The clothes have not been washed yet.

3 All the souvenirs have sold out.

4 The coat is not ready yet.

Turn to page 167 for grammar reference.

LESSON | 3

Communication activity

1 Work in two groups.

Group A: You are souvenir sellers. Look at the souvenirs, and decide a price for each item.
Group B: You have a budget of RMB200 to buy three souvenirs.

2 Imagine you are at the market. Group A stand at different "stalls" (desks) around the classroom. Group B walk around the "market".

Group A: Offer the souvenirs to customers, and bargain for the best price with them. Give reasons for your price if necessary. For example,

- 质量很好 good quality
- 颜色很漂亮 pretty colour
- 很有中国味道 very Chinese
- 很便宜 very cheap

Group B: Bargain for the best price for the items you want to buy. Give reasons for a lower price. For example,

- 不太好 not very good
- 不够漂亮 not pretty enough
- 太贵了 too expensive

3 Work with the whole class. Find out who made the most money and who got the best deals.

Turn to pages 151 and 157 for more speaking practice.

Cultural corner

Teahouses in Chengdu and *Longmen Zhen*

Teahouses are popular in many areas of China. Teahouses function as entertainment centres, community centres and as places for get-togethers and even business meetings. The city of Chengdu boasts a unique teahouse culture. You can find teahouses everywhere in Chengdu. People in the city, especially the elderly, not only enjoy drinking tea there, but also spend hours chatting, playing games, reading newspaper, eating snacks, and listening to storytellers. This kind of activity is known as "Longmen Zhen" (龙门阵). The word has its origins in the Tang dynasty, when a general named Xue Rengui (薛仁贵) invented a battle formation called "Longmen Zhen". The name implies that every teahouse in Chengdu is like a battlefield, bustling with endless activity!

Character writing

These are two common radicals in Chinese. Do you know any other characters with the same radicals?

Radicals	Meaning	Examples
走	walk	走、超
刂	knife	剧、别

1 Look at the characters and identify the radicals.

刻　赵　刷　赶

2 Match the words with the meanings.

1 拿到　　a toothbrush
2 起床　　b the more ... the more ...
3 越……越……　　c get up
4 牙刷　　d get, take to

3 Trace the characters in the boxes.

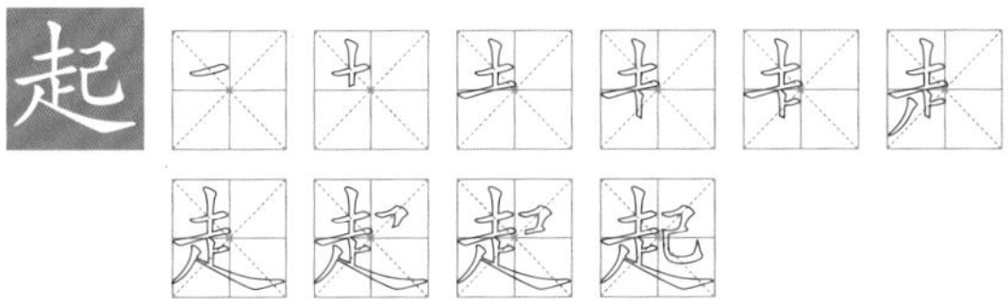

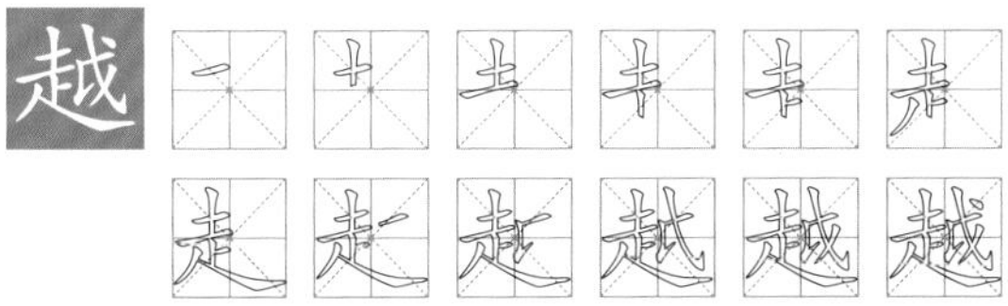

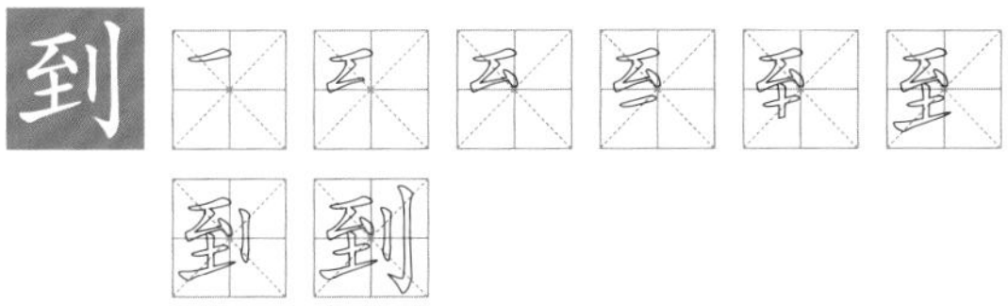

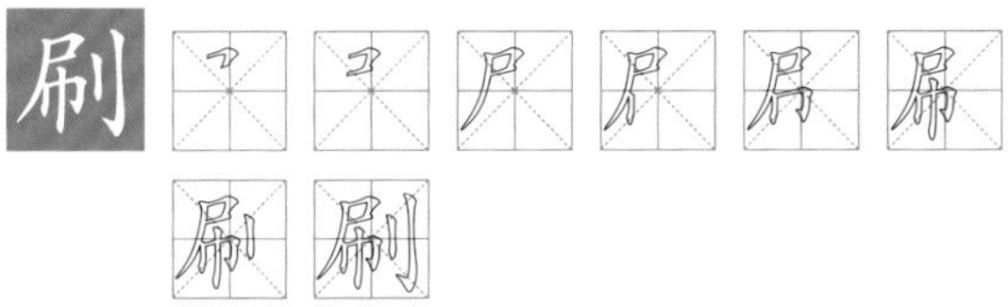

Review and practice

1 Put the sentences in the correct order to make a conversation.

a 太贵了，可以便宜一点儿吗？
b 太少了。一百块吧。
c 这件衣服多少钱？
d 再便宜一点吧。九十块，怎么样？
e 一百八。
f 那好吧。给你钱。
g 一百五卖给你吧。

2 Work in pairs. Take turns to make three suggestions with the given verbs, using a softened tone.

1 试　　2 用　　3 看

3 Rewrite the sentences using notional passive.

1 所有的菜都被他们吃光了。
2 马克填完了这张表。
3 小王准备好行李了。

4 Write two sentences to describe each picture, using 越……越…….

a

b

Vocabulary extension

Match the words with the objects in the picture.

1 皮带 pídài	2 手表 shǒubiǎo	3 领带 lǐngdài
4 钱包 qiánbāo	5 皮鞋 píxié	6 记事本 jìshìběn

Now work in pairs. Ask and answer questions about how much you have paid for these items.

Vocabulary review

Fill in the blanks.

包裹	bāoguǒ	*n.*	parcel, package
表(格)	biǎogé	*n.*	______
不得不	bùdébù		have no choice, have to
______	búguò	*conj.*	however, but
茶具	chájù	*n.*	______
地道	dìdao	*adj.*	______
______	diǎn	*v.*	order
______	dǒng	*v.*	understand
感觉	gǎnjué	*v./n.*	______
______	gàosu	*v.*	tell
______	gōngjīn	*measure word*	kilogram
光	guāng	*adj.*	used up, all gone
纪念品	jìniànpǐn	*n.*	______
______	jiā	*measure word*	(used for families or companies)
讲价	jiǎngjià	*v.*	______
空邮	kōngyóu	*v.*	air mail
______	lǎo	*adj.*	old
______	mài	*v.*	sell
毛	máo	*measure word*	Chinese currency unit; *jiao* (coll.)
明信片	míngxìnpiàn	*n.*	______
______	pà	*v.*	be afraid, fear
平邮	píngyóu	*v.*	ordinary postage, surface mail

普通话	Pǔtōnghuà	*n.*	______
其中	qízhōng	*n.*	______
______	suǒyǒu	*adj.*	all
唐装	tángzhuāng	*n.*	traditional Chinese clothes
套	tào	*n.*	set
味道	wèidào	*n.*	______
行李	xíngli	*n.*	______
样子	yàngzi	*n.*	appearance, look
______	yídìng	*adv.*	definitely, for sure
一会儿	yíhuìr	*n.*	______
邮寄	yóujì	*v.*	post, send by post
越	yuè	*adv.*	more
真丝	zhēnsī	*n.*	real silk, 100% silk
重量	zhòngliàng	*n.*	______
祝好！	Zhù hǎo		Best wishes.
______	zuótiān	*n.*	yesterday
记事本	jìshìběn	*n.*	notebook
领带	lǐngdài	*n.*	tie
毛笔	máobǐ	*n.*	writing brush
皮带	pídài	*n.*	belt
皮鞋	píxié	*n.*	leather shoes
钱包	qiánbāo	*n.*	wallet
手表	shǒubiǎo	*n.*	watch
玩具	wánjù	*n.*	toy

Review 2

Vocabulary

1 Match the activity with the place where it happens.

1 买票 a 市场
2 讲价 b 饭馆
3 登记入住 c 售票处
4 点菜 d 博物馆
5 参观文物 e 宾馆

2 Complete the phrases with the correct measure words.

1 一 ____ 衣柜
2 一 ____ 被子
3 一 ____ 毛巾
4 两 ____ 门票
5 两 ____ 米饭
6 三 ____ 汽水
7 三 ____ 筷子
8 一 ____ 唐装

3 Write three sentences to describe where the furniture is.

4 Write five sentences to describe what you usually do in the morning.

Grammar

1 Put the words in brackets in the correct places to complete the sentences.

1 你可以被子拿出来吗？（把）
2 我的书小王拿走了。（被）
3 他家的门口挂红灯笼。（着）
4 我的房间有三米，两米。(长/宽)

2 Write questions for the answers.

1 A: ____________________?
B: 古城墙有600多年的历史。

2 A: ____________________?
B: 我奶奶已经80多岁了。

3 A: ____________________?
B: 从北京到香港坐飞机要三个小时。

4 A: ____________________?
B: 因为海外的中国人称他们自己为唐人。

5 A: ____________________?
B: 这个兵马俑有两米高。

3 Complete the sentences with the words in the box.

虽然　越……越……　所以　够

1 他昨天回家了，_____没有参加派对。

2 这个宾馆的床_____大，有两米宽。

3 马克的中文_____说_____好。

4 _____这里的麻婆豆腐很好吃，但是我不舒服，不能吃辣的。

4 Make sentences using the given words.

1 桌子 / 衣柜 / 旁边

2 被子 / 不够 / 暖和

3 衣服 / 洗 / 好

4 兵马俑 / 发现 / 农民

5 冬天 / 很冷 / 穿大衣

6 因为……所以……

7 告示牌 / 安静 / 着

8 筷子 / 放 / 桌子 / 把

9 公园 / 走一走

10 是……的

11 被 / 这本书 / 借

12 体育场 / 长 / 宽

5 Write a sentence to describe each picture using 把 sentences.

1

2

3

4

Now rewrite your sentences using 被.

Integrated skills

2-17

1 Listen and choose the correct answers to the questions.

1 他什么时候去吃川菜了？

a 今天 b 昨天

2 她买了什么？

a 一条围巾 b 一套茶具

3 他觉得麻婆豆腐的味道怎么样？

a 太辣了 b 很好吃

4 她点了什么菜？

a 炒饭 b 果汁

5 中文故事书在哪里？

a 桌子的旁边 b 书柜的最上面

6 宾馆的服务怎么样？

a 很舒服 b 不够好

7 房子的门口挂着什么？

a 告示牌 b “不得进入”

8 平邮比空邮慢多少？

a 两天 b 五天

2 Work in pairs. Put the sentences in the correct order to make a conversation.

a 很好玩。成都有很多好玩的景点。

b 你最喜欢哪个景点？

c 很好。我们已经去过西安，现在我们在成都。

d 对了，你们吃川菜了吗？

e 西安怎么样？

f 很不错。到了西安，才感觉到这里是真正的历史古城。

g 你们参观了什么景点？

h 我最喜欢兵马俑。那些兵马俑看起来像真的一样！

i 成都好玩吗？

j 吃过了。川菜又麻又辣，很好吃，但是我怕辣，不能吃太多。

k 阿曼达，你们的旅游怎么样？

l 我们参观了兵马俑、古城墙、钟楼和陕西历史博物馆。

The correct order is ________________

3 **Write five sentences to describe the locations of the rooms in the flat, using 有/是, 旁边 and 对面.**

4 **Work in pairs. Write a conversation of six sentences for the people in each picture.**

a

b

Now act out the conversations.

Enjoy Chinese

Guess what these ancient Chinese characters resemble.

1  a 草

2  b 木

3  c 又

4  d 口

5  e 大

6  f 耳

Now match the ancient characters with the modern ones.

UNIT 9

Zhèlǐ de fēngjǐng měi jí le
这里的风景美极了！

The scenery here is amazing!

LESSON | 1

Vocabulary and listening

2-18 **1 Look at the picture below and check the things that you can find in it.**

hú ☐ 湖	lántiān ☐ 蓝天
shān ☐ 山	shítou ☐ 石头
niǎo ☐ 鸟	shùmù ☐ 树木

Now listen and say the words.

2-19 **2 Mark, Yeong-min and Amanda are at Jiuzhaigou Valley. Listen to the conversation and answer the questions.**

1 为什么马克说“书店应该退钱”？

2 马克喜欢这个地方吗？永民呢？

马克：今天天气真好。

永民：这里的风景美极了！

阿曼达：是啊。这个湖特别漂亮。

永民：看，湖水刚才是蓝色的，现在变成了绿色。

马克：旅游书上说这个湖叫“五彩池”，应该有五种颜色啊。我现在只看到蓝色和绿色两种。书店应该退钱！

阿曼达：哈哈，真好笑。那边的湖水有很多种颜色，看到了吗？

马克：看到了！蓝天、白云、五彩的湖水和绿色的山，真美。

阿曼达：像一幅画。

马克：我很喜欢这种自然风景。这里的山特别美，和澳大利亚的山完全不一样。

永民：和韩国的山也不一样，很特别。我第一次看到这种山水。

阿曼达：我也喜欢这里，空气又好，又安静。听到了吗？鸟儿在唱歌。

马克：哈哈，没错。在城市里听不到。

永民：看，这是我拍的照片。你们觉得怎么样？

阿曼达：不错。给我们照张相吧。

永民：没问题。一二三，笑一笑。

生词 New words

fēngjǐng 风景	scenery	hǎoxiào 好笑	funny
měi jí le 美极了	amazing	shān 山	mountain, hill
měi 美	beautiful	túhuà 图画	picture
hú pō 湖(泊)	lake	zìrán 自然	nature
tèbié 特别	especially, particularly	wánquán 完全	completely; entire
gāngcái 刚才	just now, a moment ago	shānshuǐ 山水	scenery
biànchéng 变成	change into	niǎo 鸟	bird
lǚyóu 旅游	tour; tourism	méicuò 没错	right
cǎi 彩	colour	cuò 错	wrong
chí 池	pond, pool	zhàoxiàng 照相	take a photo
zhǒng 种	kind, type	xiào 笑	smile, laugh
tuìqián 退钱	refund		

2-19

3 Listen again and check the true statements.

- ☐ 1 "五彩池" 的湖水只有蓝和绿两种颜色。
- ☐ 2 阿曼达不喜欢听到鸟叫。
- ☐ 3 永民拍的照片很漂亮。
- ☐ 4 永民让阿曼达给他拍照。

4 Work in pairs. Look carefully at the picture. You have 30 seconds to memorize as many details as possible.

Now close your book. Describe the picture to your partner from memory and see who gets the most correct details.

Pronunciation and speaking

Difference between "j" and "z"

2-20

1 Check the correct initials for the characters.

1 在	☐ j	☐ z
2 叫	☐ j	☐ z
3 就	☐ j	☐ z
4 怎	☐ j	☐ z
5 最	☐ j	☐ z

Now listen and repeat.

2-21

2 Check the correct initials for the underlined characters.

1 风景	☐ j	☐ z
2 美极了	☐ j	☐ z
3 房子	☐ j	☐ z
4 看见	☐ j	☐ z
5 安静	☐ j	☐ z
6 几个	☐ j	☐ z

Now listen and repeat.

2-22

3 Read the sentences aloud.

Zhèlǐ de fēngjǐng měi jí le
1 这里的 风景 美 极了!

Zhè tào fángzi yǒu jǐ gè fángjiān
2 这 套 房子 有 几个 房间?

Wǒ zuótiān zǒulù qù xuéxiào
3 我 昨天 走路 去 学校。

Nàge jìzhě zǒu jìn le zuǒbian de fángjiān
4 那个 记者 走 进 了 左边 的 房间。

Chūnjié shì Hànzúrén zuì zhòngyào de jiérì
5 春节 是 汉族人 最 重要 的 节日。

Now listen and repeat.

2-23

4 Listen and say the words.

1	zìrán 自然	fēngjǐng 风景	túhuà 图画	shānshuǐ 山水
2	tèbié 特别	yīnggāi 应该	wánquán 完全	gāngcái 刚才
3	zhàoxiàng 照相	ānjìng 安静	méicuò 没错	biànchéng 变成

5 Complete the table with information about a beautiful place you have visited.

在哪里	
山水的特点	

我觉得______________________

Now work in pairs. Ask and answer questions about the places you have chosen.

CHINESE TO GO

2-24

Questions to ask a tour guide

Xíngchéng shì shénme 行程 是 什么?	What's the itinerary?
Háiyǒu duō yuǎn 还有 多 远?	How far away is it?
Zài zhèlǐ dāi duō jiǔ 在这里呆 多 久?	How long are we going to stay here?
Kěyǐ zìyóu huódòng ma 可以自由 活动 吗?	Can I look around by myself?
Jǐ diǎn Zài nǎr jíhé 几点/在哪儿集合?	What time/Where do we meet up?
Yǒu shénme tèchǎn 有 什么 特产?	What special local products are there?

LESSON 2

Reading and writing

1 Work in pairs. Check the things you would expect to find at a nature reserve.

☐ gāoshān 高山	☐ sēnlín 森林
☐ pùbù 瀑布	☐ shùmù 树木
☐ héliú 河流	☐ lántiān 蓝天
☐ húpō 湖泊	☐ báiyún 白云

2-25

2 Read the flyer about the Wolong Reserves and Jiuzhaigou Valley.

生词 New words

bǎohùqū 保护区	nature reserve	pùbù 瀑布	waterfall
wèiyú 位于	be located in	sēnlín 森林	forest
zhàn 占	occupy, make up	fēicháng 非常	very, extremely
zǒngshù 总数	total number	rénjiān 人间	(human) world, the earth
bǎifēnzhī 百分之	percent	xiānjìng 仙境	paradise
xiāng 乡	hometown, countryside	qīngchè 清澈	clear
chúle 除了…… yǐwài 以外	except for, besides	dǐ 底	bottom
		shùmù 树木	trees
bǎohù 保护	protect; protection	dàoyìng 倒映	reflect, mirror
zhíwù 植物	plant	jīchǎng 机场	airport

卧龙保护区

卧龙保护区位于成都的西北，离成都大约一百三十公里。保护区里有一百多只大熊猫，占全国总数的百分之十，所以被称为“熊猫之乡”。

除了大熊猫以外，保护区里还有很多其他受国家保护的动物和植物。

交通　旅游车（成都—卧龙）三小时

九寨沟

九寨沟离成都四百多公里。这里的雪山、瀑布、湖泊和森林非常漂亮，被称为“人间仙境”。

九寨沟里有一百多个大大小小的湖泊。其中的五彩池清澈见底，蓝天、白云和树木倒映在水中，五颜六色，美极了。九寨沟里还有很多瀑布，其中最大的瀑布宽二百米，高四十多米。

交通　飞机（成都—九黄机场）45分钟
旅游车（成都—九寨沟）10小时

3 Check the true statements.

- ☐ 1 保护区里的动植物受国家保护。
- ☐ 2 从成都到卧龙坐旅游车要三个小时。
- ☐ 3 九寨沟比较远，但是可以坐飞机去。
- ☐ 4 九寨沟里有一百多个瀑布。

4 Read the flyer again and complete the table.

	卧龙保护区	九寨沟
在哪里		
被称为		
特点		
交通		

Now work in pairs. Discuss and decide which place you would like to visit together.

我想去 ________ 旅游，因为……

5 Design a travel flyer for a place you know well. Include where it is, what there is to see, how to get there and why it is special.

Language in use

Expressing result of an action with 到

1 Look at the sentences.

Subject	Adverbial	Verb	到	Object
我	第一次	看	到	这种山水。
你		找	到	书了吗？
马克		买	(不)到	火车票。

Now check the two correct explanations.

- ☐ 1 到 is used after a verb to express the result of an action.
- ☐ 2 A noun or noun phrase serving as the object must always be used after 到 to say what or who was involved in the action.
- ☐ 3 不 is used before the verb to express a negative result.

2 Complete the sentences, using 到 and the given words.

1 ________，你可以大声一点儿吗？（听）
2 你妈妈来学校了，________？（见）
3 ________，你可以帮一下我吗？（找）

Expressing percentages using 百分之……

1 Look at the sentences.

Subject	Verb	Adjective phrase	Percentage
这里的熊猫	占	全国总数的	百分之十。
中文作业	占	(所有作业的)	百分之三十。
他的朋友	占	(派对人数的)	百分之五十。

Now check the two correct explanations.

- [ ] 1 A percentage is expressed by adding the character for a number after 百分之.
- [ ] 2 The verb 占 is used before an adjective phrase to explain what it is a proportion of.
- [ ] 3 An adjective phrase must be used in a sentence expressing a percentage.

2 Write the sentences, using 百分之…… and the given words.

1 女学生 / 学校人数 / 百分之五十
2 玩游戏 / 你的时间 / 百分之三十
3 当地人 / 工作人员 / 百分之九十

除了……以外，还……

1 Look at the sentences.

除了……以外	Subject	还	Verb	Object
除了大熊猫以外，	这里	还	有	很多受国家保护的动物和植物。
除了报纸以外，	永民	还	买了	一些故事书。
除了购物以外，	她	还	喜欢	拍照。

Now check the two correct explanations.

- [ ] 1 除了……以外 means "in addition to" or "besides" when it is used together with 还.
- [ ] 2 除了……以外 means "except" or "apart from" when it is used together with 还.
- [ ] 3 The word after 除了 must express things of the same nature as the topic of the main clause after 还.

2 Complete the sentences.

除了 ________，我还喜欢 ________。
除了 ________，我每天还要 ________。
除了 ________，我们还一起 ________。

Turn to page 168 for grammar reference.

LESSON | 3

Communication activity

1 Work in groups. You are the activity coordinators for a group of Chinese students visiting your school. You are planning a day trip for them to a place of natural beauty.

- Choose a destination and write a plan. Describe the natural features and why it is so beautiful.
- Prepare a presentation about your planned trip.

2 Give your presentation to the class.

Now vote for the best plan.

Turn to pages 152 and 158 for more speaking practice.

Cultural corner

Famous mountains in China

China has many scenic mountain regions, but some peaks are better known than others, and are among the most visited sites in the country.

There are two sets of holy mountains in China: one associated with Taoism and one with Buddhism. The Four Sacred Mountains of Buddhism (四大佛教名山) are Wutai Shan 五台山, Emei Shan 峨嵋山, Jiuhua Shan 九华山 and Putuo Shan 普陀山. These mountains are home to famous Buddhist monasteries and are major sites of pilgrimage.

Each of the Taoist "Five Great Mountains" (五岳) is associated with one of the traditional Chinese cardinal directions: Tai Shan 泰山 with the east, Hua Shan 华山 with the west, Heng Shan 衡山 in Hunan with the south, Heng Shan 恒山 in Shanxi with the north and 嵩山 Song Shan with the centre. Tai Shan is therefore also known as 东岳 ("east great mountain"), Song Shan as 中岳 ("central great mountain") and so on.

Huangshan 黄山 in Anhui Province is noted for its natural beauty rather than religious significance, and ever since the Qin dynasty it has been considered one of the most beautiful locations in China. A well-known saying goes 五岳归来不看山，黄山归来不看岳 – "When you come back from the Five Great Mountains, you won't want to look at ordinary mountains any more. When you return from Huangshan, you won't want to see the Five Great Mountains."

Character writing

These are two common radicals in Chinese. Do you know any other characters with the same radicals?

Radicals	Meaning	Examples
寸	inch	寺、时
阝(left)	mound	院、阳

1 Look at the characters and identify the radicals.

对　导　阿　降

2 Match the words with the meanings.

1 除了	a tour guide
2 下降	b sorry
3 导游	c except
4 对不起	d decrease

3 Trace the characters in the boxes.

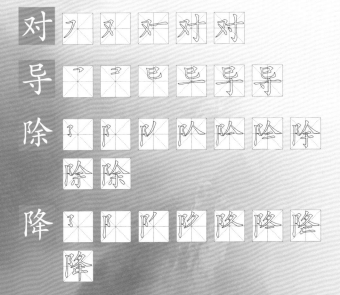

对

导

除

降

Review and practice

1 Circle the odd words out.

1 瀑布	森林	风景	雪山
2 保护	自然	变成	倒映
3 完全	特别	非常	植物
4 好笑	美极了	不错	位于

2 Write three sentences to describe the picture.

3 Write three sentences that you might say about the picture above, using 看到, 想到 and 找到.

4 Write three sentences about your school or country using 百分之…….

5 Write three sentences about yourself using 除了……以外, 还…….

Vocabulary extension

Match the words with things in the picture.

a 海滩 (hǎitān)　　b 悬崖 (xuányá)

c 岛 (dǎo)　　d 海浪 (hǎilàng)

Now work in pairs. Talk about a place you know that have the above things/features.

Vocabulary review

Fill in the blanks.

百分之	bǎifēnzhī	*n.*	percent
保护	bǎohù	*v./n.*	________
保护区	bǎohùqū	*n.*	nature reserve
____	biànchéng	*v.*	change into
彩	cǎi	*n.*	colour
池	chí	*n.*	________
除了……以外	chúle... yǐwài	*prep.*	except for, besides
____	cuò	*adj.*	wrong
倒映	dàoyìng	*v.*	reflect, mirror
底	dǐ	*n.*	bottom
____	fēicháng	*adv.*	very, extremely
风景	fēngjǐng	*n.*	scenery
____	gāngcái	*n.*	just now, a moment ago
好笑	hǎoxiào	*adj.*	________
湖(泊)	hú pō	*n.*	lake
____	jīchǎng	*n.*	airport
旅游	lǚyóu	*v.*	________
没错	méicuò		________
____	měi	*adj.*	beautiful
美极了	měi jí le		amazing
____	niǎo	*n.*	bird
瀑布	pùbù	*n.*	________
清澈	qīngchè	*adj.*	clear
人间	rénjiān	*n.*	(human) world, the earth
____	sēnlín	*n.*	forest
____	shān	*n.*	mountain, hill
山水	shānshuǐ	*n.*	________
树木	shùmù	*n.*	________
特别	tèbié	*adv.*	especially, particularly
____	túhuà	*n.*	picture
退钱	tuìqián	*v.*	________
____	wánquán	*adv./adj.*	completely; entire
位于	wèiyú	*v.*	________
仙境	xiānjìng	*n.*	paradise
乡	xiāng	*n.*	hometown, countryside
____	xiào	*v.*	________
占	zhàn	*v.*	occupy, make up
____	zhàoxiàng	*v.*	take a photo
植物	zhíwù	*n.*	________
种	zhǒng	*measure word*	kind, type
____	zìrán	*n.*	nature
总数	zǒngshù		________
岛	dǎo	*n.*	island
海浪	hǎilàng	*n.*	wave
海滩	hǎitān	*n.*	beach
河流	héliú	*n.*	river
石头	shítou	*n.*	stone
悬崖	xuányá	*n.*	cliff

UNIT 10

Tā zhǎng shénme yàngzi

她 长 什么 样子？

What does she look like?

LESSON | 1

Vocabulary and listening

2-26

1 Work in pairs. Discuss which adjectives can be used to describe the people in the picture below.

	gèzi	gāo	ǎi	zhōngděng
1	个子：	高	矮	中等
	shēncái	pàng	shòu	miáotiao
2	身材：	胖	瘦	苗条
	tóufa	cháng	duǎn	
3	头发：	长	短	
		hēisè	hèsè	jīnsè
		黑色	褐色	金色

Now listen and say the words.

2-27

2 At the hotel, Amanda talks about some new friends she has made. Listen to the conversation and answer the questions.

1 阿曼达一会儿要做什么？
2 为什么马克问她的新朋友长什么样子？
3 马克和永民会一起去酒吧吗？

阿曼达：我回来了！你们俩在做什么？
永民：我们在看电视。你买了什么纪念品？
阿曼达：我给家人买了一些丝巾和明信片。对了，我还认识了两个新朋友。
马克：真的？
阿曼达：我一会儿要去咖啡店跟她们见面。你们去不去？
永民：我不太想去，坐在这里看电视很舒服。
阿曼达：我的新朋友都是女孩。
永民：那个咖啡店在附近吗？
阿曼达：啊，现在你有兴趣了！咖啡店在宾馆后面，离这里很近，走路五分钟就到了。

生词 New words

liǎ 俩	two (coll.)	jīnsè 金色	golden, blond(e)
diànshì 电视	TV	tóufa 头发	hair
sījīn 丝巾	silk scarf	yǎnjing 眼睛	eye
duì le 对了	by the way, that's right	zhōngděng 中等	medium
kāfēi 咖啡	coffee	miáotiao 苗条	slim, slender
nǚhái 女孩	girl	lìng 另	other, another
xìngqù 兴趣	interest	duǎn 短	short (length)
zhǎng 长	grow, develop	ǎi 矮	short (height)
Déguó 德国	Germany	pàng 胖	plump, fat
liúxuéshēng 留学生	overseas student	zhòngyào 重要	important

马克：你的新朋友长什么样子？

阿曼达：一个叫丽莎，是德国留学生。她有金色的长头发，蓝色的眼睛，中等个子，很苗条。另一个叫孙玉香，是上海人。她的头发比较短，个子不高不矮，她比丽莎胖一点儿。

马克：听起来很有趣，但是你还没说最重要的。

阿曼达：什么是最重要的？

永民：马克最想知道她们漂亮不漂亮，还有她们有没有男朋友！

阿曼达：我要走了。如果你们想知道，就跟我来吧。

2-27

3 Listen again and check the true statements.

- ☐ 1 丽莎的个子不高也不矮。
- ☐ 2 丽莎比玉香瘦一点儿。
- ☐ 3 玉香的头发和丽莎的一样长。
- ☐ 4 永民想知道她们有没有男朋友。

4 Work in pairs.

Student A: Choose a person in the pictures on page 114 or 115 and answer Student B's questions.
Student B: Ask questions about the person's appearance and guess who it is.

Now change roles.

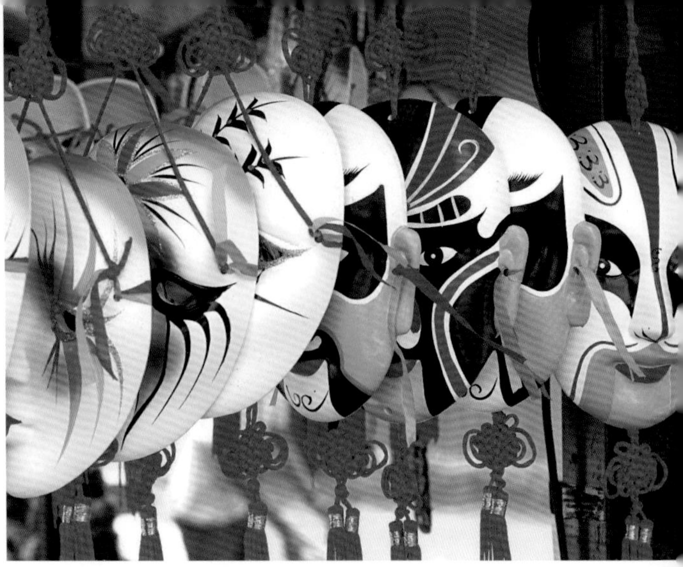

Pronunciation and speaking

The neutral tone

2-28

1 Look at the tone marks. How do they change?

1	xiǎngxiang 想想	4	kànkan 看看
2	shìshi 试试	5	shénme 什么
3	shuōshuo 说说	6	nǎli 哪里

Now listen and repeat.

2-29

2 Listen and check the pinyin with the tones you hear.

1 漂亮	☐	piàoliàng	☐ piàoliang
2 朋友	☐	péngyǒu	☐ péngyou
3 眼睛	☐	yǎnjīng	☐ yǎnjing
4 样子	☐	yàngzǐ	☐ yàngzi
5 头发	☐	tóufà	☐ tóufa

Now listen again and repeat.

2-30

3 Say the sentences aloud.

1 Nǐ de péngyou zhǎng shénme yàngzi
你的 朋友 长 什么 样子？

2 Tā hěn piàoliang cháng tóufa gāo gèzi
她 很 漂亮， 长 头发， 高 个子。

3 Wǒ kěyǐ shìshi zhè jiàn yīfu ma
我 可以 试试 这 件 衣服 吗？

4 Nǐ shuōshuo wǒ yīnggāi mǎi shénme
你 说说 我 应该 买 什么？

5 Nǐ xiǎngxiang bǎ dōngxi fàng zài nǎli le
你 想想 把 东西 放 在 哪里 了。

Now listen and repeat.

2-31

4 Listen and say the words.

1	yàngzi 样子	gèzi 个子	tóufa 头发	yǎnjing 眼睛
2	miáotiao 苗条	shòu 瘦	pàng 胖	ǎi 矮
3	jīnsè 金色	zhōngděng 中等	cháng 长	duǎn 短

5 Draw a picture of what you looked like when you were younger.

Now work in pairs. Describe how your partner's appearance has changed.

CHINESE TO GO

2-32

Expressions to describe appearance

Rén bùkě mào xiàng
人不可貌相。
Don't judge people by their appearance.

Tā zhǎng de hěn xiàng tā bàba
他长得很像他爸爸。
He looks like his father.

Nǐ liǎ yìdiǎnr yě bù xiàng
你俩一点儿也不像。
You two don't look like each other at all.

Tā hǎo shuài gāo kě'ài
他好帅/高/可爱！
He is very handsome/tall/cute!

LESSON | 2

Reading and writing

1 Work in pairs. Describe the man's appearance, what he is wearing and the size of his clothes. Use the words below.

qiúyī 球衣	yùndòngkù 运动裤
qiúxié 球鞋	wàzi 袜子
xiǎohào 小号	zhōnghào 中号
dàhào 大号	jiādàhào 加大号

生词 New words

érqiě 而且	and, but also	jiǔ 久	long (time)
tiāoxuǎn 挑选	choose	zuìjìn 最近	recently
gèng 更	more, even more	zhōnghào 中号	medium size
qiúyī 球衣	jersey, kit for ball games	Bāxī 巴西	Brazil
biǎodì 表弟	cousin (younger male)	shēncái 身材	figure, stature
shòu 瘦	thin, skinny	pífū 皮肤	skin
wèntí 问题	question, problem	kuàilè 快乐	happy
yúkuài 愉快	happy, pleasant		

2-33

2 Read Wang Yu's emails to Amanda and her cousin in Chengdu.

邮件转移至 | 确认 | 删除

邮箱 | 通讯录 | 相册 | 邮箱设置 |

阿曼达：

知道你们已经到了成都，而且玩得很开心，我很高兴。:-) 我很想看看永民穿唐装的样子，一定很帅。:-P 你挑选的两件东西都很漂亮，我觉得我妈妈可能更喜欢茶具。

另外，谢谢你帮我带球衣给我表弟。明天晚上他会去你住的宾馆拿球衣。我表弟叫王明，十七岁，个子很高，比较瘦，短头发，戴眼镜。他的手机号码是16521659870。

如果你有问题，可以给我打电话。

祝旅行愉快！ :-)

王玉

发送

邮件转移至 | 确认 | 删除

邮箱 | 通讯录 | 相册 | 邮箱设置 |

小明：

好久不见，你最近好吗？你的生日就要到了，我让朋友从英国带回来一套球衣给你，是你最喜欢的那个球队的。球衣有蓝白两种颜色，我想你应该穿中号的，希望你喜欢。*^o^*

我的朋友阿曼达去成都玩，我让她把球衣带给你。阿曼达是巴西人，个子不高，中等身材，黑皮肤，长头发。她住在成都宾馆，你可以明天晚上去宾馆找她，她的电话号码是16912764805。

祝生日快乐！ ^-^

王玉

发送

3 Check the true statements.

☐ 1 王玉觉得永民穿唐装不好看。

☐ 2 王玉的表弟会去宾馆找阿曼达。

☐ 3 王玉让阿曼达从美国带球衣给表弟。

☐ 4 阿曼达没有见过王玉的表弟。

4 Write four sentences, comparing the appearances of Amanda and of Wang Yu's cousin.

5 Write a short description of what your best friend looks like.

Now work in pairs. Listen to your partner's description and draw a picture of their friend.

Language in use

Serial verb constructions

1 Look at the sentences.

Subject	Predicate	
	Verb phrase 1	Verb phrase 2
我	去咖啡店	跟她们见面。
我	坐在这里	看电视。
我	买了一件球衣	送给你。
你	去宾馆	找她。
他们	坐火车	去成都。

Now check the two correct explanations.

☐ 1 A predicate can contain more than one verb phrase, expressing consecutive actions.

☐ 2 The order of the verb phrases can be switched around without affecting the meaning.

☐ 3 The verb phrases are related in manner or purpose.

2 Join the two sentences together, using serial verb constructions.

1 我回家。/ 我吃晚饭。

2 我晚上去学校。/ 我上中文课。

3 我坐飞机。/ 我去听音乐会。

4 我每天早上到体育场。/ 我每天早上跑步。

Affirmative-negative questions

1 Look at the sentences.

Subject	Predicate	
	Adjective/Verb	Object
你们	去不去？	
Will you go or not?		
她们	漂亮不漂亮？	
Are they pretty or not?		
这件衣服	贵不贵？	
Is this clothing expensive or not?		
你	买没买	那条裙子？
Have you bought that skirt?		
她	看没看	电影？
Has she seen the movie?		

Now check the two correct explanations.

☐ 1 Affirmative-negative questions are used to get a straight yes or no answer.

☐ 2 These questions always contain a verb or an adjective and their negative form.

☐ 3 Affirmative-negative questions must contain the negative adverb 不.

2 Rewrite the sentences using affirmative-negative questions.

1 你明天去学校吗？
2 安娜买了那件大衣吗？
3 这个菜好吃吗？
4 你喜欢打网球吗？

Expressing immediate actions with (就) 要……了

1 Look at the sentences.

Subject	Adverb	Predicate
我	（就）要	走了。
你的生日	（就）要	到了。
我们	（就）要	去上海了。
她	（就）要	二十一岁了。

Now check the two correct explanations.

☐ 1 (就) 要……了 is used to express an action or event that is going to happen soon.

☐ 2 了 is used at the end of the sentence to indicate that something has happened.

☐ 3 就 can be left out, whereas 要 must be used.

2 Write the sentences in Chinese.

1 Will you go to Shanghai soon?
2 I'm going to the hospital tomorrow.
3 My mother is turning 60.
4 We're about to get off the train.
5 The summer vacation is coming.

Turn to page 169 for grammar reference.

LESSON | 3

Communication activity

1 **Choose a student from the class and write five sentences to describe their appearance.**
For example,

她是女的。
她个子不高。
她的头发是红色的。
她比我瘦。
她和我一样漂亮。

2 **Work in groups. Take turns to say the descriptions to the group one sentence at a time. Don't say the name of the student you are describing.**

Other students in the group guess who is being described. The winner is the person who makes the most correct guesses.

Turn to pages 152 and 158 for more speaking practice.

Cultural corner

Who is beautiful?

The standards of beauty have changed many times over the centuries in China, and the great beauties of one age might be considered quite plain in other eras.

In general, looks were considered more important for women than for men, since society permitted women few opportunities to distinguish themselves by other means.

For women, in most eras, a slim, willowy figure was considered desirable. Zhao Feiyan, wife of the Han Emperor Cheng, was said to be so petite she could dance on the palm of a man's hand. She was often compared and contrasted with Yang Guifei, the beautiful concubine of the Tang Emperor Xuanzong, because Zhao was known for her slender build while Yang was known for being rather plump. This is the source of the Chinese expression *yanshou huanfei* (燕瘦环肥), describing how people can differ, yet still be attractive.

Character writing

These are two common radicals in Chinese. Do you know any other characters with the same radicals?

Radicals	Meaning	Examples
目	eye	看、睡
子	child	孙、好

1 Look at the characters and identify the radicals.

孩 省 睛 学

2 Match the words with the meanings.

1 女孩 a watch TV
2 眼睛 b girl
3 看电视 c overseas student
4 留学生 d eye

3 Trace the characters in the boxes.

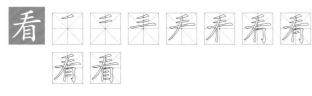

看

眼

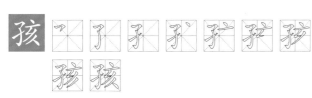

孩

学

Review and practice

1 Write sentences with the given phrases, using serial verb constructions.

1 去英国 / 看足球比赛
2 坐地铁 / 上班
3 到市中心 / 找房子
4 买东西 / 送给朋友
5 到朋友家 / 庆祝生日

2 Work in pairs. Ask and answer three affirmative-negative questions about each other.

3 Write five sentences to describe the appearance of the people in the picture, including their age, height, build and hair.

4 Work in pairs. Talk about three things that are going to happen soon, using （就）要.

Vocabulary extension

Match the words with the facial features of the man in the picture.

a liǎn 脸	b bízi 鼻子	c zuǐ 嘴
d ěrduo 耳朵	e méimao 眉毛	f húzi 胡子

Now work in pairs. Describe the man's appearance using these words. Discuss whether you think he is good-looking and explain why.

Vocabulary review

Fill in the blanks.

矮	ǎi	*adj.*	short (height)
巴西	Bāxī	*n.*	Brazil
______	biǎodì	*n.*	cousin (younger male)
德国	Déguó	*n.*	______
______	diànshì	*n.*	TV
短	duǎn	*adj.*	______
______	duì le		by the way, that's right
而且	érqiě	*conj.*	and, but also
更	gèng	*adv.*	more, even more
金色	jīnsè	*n.*	golden, blond(e)
久	jiǔ	*adj.*	long (time)
______	kāfēi	*n.*	coffee
______	kuàilè	*adj.*	happy
俩	liǎ	*num.*	two (coll.)
另	lìng	*pron.*	other, another
______	liúxuéshēng	*n.*	overseas student
苗条	miáotiao	*adj.*	______
______	nǚhái	*n.*	girl
胖	pàng	*adj.*	______
皮肤	pífū	*n.*	skin
球衣	qiúyī	*n.*	jersey, kit for ball games
让	ràng	*v.*	let, allow
______	shēncái	*n.*	figure, stature

瘦	shòu	*adj.*	______
丝巾	sījīn	*n.*	silk scarf
挑选	tiāoxuǎn	*v.*	______
______	tóufa	*n.*	hair
______	wèntí	*n.*	question, problem
兴趣	xìngqù	*n.*	______
眼睛	yǎnjing	*n.*	eye
愉快	yúkuài	*adj.*	happy, pleasant
长	zhǎng	*v.*	______
中等	zhōngděng	*adj.*	medium
______	zhōnghào		medium size
重要	zhòngyào	*adj.*	______
最近	zuìjìn	*n.*	______
鼻子	bízi	*n.*	nose
耳朵	ěrduo	*n.*	ear
褐色	hèsè	*n.*	brown
胡子	húzi	*n.*	moustache
加大号	jiādàhào	*n.*	extra large size
脸	liǎn	*n.*	face
眉毛	méimao	*n.*	eyebrow
球鞋	qiúxié	*n.*	sports shoes
袜子	wàzi	*n.*	socks
嘴	zuǐ	*n.*	mouth

UNIT 11

Wǒ juéde bù shūfu
我 觉得 不 舒服。

I'm not feeling well.

LESSON | 1

Vocabulary and listening

2-34

1 Match the medicine labels with the meanings.

1 měi rì sān cì
每日三次

2 měi cì liǎng piàn
每次两片

3 fàn hòu fúyòng
饭后服用

4 yǐnqǐ shuìyì
引起睡意

a cause drowsiness

b three times a day

c take after meals

d two tablets each time

Now listen and say the phrases.

2-35

2 Work in pairs. Check the symptoms of a cold.

☐ tóutòng 头痛

☐ késou 咳嗽

☐ fāshāo 发烧

☐ hóulóng tòng 喉咙痛

☐ bísè 鼻塞

☐ lādùzi 拉肚子

Now listen and say the words.

2-36

3 Back in Beijing, Mark goes to see the doctor. Listen to the conversation and answer the questions.

1 马克得了什么病？

2 马克为什么病了？

3 马克的病应该怎么治？

医生：请坐！你叫什么名字？

马克：我叫马克。

医生：你觉得哪里不舒服？

马克：我有一点儿头痛，发烧，还拉肚子。

医生：多长时间了？

马克：两天了。

医生：你最近有没有离开过本地？

马克：有。我跟两个朋友去成都旅行，刚回来。

医生：先检查一下吧。张大嘴，让我看看你的喉咙。

马克：啊——

医生：再听听肺。

马克：医生，我得了什么病？

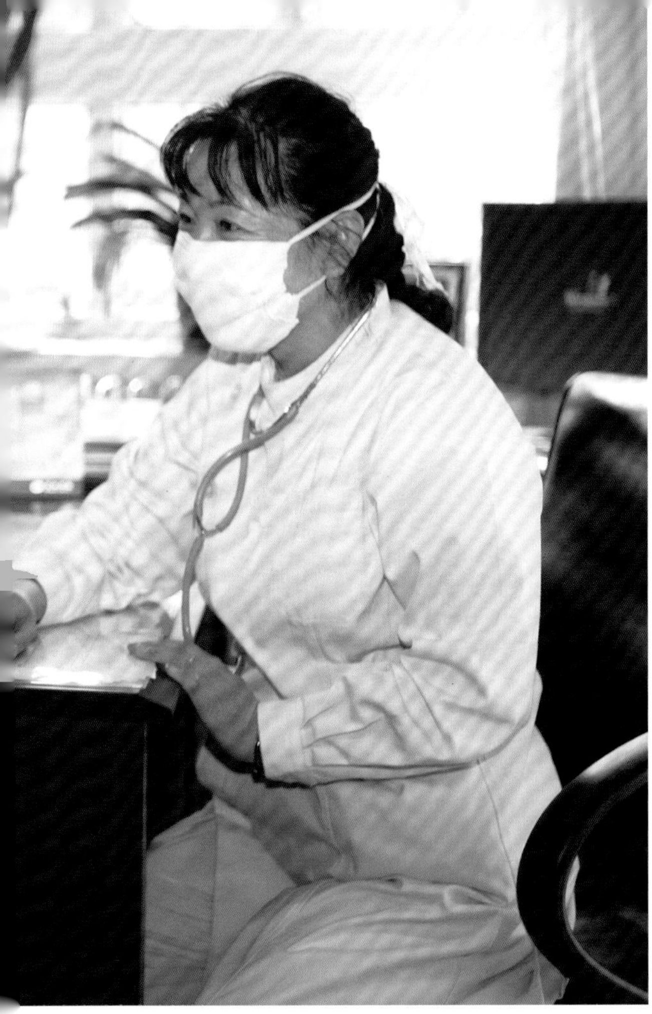

医生：没什么大问题，只是普通的感冒。你生病是因为没休息好，又着凉了。

马克：那应该怎么治？要打针吗？

医生：不用打针，我给你开一些药。好好休息，不要吃太辣的东西，很快就会好的。

马克：谢谢医生。

[在药房]

护士：马克，这是你的药。这是感冒和退烧药，每天三次，每次两片，饭前或者饭后服用都可以。请注意，吃药以后可能会想睡觉。

马克：谢谢你，再见。

生词 New words

tóutòng 头痛	headache	
fāshāo 发烧	fever; have a fever	
lādùzi 拉肚子	suffer from diarrhoea	
běndì 本地	local area, place	
jiǎnchá 检查	check up, examine	
zuǐ 嘴	mouth	
hóulóng 喉咙	throat	
ā 啊	ah	
fèi 肺	lung	
débìng 得病	acquire/get disease	
pǔtōng 普通	ordinary, common	
gǎnmào 感冒	cold	
shēngbìng 生病	get sick	
xiūxi 休息	rest	
zháoliáng 着凉	catch a cold	
zhì 治	treat (disease)	
dǎzhēn 打针	have/give an injection	
yào 药	medicine	
hùshi 护士	nurse	
tuìshāo 退烧	bring down a fever	
piàn 片	tablet	
fúyòng 服用	take (medicine)	
zhùyì 注意	note, pay attention to	

2-36

4 Listen again and check the true statements.

☐ 1 马克病了两天了。

☐ 2 医生先听肺，然后检查喉咙。

☐ 3 马克的药只能饭后服用。

☐ 4 感冒药可能会让人想睡觉。

5 Complete the sentences.

1 马克有一点 ______，______，还 ______。

2 医生叫马克好好 ______，不要 ______。

3 马克的药每天要吃 ______ 次。

6 Work in pairs. Act out a conversation between a doctor and a patient who has got a stomach ache.

Pronunciation and speaking

Tone sandhi: 不 and 一

2-37

1 **Look at the tone marks for 一 and 不. How do they change when the following character carries a fourth tone?**

不用 búyòng	一片 yípiàn
不是 búshì	一件 yíjiàn
不要 búyào	一次 yícì
不错 búcuò	一共 yígòng

How do they change when the following character carries other tones?

不舒服 bùshūfu	一些 yìxiē
不能 bùnéng	一天 yìtiān
不来 bùlái	一年 yìnián
不好 bùhǎo	一点儿 yìdiǎnr

Now listen and repeat.

2-38

2 **Write pinyin with the correct tones for the words.**

1 一个 ____________________

2 一瓶 ____________________

3 不辣 ____________________

4 不咸 ____________________

Now listen and repeat.

2-39

3 **Say the sentences aloud, using the correct tones.**

Wǒ de tóu bú tòng le, búyòng chīyào le.
1 我的头不痛了，不用吃药了。

Wǒ zhīdào yì zhǒng yào, zhì gǎnmào búcuò.
2 我知道一种药，治感冒不错。

Wǒ bù zhīdào tā qù bú qù
3 我不知道他去不去？

Yí gè píngguǒ hé yì bēi niúnǎi duōshao qián
4 一个苹果和一杯牛奶，多少钱？

Now listen and repeat.

2-40

4 **Listen and say the words.**

1	tóutòng 头痛	fāshāo 发烧	lādùzi 拉肚子	gǎnmào 感冒
2	débìng 得病	kànbìng 看病	chīyào 吃药	dǎzhēn 打针
3	xiūxi 休息	zháoliáng 着凉	tuìshāo 退烧	zhùyì 注意
4	jiǎnchá 检查	fúyòng 服用	kāiyào 开药	zhìbìng 治病

5 **Work in pairs. Ask and answer questions about your last visit to the doctor.**

CHINESE TO GO

2-41

Expressions related to sickness

Bìng cóng kǒu rù 病从口入。	Illness finds its way in by the mouth.
Nǐ de qìsè bú tài hǎo 你的气色不太好。	You don't look well.
Hǎo yìdiǎnr le ma 好一点儿了吗？	Are you feeling any better?
Duō bǎozhòng 多保重。	Take care.
Zǎorì kāngfù 早日康复。	Get well soon.

LESSON | 2

Reading and writing

1 Match the words with the pictures.

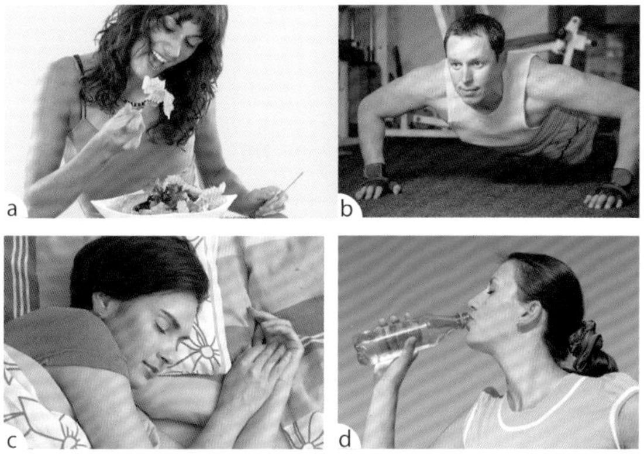

hēshuǐ　chī shūcài　shuìjiào　yùndòng
1 喝水　2 吃 蔬菜　3 睡觉　4 运动

Now work in pairs. Put the words in order of their importance for a healthy life.

2 Read the poster and answer the questions.

1 想健康地生活，应该做什么？

2 想健康地生活，不应该做什么？

生词　New words

jiànkāng 健康	healthy; health	dìngshí 定时	at a fixed time
shēnghuó 生活	live; life	dìngliàng 定量	with fixed quantity
chángshí 常识	general knowledge, common sense	ànshí 按时	on time
de 地	(used to indicate an adverbial phrase)	bǎo 饱	full, replete
shūcài 蔬菜	vegetable	jīngcháng 经常	often
		zhěngtiān 整天	whole day, all day
yán 盐	salt	wǎn 晚	late

健康
生活
小常识

健康的身体对每个人都很重要。你知道怎样才能健康地生活吗？这些生活小常识可能会帮到你！

你吃的东西健康吗？

要多吃蔬菜和水果，少吃多油多盐的饭菜。

你的早、午、晚饭定时定量吗？

要按时吃饭，早饭要吃好，午饭要吃饱，晚饭要吃少。

你每天喝的水够不够？

要多喝水，每天最少喝八杯水。

你经常做运动吗？

要多做运动，每天最好运动半个小时。不要整天在家看电视和上网玩电子游戏。

你每天睡觉的时间够吗？

要早睡早起，每天最少要睡八个小时。不要很晚才上床睡觉。

3 **Read again and complete the sentences.**

1 应该多吃 ________，少吃 ________。
2 早饭应该 ________，午饭应该 ________，晚饭应该 ________。
3 每天最少要喝 ________ 杯水。
4 每天最好做 ________ 个小时运动。
5 每天睡觉最少要 ________ 个小时。

4 **Work in pairs. Write five things you must or must not do in order to lead a healthy life.**

Language in use

The auxiliary word 地

1 **Look at the sentences.**

Subject	Modal verb	Adverbial phrase		Verb
人们	想	健康	地	生活。
她		高兴	地	回家了。
你	要	好好	地	休息。
他		慢慢	地	走了。

Now check the two correct explanations.

☐ 1 地 is used between an adjective and a verb to denote the manner of an action.

☐ 2 地 is used between a verb and its subject to denote the manner of the action.

☐ 3 地 cannot be used after the verb that the adverbial phrase describes.

2 **Make sentences using 地 and the given words.**

1 慢慢 / 吃着早餐
2 开心 / 唱着歌
3 很快 / 离开学校
4 愉快 / 去旅行

多 and 少

1 Look at the sentences.

Modal verb	多/少	Verb	Object
要	多	吃	水果和蔬菜。
	多	吃了	两碗饭。
要	多	喝	水。
要	多	做	运动。
	少	看	电视。
	少	写	一个字。

Now check the two correct explanations.

☐ 1 多 is used before a verb to mean doing something more, while 少 is used before a verb to mean doing something less.

☐ 2 多 or 少 can be used between the verb they modify and the object to express more or less in quantity.

☐ 3 When a verb is used with 多 or 少, the additional or lesser quantities can be specified by placing a number and measurement word after the verb.

2 Work in pairs. Make two suggestions to each other, using 多 and 少 respectively.

Expressing the duration of action

1 Look at the sentences.

Subject	Adverbial	Verb phrase	Verb	了	Duration
马克	每天	做运动	做		半个小时。
她	下午	打网球	打	了	两个小时。
永民	中午	吃饭	吃	了	十五分钟。
他			走	了	半个小时。

Now check the two correct explanations.

☐ 1 A noun phrase for the duration of an action is used at the end of the sentence.

☐ 2 When the verb phrase contains an object, it needs to be followed by a repetition of the verb.

☐ 3 了 must be used before the verb to indicate that something has already happened.

2 Write the sentences in Chinese.

1 I went shopping for three hours last Saturday.
2 He has been waiting for me for two hours.
3 She eats lunch for one hour every day.
4 Mark spent half an hour writing his blog last night.

▶ Turn to page 170 for grammar reference.

LESSON | 3

Communication activity

1 **Work in pairs. You are planning to write an article for a school newspaper about a common health problem. Brainstorm problems that you could write about.**

Now discuss and choose one problem to write about.

2 **Do research on the following questions, and then write the article together.**

生病时会有什么感觉?
为什么会得病?
什么人容易得这种病?
这种病怎么治?

3 **Work with another pair. Present your article to each other and answer questions.**

Turn to pages 153 and 159 for more speaking practice.

Cultural corner

Traditional Chinese medicine (中医中药)

Not only does traditional Chinese medicine still have a big presence in China and in other Asian countries, it is also gaining popularity in the West as an alternative to standard medical practice. The most well-known forms of Chinese medical treatment include Chinese herbs, acupuncture, *tui na* massage and cupping. The underlying philosophy of Chinese medicine, upon which its models of human body and medical theories are built, is quite different from that of contemporary western medicine. Chinese medicine treats the human body as a balanced system and views any specific illness as the result of that delicate balance being broken. Hence, Chinese medicine aims at restoring that balance and focuses more on prevention than treatment. A traditional Chinese medicine practitioner uses four techniques for diagnosis, referred to as observation (望), smelling (闻), asking (问) and touching (切).

Character writing

These are two common radicals in Chinese. Do you know any other characters with the same radicals?

Radicals	Meaning	Examples
疒	sickness	病、瘦
火	fire	焚、炒

1 Look at the characters and identify the radicals.

痛　疼　烧　烦

2 Match the words with the meanings.

1 得病　　a fever
2 发烧　　b headache
3 头痛　　c bother
4 麻烦　　d get sick

3 Trace the characters in the boxes.

病
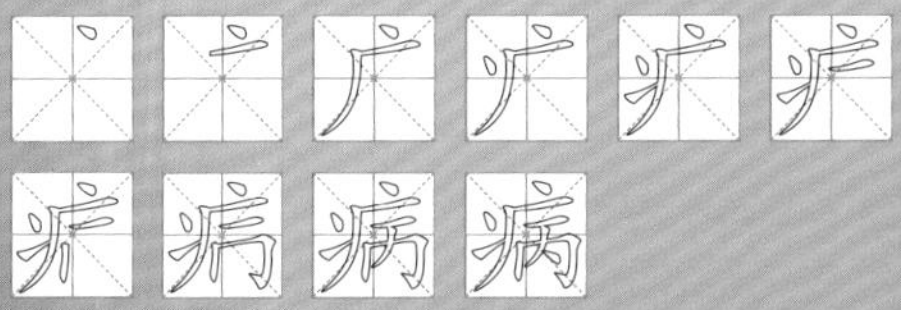

痛
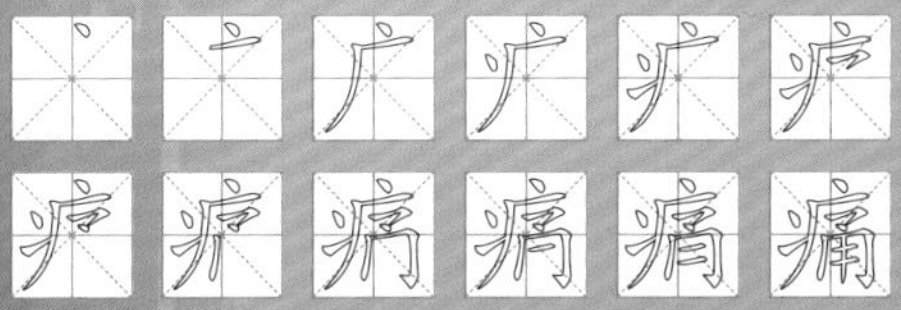

烧
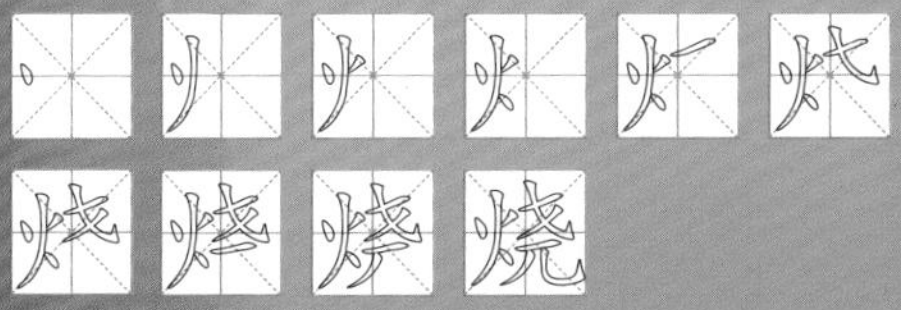

烦
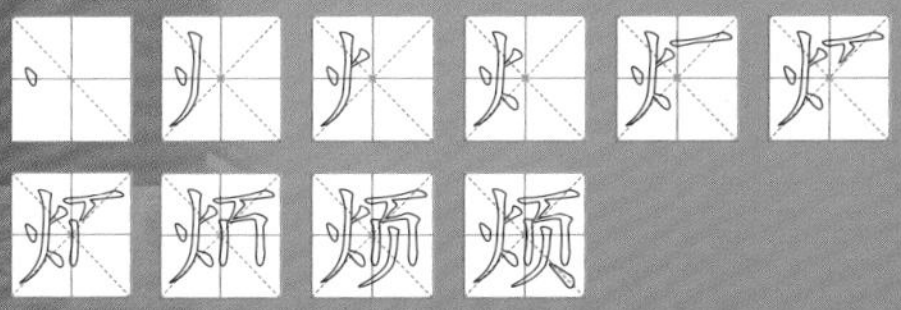

Review and practice

1 Circle the odd words out.

1 头痛　感冒　发烧　拉肚子
2 打针　吃药　休息　着凉
3 健康　身体　常识　经常
4 水果　饭菜　蔬菜　按时

2 Write sentences using 地 and the given words.

1 愉快 / 生活
2 很快 / 走去
3 慢慢 / 停下
4 开心 / 告诉

3 Write a sentence to describe each picture.

a

b

Now write two suggestions you would give to the people in the pictures.

4 Work in pairs. Tell each other how long you spent studying, sleeping and eating yesterday.

Vocabulary extension

Match the words for symptoms with the meanings.

1	dǎ pēntì 打喷嚏	a dizzy
2	liú bítì 流鼻涕	b stomach ache
3	ǒutù 呕吐	c sore throat
4	tóuyūn 头晕	d sneeze
5	sǎngzi téng 嗓子疼	e runny nose
6	dǔzi tòng 肚子痛	f vomit

Now work in pairs. Tell each other when you had any of these symptoms before and try to explain why.

Vocabulary review

Fill in the blanks.

啊	ā	interj.	ah
按时	ànshí	adv.	________
____	bǎo	adj.	full, replete
本地	běndì	n.	local area, place
____	chángshí	n.	general knowledge, common sense
打针	dǎzhēn	v.	________
得病	débìng	v.	acquire/get disease
____	de	particle	(used to indicate an adverbial phrase)
定量	dìngliàng	v.	with fixed quantity
____	dìngshí	v.	at a fixed time
发烧	fāshāo	v.	________
肺	fèi	n.	lung
服用	fúyòng	v.	take (medicine)
____	gǎnmào	n./v.	cold
喉咙	hóulóng	n.	________
____	hùshi	n.	nurse
检查	jiǎnchá	v.	check up, examine
健康	jiànkāng	adj.	________
____	jīngcháng	adv.	often
拉肚子	lādùzi	v.	________
____	piàn	measure word	tablet
普通	pǔtōng	adj.	ordinary, common
____	shēntǐ	n.	body

生病	shēngbìng	v.	________
____	shēnghuó	v./n.	live; life
蔬菜	shūcài	n.	________
____	tóutòng	v.	headache
退烧	tuìshāo	v.	________
____	wǎn	adv.	late
____	xiūxi	v.	rest
盐	yán	n.	________
药	yào	n.	medicine
着凉	zháoliáng	v.	catch a cold
整天	zhěngtiān	n.	whole day, all day
____	zhì	v.	treat (disease)
注意	zhùyì	v.	________
嘴	zuǐ	n.	________
鼻塞	bísè	n.	stuffy nose
打喷嚏	dǎ pēntì	v.	sneeze
肚子痛	dǔzi tòng	v.	stomach ache
咳嗽	késou	v.	cough
流鼻涕	liú bítì	v.	runny nose
呕吐	ǒutù	v.	vomit
嗓子疼	sǎngzi téng	v.	sore throat
头晕	tóuyūn	v.	dizzy
引起睡意	yǐnqǐ shuìyì	v.	cause drowsiness

UNIT 12

Nǐ huì xǐhuan tā de
你会喜欢她的！
You'll really like her!

LESSON 1

Vocabulary and listening

2-43

1 Work in pairs. Tell each other about your best friend's personality, using the words below.

xìnggé 性格	character
píqi 脾气	temper, disposition
lèguān 乐观	optimistic
zìxìn 自信	self-confident
jí píqi 急脾气	hot-tempered
guānxīn 关心	caring, considerate

2-44

2 Wang Yu, Amanda and Mark are at karaoke, chatting about a friend of Wang Yu's. Listen to the conversation and check the correct answers.

1 王玉的朋友凯特是 _______ 人。

- ☐ a 美国
- ☐ b 英国
- ☐ c 加拿大

2 凯特现在在北京 _______。

- ☐ a 工作
- ☐ b 学中文
- ☐ c 唱歌

3 阿曼达的性格 _______。

- ☐ a 不乐观
- ☐ b 急脾气
- ☐ c 不自信

阿曼达：王玉，今天还有什么人来？
王玉：还有我的一个好朋友。你们可以认识一下。我觉得你会喜欢她的。
马克：太好了！她叫什么名字？
王玉：她叫凯特，是加拿大人。上个星期刚开始在北京工作。
阿曼达：你们是怎么认识的？
王玉：凯特去年来北京学中文的时候，我是她的老师。
马克：她长什么样子？
王玉：她中等身材，有双蓝色的大眼睛，金色的长卷发，跟我一样高。
阿曼达：是个美女啊！我们应该把她介绍给史蒂夫、永民他们。对了，她的性格怎么样？
王玉：她跟你很像——很乐观、很自信。虽然脾气有一点儿急，但是很关心朋友。凯特喜欢交朋友，喜欢唱歌、跳舞。流行

歌曲和民歌她都会唱，特别是中国民歌“半个月亮爬上来”唱得特别好听。

马克：让我猜一猜，她是不是白羊座的？

王玉：你怎么知道？

马克：我喜欢研究星座，她的性格跟白羊座的很像。

王玉：等她来了，你可以问问她。希望你猜对了。

阿曼达：史蒂夫是狮子座的，听说白羊座跟狮子座很配。

王玉：那一定要把凯特介绍给史蒂夫认识。对了，你们知道中国的属相吗？很多人相信属相跟性格也有关系。

凯特：对不起，我来迟了。

生词 New words

qùnián 去年	last year	míngē 民歌	folk song
juǎnfà 卷发	curly hair	yuèliang 月亮	moon
xìnggé 性格	character	cāi 猜	guess
lèguān 乐观	optimistic	Báiyángzuò 白羊座	Aries
zìxìn 自信	self-confident	yánjiū 研究	research, study
píqi 脾气	temper, disposition	xīngzuò 星座	constellation, star sign
jí 急	irritable; fast, quick	shīzi 狮子	lion
guānxīn 关心	care about; care	pèi 配	match
liúxíng 流行	popular	shǔxiang 属相	Chinese zodiac
gēqǔ 歌曲	song	xiāngxìn 相信	believe
		guānxi 关系	relationship, connection

2-44

3 Listen again and answer the questions.

1 凯特的性格怎么样？
2 凯特喜欢做什么？
3 王玉说要把凯特介绍给谁？

4 Work in pairs. Try to match the characteristics with the Chinese zodiac signs.

a

b

c

d

1 自信　2 乐观　3 关心人　4 急脾气

5 Work in groups of four. Discuss who in the class has the characteristics in Activity 4.

Pronunciation and speaking

Difference between "s" and "sh"

2-45

1 Check the correct initials for the underlined characters.

1 什么	☐ s	☐ sh
2 认识	☐ s	☐ sh
3 森林	☐ s	☐ sh
4 开始	☐ s	☐ sh
5 老师	☐ s	☐ sh
6 蓝色	☐ s	☐ sh

Now listen and repeat.

2-46

2 Check the correct pinyin for the words.

1 身材	☐ sēncái	☐ shēncái
2 时候	☐ síhou	☐ shíhou
3 金色	☐ jīnsè	☐ jīnshè
4 虽然	☐ suīrán	☐ shuīrán
5 狮子	☐ sīzi	☐ shīzi
6 属相	☐ sǔxiang	☐ shǔxiang

Now listen and repeat.

2-47

3 Say the sentences aloud.

Wǒ zài Shíshī Shì de shíhou rènshi tā
1 我在石狮市的时候认识她。

Shǐdìfū xǐhuan de diànshìjù shí diǎn kāishǐ
2 史蒂夫 喜欢 的 电视剧 十 点 开始。

Sì shì sì shí shì shí shísì shì shísì
3 四是四，十是十，十四是十四，

sìshí shì sìshí
四十是四十。

Now listen and repeat.

2-48

4 Listen and say the words.

1	yàngzi 样子	shēncái 身材	yǎnjing 眼睛	juǎnfà 卷发
2	xìnggé 性格	píqi 脾气	lèguān 乐观	zìxìn 自信
3	xīngzuò 星座	shǔxiang 属相	guānxīn 关心	liúxíng 流行

5 Work in pairs. Ask and answer the questions.

问题	Yes	No
你唱歌唱得好听吗？		
你长得很漂亮/帅吗？		
你走路走得快吗？		
你知道朋友的生日吗？		
你有宠物吗？		
你喜欢红色吗？		

Now decide which word best describes your partner's character.

☐ 自信 ☐ 关心人 ☐ 急脾气

2-49

CHINESE TO GO

Expressions to describe personality

Tā bú shànyú jiāojì
她（不）善于交际。
She is (not) good at socializing.

Tā bú hǎo xiāngchǔ
他（不）好相处。
He is (not) easy to get along with.

Tā de rénpǐn hěn hǎo
她的人品很好。
She has a nice personality.

Nàgè rén hěn chīxiāng
那个人很吃香/
xiǎoxīnyǎn zhíxīnyǎn
小心眼/直心眼。
That person is very popular / narrow-minded / straightforward.

Báimǎ wángzǐ
白马王子
Prince Charming

LESSON 2

Reading and writing

1 **Work in pairs. Discuss and agree on the three most important characteristics of a good friend, using the words below.**

cōngming 聪明	clever	zìxìn 自信	self-confident
chéngshí 诚实	honest	lèguān 乐观	optimistic
yǒnggǎn 勇敢	brave	dúlì 独立	independent

2-50

2 **Read and complete the quiz.**

生词 New words

hèsè 褐色	brown	chǒngwù 宠物	pet
huīsè 灰色	grey	māo 猫	cat
zhíjiē 直接	direct	gǒu 狗	dog
yìjiàn 意见	advice	shíjì 实际	practical
bùtóng 不同	different	xiǎoxīn 小心	careful
shāngdiàn 商店	shop	xíngdòng 行动	act; action
dǎgōng 打工	work, labour	zǒngshì 总是	always
zhèngqián 挣钱	make money	kǎolǜ 考虑	consider
mǎshàng 马上	immediately, at once	dúlì 独立	independent
zīliào 资料	information, data	cìjī 刺激	exciting
yǎng 养	raise, feed		

Who am I?

1 我最喜欢的颜色是

a 红色或者黄色。

b 褐色或者灰色。

c 蓝色或者绿色。

2 购物的时候，我会

a 直接去买想要的东西。

b 问朋友的意见。

c 去很多不同的商店，比较东西和价钱。

3 放暑假的时候，我会

a 去打工挣钱。

b 和朋友们一起去旅行、爬山或者潜水。

c 在家里看书或者听音乐。

4 生病的时候，我会

a 马上看医生。

b 打电话给我妈妈，问问应该怎么做。

c 上网找资料，试新药。

5 我最想养的宠物是

a 一只猫。

b 一只狗。

c 几条鱼。

10–16	18–22	24–30
你很实际，又很小心。你行动前总是会好好考虑。	你很喜欢交朋友，对朋友很关心，不太独立。	你很独立、自信和乐观，喜欢刺激的生活。

①a 6 b 2 c 4 ②a 6 b 4 c 2 ③a 2 b 6 c 4 ④a 2 b 4 c 6 ⑤a 4 b 6 c 2

3 Read again and answer the questions.

1 喜欢刺激生活的人可能会喜欢什么颜色？
2 喜欢交朋友的人可能会养什么宠物？
3 你是什么性格的人？

4 Choose a person in the class and guess what Chinese zodiac sign they might have. Write a description of their characteristics and hobbies, and explain the reasons for your guess.

Now work with the whole class. Find out whether your guesses are correct.

Language in use

Wh-questions

1 Look at the sentences.

Question Type				
What	她		叫	什么名字？
	她		叫	凯特。
Who	她		是	谁？
	她		是	我姐姐。
	谁		会来？	
	永民		会来。	
Where	你		住	在哪里？
	我		住	在北京。
When	你	什么时候	去	我家？
	我	周末	去	你家。
Why	马克	为什么	不能来？	
	马克	病了	不能来。	
How	你们	怎么	去	西安？
	我们	坐火车	去	西安。

Now check the two correct explanations.

☐ 1 The position of question words in Chinese sentences is usually the same as in English.

☐ 2 The position of question words in Chinese sentences is usually different from English.

☐ 3 In replies in Chinese, the answering information usually appears where the question words were.

2 Answer the questions.

1 周末你喜欢做什么？
2 你最喜欢的明星是谁？
3 你喜欢去哪里旅行？为什么？
4 你什么时候放暑假？
5 你怎样认识新朋友？

Difference between 有一点 and 一点儿

1 Look at the sentences.

Subject	Predicate	
	Adverb	Adjective
她的脾气	有一点	急。
火车	有一点	不方便。
这个菜	有一点	辣。

Subject	Predicate		
	Verb	Adjective	Complement
丽莎	需要	独立	一点儿。
他	应该	自信	一点儿。
你	说	慢	一点儿。

Now check the two correct explanations.

☐ 1 有一点 is often used before an adjective to indicate a positive tone.

☐ 2 一点儿 is used after an adjective to indicate the need for more of something.

☐ 3 有一点 is used before an adjective, while 一点儿 is used after an adjective.

2 Write the sentences in Chinese.

1 Xi'an's winter is a little cold.
2 You should get up earlier.
3 This dress is a bit too expensive.
4 Could you speak a bit louder?

The auxiliary words 的/地/得

1 Look at the sentences.

Subject	Predicate
永民拍的照片	很漂亮。
凯特	有双蓝色的大眼睛。
他	慢慢地放下了书。
大家	都想快乐地生活。
她	高兴得跳起来。
王玉	打网球打得很好。

Now check the two correct explanations.

☐ 1 的 is used with an adjective phrase to modify a noun.

☐ 2 地 is used between an adverb or adjective and a verb describing the purpose of an action.

☐ 3 得 is used between an adjective or a verb and its complement expressing result or degree.

2 Complete the sentences with 的, 地 and 得.

1 他跳舞跳 ___ 很好。
2 小明开心 ___ 跳了起来。
3 我很喜欢王玉买 ___ 新裙子。
4 马克在公园拍 ___ 照片很漂亮。
5 她小心 ___ 把电脑放在桌子上面。

Turn to page 171 for grammar reference.

LESSON 3

Communication activity

1 Work in groups of four.

Student A: You are a matchmaker, trying to find the ideal partner for your client. Create a profile for your client, including their name, appearance, personality, background and Chinese zodiac sign. Draw a picture of your client.

Students B, C and D: You will each play a suitor for Student A's client. Create a profile of your character, including background, appearance, personality and hobbies. Be creative!

2 Play the Match-making Game.

- **Student A:** Introduce your client to the suitors.
- **Students B, C and D:** As your character, introduce yourself to the matchmaker, emphasizing your good points.
- **Student A:** Ask the suitors questions to find out more about them, and decide which suitor is the best match for your client.

Turn to pages 153 and 159 for more speaking practice.

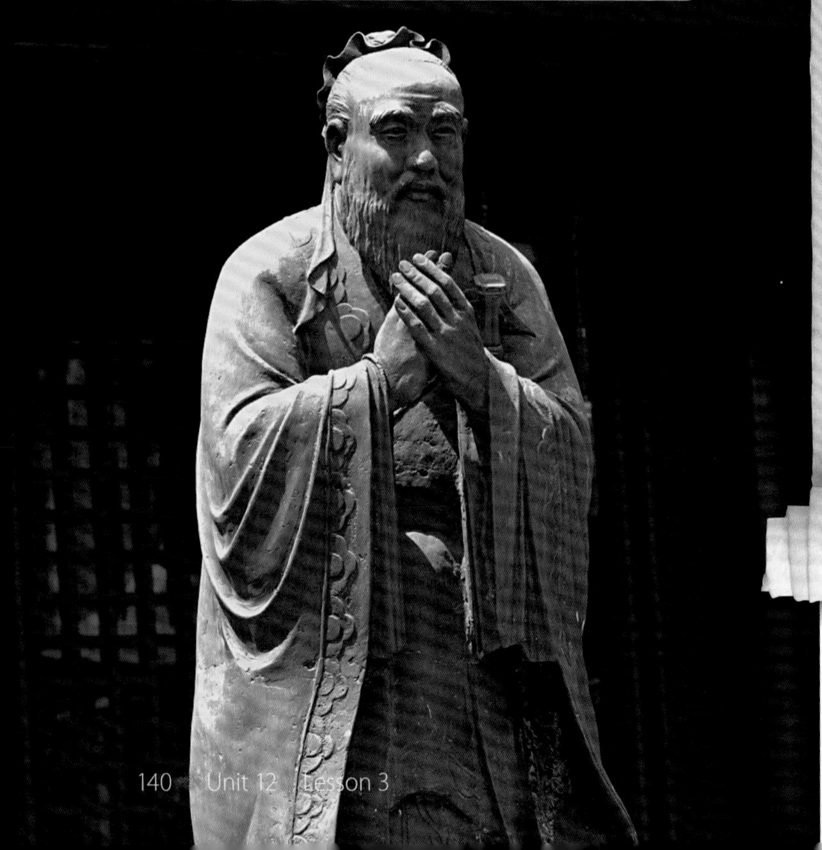

Cultural corner

The Confucian personality

Confucius (孔子, 551—479BC) was a philosopher who lived during the Spring and Autumn Period. His teachings were required reading for imperial officials from the Han dynasty onwards. Confucian beliefs have been admired and followed for a long time in China. Even today you can still see elements of Confucian belief in Chinese people's perception of personality.

Ren 仁 and *li* 礼 are two important concepts in Confucian thought.

Ren, sometimes translated as "humaneness" or "benevolence", is the inward expression of the Confucian ideal. Confucius described this personality trait as love for others and an understanding of how important your relationships with other people are.

Li literally means "ritual", and in Confucianism means correct behaviour in society. Confucius taught that correctly following *li* in all social relationships would lead to a harmonious society, with everyone knowing their place and showing one another the appropriate respect – a father should show kindness to his son, and the son should be obedient. A ruler should be benevolent and his subjects loyal. Social elders should be considerate of their juniors, and the young should defer to them. A husband should be loving and a wife attentive.

Confucius taught that in order to truly follow *li*, one must not only behave outwardly in the proper fashion but also cultivate *ren* within oneself, so right behaviour will come naturally.

Character writing

These are two common radicals in Chinese. Do you know any other characters with the same radicals?

Radicals	Meaning	Examples
忄	heart	忙、快
马	horse	马、闯

1 Look at the characters and identify the radicals.

骑　验　怕　慢

2 Match the words with the meanings.

1 测验　　a be afraid
2 性格　　b ride a bike
3 怕　　c quiz
4 骑车　　d character

3 Trace the characters in the boxes.

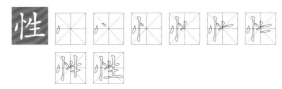

性

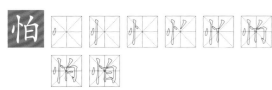

怕

验

骑

Review and practice

1 Match the words with the meanings.

1 乐观　　a independent
2 自信　　b clever
3 实际　　c optimistic
4 独立　　d practical
5 聪明　　e self-confident

2 Complete the sentences with 有一点 or 一点儿.

1 白羊座的人脾气 __________ 急。
2 今天天气 __________ 热。
3 他应该独立 __________。
4 你能不能快 __________？

3 Work in pairs. Ask and answer five wh- questions about each other, using 谁, 什么, 哪里, 什么时候 and 为什么.

4 Work in pairs. Tell each other about your hobbies using 得.

Now tell each other how you do certain things using 地.

5 Imagine you are stranded on a desert island. Write a description of the type of person you would prefer to be with.

Now work in pairs. Ask and answer questions about your partner's description.

Vocabulary extension

1 Look at the words for personality and check the words that can be used to describe the man on the right.

nàixīn 耐心 patient	xiūqiè 羞怯 shy
rènzhēn 认真 careful	gùzhi 固执 stubborn
dàfang 大方 generous	bēiguān 悲观 pessimistic

2 Work in pairs. Talk about two people you both know. Try to use the words above.

Vocabulary review

Fill in the blanks.

白羊座	Báiyángzuò	n.	Aries
______	bùtóng	adj.	different
猜	cāi	v.	______
宠物	chǒngwù	n.	______
刺激	cìjī	v.	exciting
______	dǎgōng	v.	work, labour
独立	dúlì	adj.	______
歌曲	gēqǔ	n.	song
______	gǒu	n.	dog
关系	guānxi	n.	relationship, connection
______	guānxīn	v.	care about; care
褐色	hèsè	n.	brown
灰色	huīsè	n.	______
______	jí	adj.	irritable; fast, quick
卷发	juǎnfà	n.	curly hair
考虑	kǎolǜ	v.	______
乐观	lèguān	adj.	______
流行	liúxíng	adj.	popular
______	mǎshàng	adv.	immediately, at once
______	māo	n.	cat
民歌	míngē	n.	folk song
配	pèi	v.	match
脾气	píqi	n.	______
______	qùnián	n.	last year
______	shāngdiàn	n.	shop
狮子	shīzi	n.	______
实际	shíjì	adj.	practical
属相	shǔxiang	adv.	Chinese zodiac
______	xiǎoxīn	adj.	careful
相信	xiāngxìn	v.	______
星座	xīngzuò	n.	constellation, star sign
行动	xíngdòng	v./n.	act; action
______	xìnggé	n.	character
研究	yánjiū	v.	research, study
______	yǎng	v.	raise, feed
意见	yìjiàn	n.	______
______	yuèliang	n.	moon
挣钱	zhèngqián	v.	______
直接	zhíjiē	adj.	direct
资料	zīliào	n.	______
______	zìxìn	adj.	self-confident
总是	zǒngshì	adv.	always
悲观	bēiguān	adj.	pessimistic
诚实	chéngshí	adj.	honest
聪明	cōngming	adj.	clever
大方	dàfang	adj.	generous
固执	gùzhi	adj.	stubborn
耐心	nàixīn	adj.	patient
认真	rènzhēn	adj.	careful, serious
羞怯	xiūqiè	adj.	shy
勇敢	yǒnggǎn	adj.	brave

Review 3

Vocabulary

1 Match the adjectives with the nouns.

1 短	a 脾气
2 矮	b 身材
3 急	c 头发
4 苗条	d 性格
5 乐观	e 个子

2 Circle the odd words out.

1 动物	植物	自然	保护
2 流行	刺激	普通	经常
3 生病	休息	受凉	身体
4 头发	眼睛	个子	眼镜
5 湖泊	瀑布	森林	图画

3 Match the verbs with the nouns to make phrases.

1 打	a 朋友
2 吃	b 病
3 检查	c 针
4 治	d 身体
5 关心	e 药

Now write five sentences using the phrases above.

4 Put the words in the correct categories.

a 胖	d 拉肚子	g 雪山
b 发烧	e 卷发	h 树木
c 山水	f 头痛	i 瘦

风景	生病	外表 / 样子

Grammar

1 Complete the sentences with the correct words.

1 我的作业 ______ 做完了。

a 已经　　b 刚才

2 我比我妹妹胖 ______。

a 有一点　　b 一点儿

3 明天 ______ 下雪吗？

a 要　　b 会

4 我不发烧了，______ 感觉也好多了。

a 而且　　b 另外

5 我 ______ 我的手套了。

a 找　　b 找到

2 Put the words in the correct order to make sentences.

1 九寨沟 / 我们 / 了 / 到 / 马上 / 就要 / 。

2 我奶奶 / 上海 / 看 / 会 / 去 / 暑假 / 我 / 。

3 吃饭 / 和永民 / 正在 / 马克 /呢 / 。

4 里 / 围巾 / 那条 / 放在 / 把 / 衣柜 / 。

5 吃 / 不能 / 所以 / 怕 / 我 / 辣 / 川菜 / ，/ 。

6 他 / 一样 / 瘦 / 他爸爸 / 跟 / 。

3 Complete the sentences with the words in the box.

地	的	得	不	没

1 我不太喜欢吃甜 ______。

2 王玉说英语说 ______ 很好。

3 她开心 ______ 跳起来。

4 他跑 ______ 很快。

5 这里五彩 ______ 湖水真美！

6 每个人都想健康 ______ 生活。

7 你想 ______ 想去听音乐会？

8 永民买 ______ 买那件唐装？

9 你有 ______ 有吃过午饭？

10 这个假期你回 ______ 回家？

4 Make sentences using the given words.

1 看电视时间 / 百分之……

2 除了……以外，还……

3 去美国 / 看朋友

4 参加除夕派对 / 庆祝新年

5 今天下午 / 就要……了

6 明年 / 就要……了

7 多 / 吃健康的饭菜

8 少 / 玩电子游戏

9 跑步 / 半个小时

Integrated skills

2-51

1 Listen and choose the most appropriate responses.

1 a 没问题。 b 没错。

2 a 不错。 b 很有趣！

3 a 有，我去旅行了。

b 有，我在这里住了两年。

4 a 听不到，你在说话吗？

b 听不到，你可以大声一点儿吗？

5 a 她又高又瘦。

b 她很乐观也很自信。

6 a 你应该多喝水，好好休息。

b 你应该去跑步，好好吃饭。

2 **Complete the sentences with the words in the brackets.**

1 我觉得肚子不舒服，

____________________。（可能）

2 我在派对上玩得很开心，

____________________。（而且）

3 如果你去成都旅游，

____________________。（一定）

4 凯特很关心朋友，

____________________。（经常）

5 想病早一点儿好，

____________________。（按时）

3 **Work in pairs. Complete the conversation.**

王玉：这几天我怎么没有看到你？

马克：________________________。

王玉：你为什么会生病？

马克：________________________。

王玉：你去看医生了吗？

马克：________________________。

王玉：医生给你开药了吗？

马克：________________________。

王玉：希望你很快好起来。

4 **Write three sentences to describe each of the following items.**

1 我的好朋友（样子，身材，性格）

____

2 我的学校（在哪里，有多大，女学生占百分之几）

____

3 我家附近的公园（多大，有什么，风景特点）

____

Enjoy Chinese

马

马	horse
马车	horse-drawn cart or carriage
骑马	ride a horse
兵马俑	Terracotta Warriors
马上	in no time; immediately

In its ancient form, the character 马 looks like a standing horse. It has a head, four feet, and a tail. As time went on, the character was simplified into its current form. Some Chinese characters are also formed by putting different characters together. Can you guess the meaning of the character 闯?

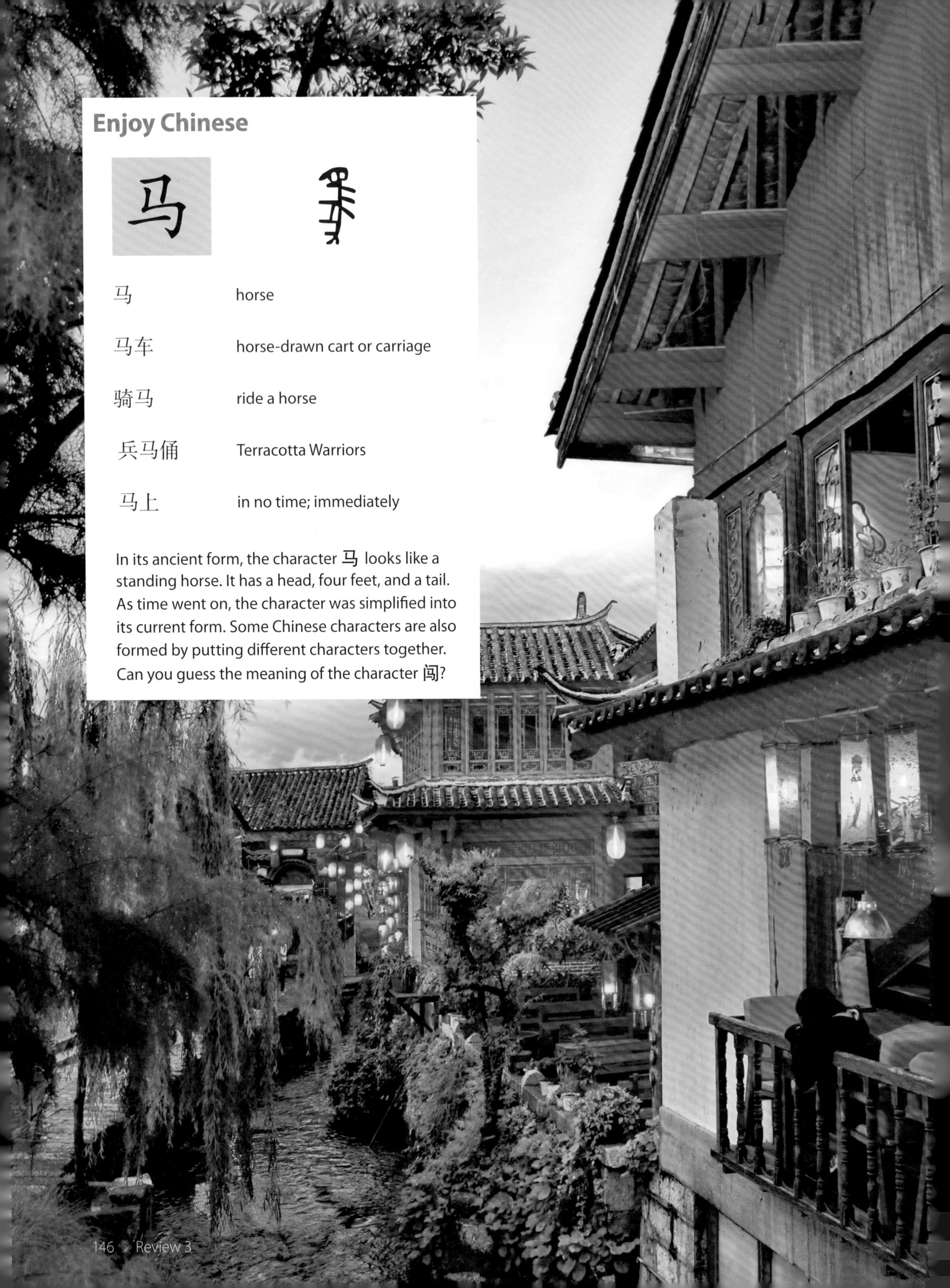

Pinyin pronunciation guide

Sound	Words	Example 1	Example 2
Initials			
b	bed	bō 玻	bēi 杯
p	pin	pō 坡	pāi 拍
m	moon	mō 摸	mái 埋
f	fun	fó 佛	fā 发
d	day	dé 得	dā 搭
t	tin	tè 特	tā 他
n	nose	ne 呢	nà 纳
l	long	lè 勒	lā 拉
g	good	gē 哥	gāi 该
k	kind	kē 科	kāi 开
h	hat	hē 喝	hā 哈
j	jug	jī 基	jiāo 交
q		qī 欺	qià 恰
x		xī 希	xiāo 消
zh	bridge	zhī 知	zhā 渣
ch	chin	chī 吃	chá 茶
sh	shirt	shī 诗	shā 沙
r	reduce	rì 日	rén 人
z	"ds" in reads	zī 资	zá 杂
c	"ts" in hats	cí 雌	cā 擦
s	say	sī 思	sè 色
Finals			
a	far	ā 啊	bā 八
o	saw	wō 喔	mò 墨
e	her	é 鹅	chē 车
i	bee	yī 衣	bǐ 比
u	rude	wū 乌	wū 屋
ü	German Fühlen	yū 迂	nǚ 女
ai	eye	āi 哀	bái 白
ei	eight	ēi 欸	féi 肥
ao	cow	áo 熬	bāo 包
ou	oh	ōu 欧	pōu 剖
an	enhance	ān 安	bān 班
en	taken	ēn 恩	běn 本
ang	gang	áng 昂	bāng 邦
eng	sung	hēng 亨	bēng 崩
ong	German Lunge	hōng 轰	dōng 东
ia	yard	ya 呀	ph
ie	yes	yē 耶	bié 别
iao	meow	yāo 腰	jiāo 交
iu	yoga	yōu 优	diū 丢
ian	yen	yān 烟	piān 偏
in	in	yīn 因	bīn 宾
iang	e + yang	yāng 央	niáng 娘
ing	sing	yīng 英	bǐng 丙
iong	German Jünger	yōng 雍	qióng 穷
ua	guano	wā 蛙	guā 瓜
uo	wall	wō 窝	duō 多
uai	why	wāi 歪	guài 怪
uei		wēi 威	wéi 围
uan	wan	wān 弯	duǎn 短
un	won	wēn 温	kūn 昆
uang	u + ongoing	wāng 汪	guāng 光
ueng		wēng 翁	wèng 瓮
üe	ü + eh	yuē 约	quē 缺
üan	ü + an	yuān 冤	xuān 宣
ün	German grün	yūn 晕	qún 群

Combinations of pinyin initials and simple finals

Initials \ simple finals	a	o	e	i	u	ü
b	ba	bo		bi	bu	
p	pa	po		pi	pu	
m	ma	mo	me	mi	mu	
f	fa	fo			fu	
d	da		de	di	du	
t	ta		te	ti	tu	
n	na		ne	ni	nu	nü
l	la		le	li	lu	lü
g	ga		ge		gu	
k	ka		ke		ku	
h	ha		he		hu	
j				ji		jü (ju)
q				qi		qü (qu)
x				xi		xü (xu)

Pair work activities for Student A

Unit 1

1 You are planning to meet Student B tomorrow to return some books you borrowed. Look at your timetable for tomorrow below.

8:00 – 10:00	中文课
10:10 – 11:00	中文考试
11:00 – 12:00	______________
12:00 – 1:00	吃午饭
1:00 – 2:00	去图书馆看书
3:00 – 4:00	______________
4:00 – 5:00	踢足球
5:00 – 6:00	______________
6:00 – 7:00	跟朋友看电影

2 Discuss and agree on a good time for you to meet.

Unit 2

1 Describe the scene shown in the picture below, including the sorts of clothes you could wear in that kind of weather, and the activities you could do.

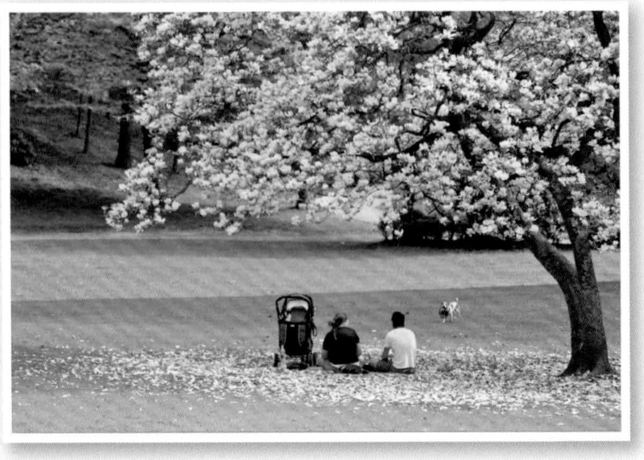

2 Look at the three pictures below. Listen to Student B's description and say which picture is being described.

Unit 3

1 Label Plan A with the different rooms and features of your ideal home.

Plan A

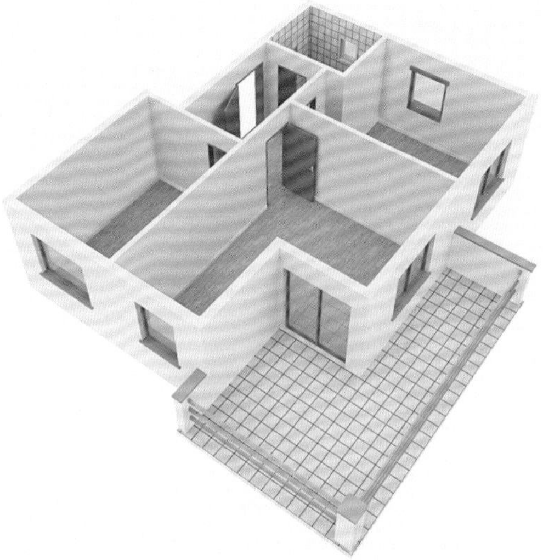

2 Answer Student B's questions about your ideal home.

3 Ask Student B questions and label Plan B with the rooms and features of their dream home.

Plan B

4 Compare your plans to find out whose Plan B contains the most accurate details.

Unit 4

1 Mark the following places on Map A.

医院　邮局　火车站　出租车站

Map A

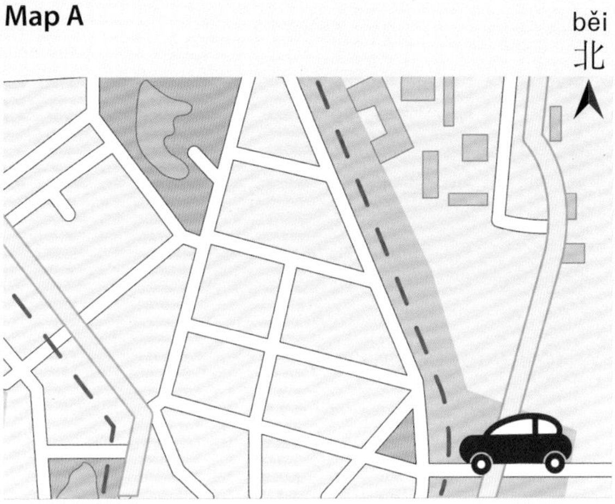

2 Answer Student B's questions about how to get to the places you marked on Map A.

3 Ask Student B questions about how to get to the following places and mark them on Map B.

宾馆　银行　博物馆　地铁站

Map B

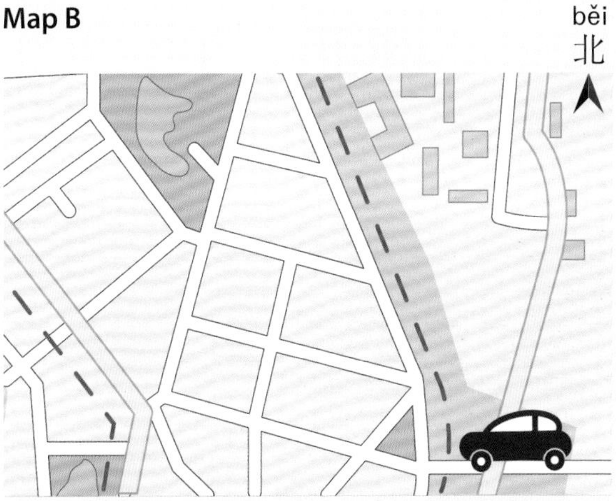

4 Compare your maps to find out whose Map B contains the most accurate details.

Unit 5

1 Look carefully at the picture. You have one minute to memorize as many details as possible.

2 Close your book. Describe the picture from memory, using 旁边, 对面, 上面, 下面 when necessary.

3 Listen to Student B describing a room, and draw it.

4 Compare your drawings with the original pictures to find out whose drawing contains the most accurate details.

Unit 6

1 Mime the following signs to Student B.

2 Guess what Student B is miming, in Chinese.

Unit 7

1 Look at the ingredients and choose three to make a dish. Add two ingredients of your own choice.

zhūròu	yángròu	niúròu	jīròu
猪肉	羊肉	牛肉	鸡肉
yúròu	jīdàn	mǐfàn	Yìdàlì miàn
鱼肉	鸡蛋	米饭	意大利 面

2 Write a recipe for your dish, including the ingredients and the cooking steps.

3 Explain to Student B how to make your dish, without saying its name.

4 Listen and guess the name of the dish that Student B is describing.

Unit 8

1 Choose three souvenirs of a trip to China from the objects below — two as gifts for friends and one to keep for yourself.

2 Ask Student B about the colour, size and use of the souvenirs and guess which they have chosen. Do not ask what they are.

3 Answer Student B's questions about your souvenirs. Do not say what they are.

Unit 9

1 Describe the scenery in the picture.

2 Listen to Student B's description of their picture.

3 Ask each other questions to find out the differences between your pictures.

Unit 10

1 Describe the appearance of the girl in the picture.

2 Listen to Student B's description of the girl in the picture when she was 30 years old.

3 Ask each other questions to find out how her appearance has changed.

Unit 11

1 You have a headache, a blocked nose and a cough, and you want to buy some medicine at a pharmacy. Prepare some questions to ask the pharmacist about the medicine they give you. Use the words below.

yàomíng 药名	medicine name
bùliáng fǎnyìng 不良　反应	side effects

2 Answer Student B's questions about your symptoms.

3 Ask Student B questions about the details of the medicine.

Unit 12

1 Describe the two candidates who are applying for the post of Student Events Manager at your school.

姓名: Jessica
国籍: 巴西
性格: 自信、乐观
爱好: 跳舞、潜水

姓名: Jean-Philippe
国籍: 法国
性格: 独立、自信
爱好: 唱民歌、购物

2 Listen to Student B's description of their candidates.

3 Ask each other questions about the candidates. Choose the best person for the job from the four candidates.

Pair work activities for Student B

Unit 1

1 You are planning to meet Student A tomorrow to get some books. Look at your timetable for tomorrow below.

8:00 – 10:00	英文课
10:10 – 11:00	______________
11:00 – 12:00	复习准备考试
12:00 – 1:00	______________
1:00 – 2:00	跟朋友们一起吃午饭
2:00 – 4:00	______________
4:00 – 5:00	去超市买东西
5:00 – 6:00	做作业
6:00 – 7:00	______________

2 Discuss and agree on a good time for you to meet.

Unit 2

1 Look at the three pictures below. Listen to Student A's description and say which of the three is being described.

2 Describe the scene shown in the picture below, including the sorts of clothes you could wear in that kind of weather, and the activities you could do.

Unit 3

1 Label Plan A with the different rooms and features of your ideal home.

Plan A

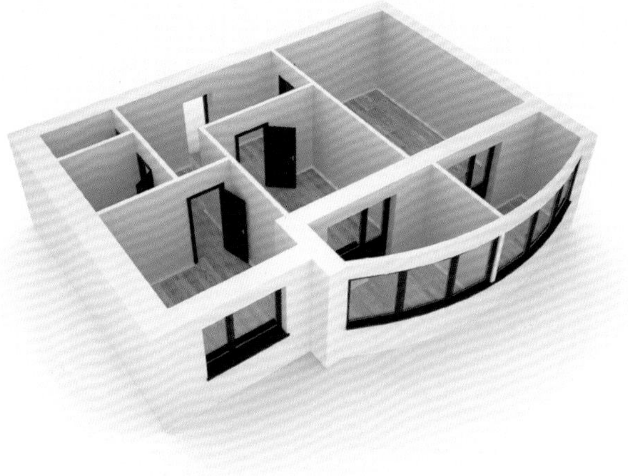

2 Ask Student A questions and label Plan B with the rooms and features of their dream home.

Plan B

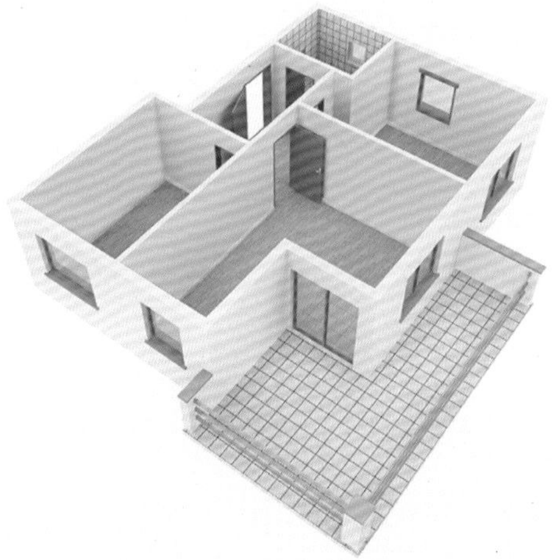

3 Answer Student A's questions about your ideal home.

4 Compare your plans to find out whose Plan B contains the most accurate details.

Unit 4

1 Mark these places on Map A.

宾馆　银行　博物馆　地铁站

Map A

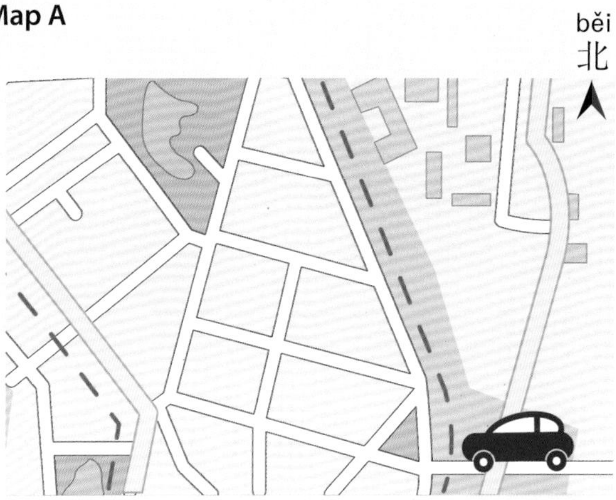

2 Ask Student A questions about how to get to the following places and mark them on Map B.

医院　邮局　火车站　出租车站

Map B

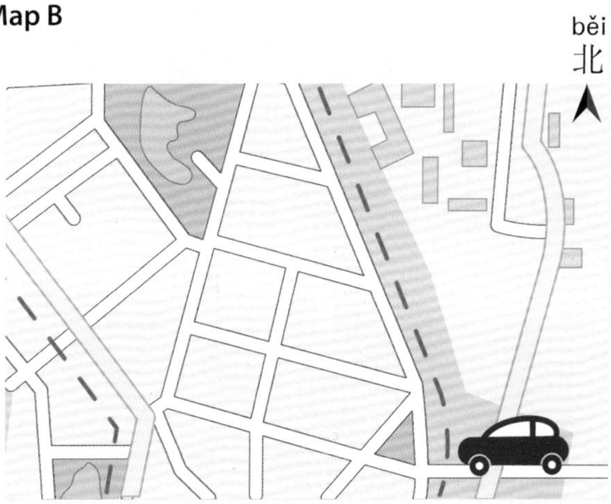

3 Answer Student A's questions about how to get to the places you marked on Map A.

4 Compare your maps to find out whose Map B contains the most accurate details.

Unit 5

1. Listen to Student A describing a room, and draw it.

2. Look carefully at the picture. You have one minute to memorize as many details as possible.

3. Close your book. Describe the picture from memory, using 旁边, 对面, 上面, 下面 when necessary.

4. Compare your drawings with the original pictures to find out whose drawing contains the most accurate details.

Unit 6

1. Guess what Student A is miming, in Chinese.

2. Mime the following signs to Student A.

Unit 7

1 Look at the ingredients and choose three to make a dish. Add two ingredients of your own choice.

zhūròu 猪肉	yángròu 羊肉	niúròu 牛肉	jīròu 鸡肉
yúròu 鱼肉	jīdàn 鸡蛋	mǐfàn 米饭	Yìdàlì miàn 意大利 面

2 Write a recipe for your dish, including the ingredients and the cooking steps.

3 Listen and guess the name of the dish that Student A is describing.

4 Explain to Student A how to make your dish, without saying its name.

Unit 8

1 Choose three souvenirs of a trip to China from the objects below — two as gifts for friends and one to keep for yourself.

2 Answer Student A's questions about your souvenirs. Do not say what they are.

3 Ask Student A about the colour, size, and use of the souvenirs, and guess which they have chosen. Do not ask what they are.

Unit 9

1 Listen to Student A's description of their picture.

2 Describe the scenery in the picture.

3 Ask each other questions to find out the differences between your pictures.

Unit 10

1 Listen to Student A's description of the woman in the picture below when she was seven years old.

2 Describe the appearance of the woman in the picture.

3 Ask each other questions to find out how her appearance has changed.

Unit 11

1 **You are a pharmacist. Read the medicine label and prepare to answer questions about it.**

yàomíng 药名：	gǎnmào qīng 感冒清
zhǔzhì 主治：	gǎnmào fāshāo bísāi 感冒，发烧，鼻塞
bùliáng fǎnyìng 不良反应：	kǒu gān wèibù bù shūfu wúlì tóuyūn děng 口干、胃部不舒服、无力、头晕等
yòngfǎ yòngliàng 用法用量：	kǒufú měi shí' èr xiǎoshí fú yí piàn èrshísì xiǎoshí nèi bù néng duō yú liǎng piàn 口服，每 12 小时服 1 片，24 小时内不能多于两片
zhùyì shìxiàng 注意事项：	fú yào shí bù néng hē jiǔ 服药时不能喝酒

2 **Ask Student A questions about their symptoms.**

3 **Answer Student A's questions about the medicine.**

Unit 12

1 **Listen to Student A's description of their candidates who are applying for the post of Student Events Manager at your school.**

2 **Describe these two candidates who are applying for the same post.**

姓名：Pak Jimin
国籍：韩国
性格：关心别人、诚实
爱好：在家看书、听音乐

姓名：Stefan
国籍：德国
性格：急脾气、勇敢
爱好：蹦极、滑雪

3 **Ask each other questions about the candidates. Choose the best person for the job from the four candidates.**

Grammar reference

Unit 1

The auxiliary word 得 (de)

The auxiliary word 得 is used between a verb and its complement to indicate result or degree. An adjective phrase is used after 得 as the verb complement. There can be two verbs in a sentence with 得 to indicate the complement. The first verb phrase expresses an event, while the second verb expresses the exact action involved in the event. The second verb should be the same as the verb included in the first verb phrase. To negate the sentence, the adverb 不 is used at the beginning of the adjective phrase as part of the complement. For example,

Subject	Verb phrase	Verb	de 得	Complement
Mǎkè 马克	tiào 跳		de 得	hěn gāo 很高。
Mark jumps very high.				
Tā 他	pǎo 跑		de 得	kuài 快。
He runs quickly.				
Nǐ 你	chànggē 唱歌	chàng 唱	de 得	hěn hǎotīng 很好听。
You sing very well.				
Tā 她	tiàowǔ 跳舞	tiào 跳	de 得	bù hǎo 不好。
She does not dance well.				
Mèimei 妹妹	chīfàn 吃饭	chī 吃	de 得	hěn màn 很慢。
My little sister eats slowly.				
Wǒ 我	kànshū 看书	kàn 看	de 得	bú kuài 不快。
I don't read books very quickly.				

Topic-comment sentences

When a piece of information is already known to the speakers, it is often put at the beginning of a sentence as the subject. This structure is called a topic-comment sentence, which is different from the usual word order of Chinese sentences.

For example,

Topic	Comment
Xīngqīsān de kǎoshì 星期三的考试	wǒ zhǔnbèi hǎo le 我准备好了。
I have finished preparing for Wednesday's test.	
Xīngqītiān yìqǐ qù chīfàn 星期天一起去吃饭	tā hái bù zhīdào 她还不知道。
She still doesn't know about going to eat together on Sunday.	
Míngtiān jiāo zuòyè 明天交作业	dāngrán bù kěnéng 当然不可能。
Of course it's impossible to hand in the homework tomorrow.	
Yìbiān gōngzuò yìbiān dúshū 一边工作一边读书	tài nán le 太难了。
Working and studying at the same time is too difficult.	

了 (le) as a particle and an auxiliary word

Besides being used as an auxiliary word placed after a verb to express past actions, 了 can also be used as a particle placed at the end of a sentence to indicate a statement, showing a change of situation or state. For example,

Subject	Predicate
Tā 他	qùle Běijīng 去了北京。
He went to Beijing.	
Nǐ 你	chīfàn le ma 吃饭了吗?
Have you eaten?	
Wǒ 我	zhīdào zhè jiàn shì le 知道这件事了。
I know (now) about this whole thing.	
Wáng Yù 王玉	qù shàngkè le 去上课了。
Wang Yu went to class.	

Expressing succession using 一 (yī)……就 (jiù)……

一……就…… is used to connect two events or actions that happen one right after the other. It means "as soon as". The subjects of the two actions or events can be the same or different.

For example,

Tā yí shàngkè jiù xiǎng shuìjiào
他一上课就想睡觉。

As soon as he began class he wanted to sleep.

Wǒ yí dào Xī'ān jiù gěi nǐ dǎ diànhuà
我一到西安，就给你打电话。

As soon as I reach Xi'an, I'll give you a call.

Wǒ yì huílai tā jiù chūqu
我一回来，他就出去。

As soon as I came back, he went out.

一……就…… can also be used to connect a time phrase and an action or event, meaning something will happen as soon as the time comes. For example,

Yí dào zhōumò tā jiù qù kàn yéye
一到周末，她就去看爷爷。

As soon as the weekend comes, I'll go to see Grandpa.

Yí dào shǔjià wǒ jiù qù lǚxíng
一到暑假，我就去旅行。

Once it's the summer holidays, I'm going travelling.

Yí dào wǎnshang jiǔ diǎn wǒ jiù shàngchuáng shuìjiào
一到晚上九点，我就上床睡觉。

When it gets to 9 pm, I'll go to bed.

Unit 2

Expressing similarity using A和B + 差不多/一样 (hé chàbuduō yíyàng)

"A和B + 差不多 / 一样" is used to express similarity between two things. 差不多 is often used alone as the predicate, meaning "almost the same". 一样 means "the same" or "identical". It can stand alone, or be followed by an adjective as its complement stating the specific details of the similarity. For example,

A	hé 和	B	Adjective	Complement
Zhè jiàn yīfu de jiàqián 这件衣服的价钱	hé 和	nà jiàn yīfu de jiàqián 那件（衣服的价钱）	chàbuduō 差不多。	
The prices of this item of clothing and that one are almost the same.				

A	hé 和	B	Adjective	Complement
Běijīng de tiānqì 北京的天气	hé 和	Niǔyuē de tiānqì 纽约的（天气）	chàbuduō ma 差不多吗？	
Is the weather in Beijing and New York similar?				
Zhèlǐ de wēndù 这里的温度	hé 和	nàlǐ de wēndù 那里的（温度）	yíyàng 一样。	
The temperature here is the same as there.				
Mèimei 妹妹	hé 和	jiějie 姐姐	yíyàng 一样	piàoliang 漂亮。
The younger and elder sisters are equally pretty.				

Making comparisons using A 比/没有 B + adjective (bǐ méiyǒu)

"A比B + adjective" is used to make the comparison between two things, meaning the former is higher in degree than the latter. 没有 is used to express that A is less or lower in degree than B. When the same head noun is used in both A and B, the head noun in B can be left out to avoid repetition. For example,

A	bǐ méiyǒu 比/没有	B	Adjective
Zhōngguó dàxué de shàngkè shíjiān 中国大学的上课时间	bǐ 比	Yīngguó dàxué de shàngkè shíjiān 英国大学的（上课时间）	zǎo 早。
Classes in Chinese universities start earlier than those in British universities.			
Jīntiān de tiānqì 今天的天气	bǐ 比	zuótiān de tiānqì 昨天的（天气）	hǎo 好。
Today's weather is nicer than yesterday's.			
Zhèxiē zhàopiàn 这些照片	méiyǒu 没有	nàxiē zhàopiàn 那些（照片）	piàoliang 漂亮。
These photographs are not as pretty as those.			
Xī'ān 西安	méiyǒu 没有	Běijīng 北京	dà 大。
Xi'an is not as big as Beijing.			

Expressing future actions with 要/会 (yào huì)

要 can be a modal verb, meaning 需要 (need). For example, 我要买一件大衣。(I need to buy a coat.)

When 要 is used to express future actions, it usually indicates something that the speaker intends to do. For example, 我要去看电影。(I'm going to go and see a film.)

Besides expressing ability (e.g. 她会说日语), the modal verb 会 can also be used to express a future event, indicating a high probability. 不 is used before 会 to negate sentences about future events. Sometimes 的 is used at the end of the sentences to strengthen the certainty.

Adverbial of time	Subject	Modal verb	Verb phrase
Jīntiān wǎnshang 今天 晚上	Yǒngmín 永民	huì 会	lái ma 来吗？
Will Yeong-min come tonight?			
	Tā 他	bú huì 不会	lái le 来了。
He won't come.			
	Wǒ 我	huì 会	gěi nǐ dǎ diànhuà de 给你打电话的。
I'm going to phone you.			
Zhōumò 周末	wǒ 我	huì 会	qù kàn nǐ de 去看你的。
I'm going to go and see you at the weekend.			

Unit 3

Expressing actions in progress using 正在 (zhèngzài)

正在 is an adverb used before a verb phrase to indicate that something is taking place or someone is right in the middle of doing something at the time mentioned. Either 正 or 在 can be left out if the emphasis is on the event as a whole instead of something happening at that moment. Sometimes, 呢 can be used at the end of a progressive sentence to emphasize the continuousness of the action or event. For example,

Adverbial	Subject	zhèngzài 正在	Verb phrase	ne 呢
	Wǒ 我	zhèngzài 正在	mǎi dōngxi 买东西。	
I am in the middle of shopping.				
Zuótiān xiàwǔ sì diǎn 昨天 下午 四点	Yǒngmín 永民	zhèng zài （正）在	dǎ lánqiú 打篮球	ne 呢。
At four yesterday afternoon, Yeong-min was playing basketball.				
Nǐ dǎ diànhuà de shíhou 你打电话的时候，	wǒ 我	zhèng zài 正（在）	kàn diànshì 看电视	ne 呢。
I was watching TV when you phoned.				

Expressing "both… and…" with 又……又…… (yòu yòu)

又……又…… is used to express equal characteristics of a person or entity, and concurrent actions, events or circumstances. It can be used to link verb phrases and adjective phrases. The words connected by 又……又…… should be of the same structure or part of speech, stating things that do not contradict with each other. When adjective phrases are linked, the adverb 很, meaning "very" and usually placed before the adjectives, can be left out. For example,

Time/Place/Manner	First condition/quality	Second condition/quality
	Dìtiě hěn kuài 地铁很快。	Dìtiě hěn piányi 地铁很便宜。
Dìtiě yòu kuài yòu piányi 地铁又快又便宜。		
The subway is both quick and cheap.		
Zài pàiduì shang 在派对上，	tā chànggē 他唱歌，	tā tiàowǔ 他跳舞。
Zài pàiduì shang, tā yòu chànggē yòu tiàowǔ 在派对上，他又唱歌又跳舞。		
At the party, he was singing and dancing.		

xiān ránhòu

Expressing sequences with 先……然后……

先……然后…… expresses a succession of actions or sequence of events. 先 must be placed after the subject of the first action or event, while 然后 is usually placed before the subject of the following action or event. The second subject is often left out if it is the same as the first subject. For example,

First event / action	Second event / action
Wǒ xiān kàn shū 我 先 看 书，	ránhòu qù dǎ wǎngqiú 然后 去 打 网球。
First I read, then I go to play tennis.	
Wáng Yù xiān qù kàn yéye 王 玉 先 去 看 爷爷，	ránhòu hé Shǐdìfū kàn diànyǐng 然后 和史蒂夫 看 电影。
First Wang Yu went to see her grandfather, then she watched a film with Steve.	
Míngtiān wǒ yào xiān qù yínháng 明天 我 要 先 去 银行，	ránhòu qù chāoshì mǎi dōngxi 然后 去 超市 买 东西。
Tomorrow I'm going to go to the bank first, then I'll go shopping at the supermarket.	

Unit 4

lí duōyuǎn

Talking about distance using 离/ 多 远

离 is used to express how far away one place is from the other. The subject takes the form of A离B. The distance can be described simply with an adjective, precisely with physical distance, or approximately with time spent on transportation. For example,

Subject	Predicate
Wǒ jiā lí xuéxiào 我 家 离 学校	hěn jìn 很 近。
My home is very close to the college.	
Xīní lí Mò'ěrběn 悉尼 离 墨尔本	dàyuē gōnglǐ 大约 900 公里。
Sydney is about 900km from Melbourne.	
Niǔyuē lí Bōshìdùn 纽约 离 波士顿	kāi chē sì gè xiǎoshí 开 车 四 个 小时。
New York is four hours' drive from Boston.	

If the starting or ending point of a distance is obviously known in the context, 离 and the known point can be left out of the sentence. For example,

Nǐ jiā duō yuǎn
你 家 多 远？ How far away is your home?

Zǒulù shí fēnzhōng
走路 十 分钟 。It takes ten minutes on foot.

cóng dào

Expressing distance using 从 A 到 B

"从A到B" is used to describe the distance between two places, with A being the starting point and B the ending point. The topic takes the form "从A到B", which is often followed by a comment including a verb phrase and the duration of time.

Topic				Comment	
cóng 从	A	dào 到	B	Verb phrase	Duration
Cóng 从	Lúndūn 伦敦	dào 到	Bālí 巴黎，	zuò gāosù huǒchē 坐 高速 火车	zuì fāngbiàn 最 方便 。
High-speed train is the most convenient way from London to Paris.					
Cóng 从	xuéxiào 学校	dào 到	wǒ jiā 我 家	zǒu lù 走 路	shí fēnzhōng 十 分钟 。
It takes ten minutes to walk from the college to my house.					
Cóng 从	Xī'ān 西安	dào 到	Běijīng 北京	kāi chē 开 车	shíjiān hěn cháng 时间 很 长 。
It takes a long time to drive from Xi'an to Beijing.					

"从A到B" can also be used to express the starting and ending points of a period of time. For example,

Cóng Xīngqīyī dào Xīngqīwǔ měitiān wǒ dōu yǒu hěn duō zuòyè
从 星期一 到 星期五， 每天 我 都 有 很 多 作业。

I have a lot of homework from Monday to Friday.

Cóng xiǎo dào dà wǒ dōu hěn xǐhuan chànggē
从 小 到 大， 我 都 很 喜欢 唱歌 。

I have liked singing very much since childhood.

yǐhòu de shíhou
Using 以后 / ……的 时候

以后 is used together with a verb phrase or time phrase to express a sequence of actions or events, meaning "after". It is used at the end of an adverbial phrase or clause stating time, which can be put before or after the subject of the sentence. For example,

Adverbial clause	Subject	Adverbial	Predicate
Huíjiā yǐhòu 回家 以后，	wǒ 我		gěi Ānnà dǎ diànhuà 给 安娜 打 电话。
After I got home, I telephoned Anna.			
Liǎng nián yǐhòu 两 年 以后，	Xiǎomíng 小明		yào qù Měiguó 要 去 美国。
After two years, Xiao Ming will go to America.			
	Wǒ māma 我 妈妈	sān tiān 三 天 yǐhòu 以后	lái kàn wǒ 来 看 我。
My mother came to see me three days later.			

……的时候 is also used at the end of an adverbial phrase or clause stating time, meaning "when".

Adverbial clause	Subject	Predicate
Fàngxué de shíhou 放学 的 时候，	Mǎkè 马克	hái méiyǒu zuòwán zuòyè 还 没有 做完 作业。
When class finished, Mark had still not finished his homework.		
Chī wǎnfàn de shíhou 吃 晚饭 的时候，	wǒ 我	qùle diànyǐngyuàn 去了 电影院 。
At dinner time, I went to the cinema.		

Unit 5

yǒu
Expressing possession, existence or location with 有

有 is used to express possession. The subject of the possession sentence with 有 can be a person or something. For example,

Wǒ yǒu hěn duō gùshishū
我 有 很 多 故事书。 I have a lot of story books.

Bówùguǎn yǒu hěn duō wénwù
博物馆 有 很 多 文物。 The museum has many artefacts.

Xī'ān yǒu jǐ qiān nián de lìshǐ
西安 有 几 千 年 的 历史。

Xi'an has several thousand years of history.

有 can also be used to describe the existence or location of one thing in relation to another. The subject is usually a locative phrase, which contains or is equal in size to the object. For example,

Locative phrase		Verb	Noun phrase
Wǒ de yīguì 我 的 衣柜	li 里	yǒu 有	hěn duō yīfu 很 多 衣服。
There are a lot of clothes in my wardrobe.			
Zhuōzi 桌子	xiàmian 下面	yǒu 有	yì shuāng xié 一 双 鞋。
There's a pair of shoes under the table.			
Wǒ de gōngyù 我 的 公寓	qiánmiàn 前面	yǒu 有	yí gè chāoshì 一 个 超市。
There is a supermarket in front of my building.			
Xuéxiào 学校	dōngbian 东边	yǒu 有	yí gè diànyǐngyuàn 一 个 电影院。
There is a cinema to the east of the college.			

gòu búgòu
Expressing adequacy with 够/不够

够 is used as a verb with its own complement, meaning "be enough / sufficient" or "reach (a standard)". Its negative form is 不够.

For example,

Wǒmen diǎn de cài gòu ma
我们 点 的 菜 够 吗？

Have we ordered enough food?

Wǒ de shíjiān bú gòu yòng
我 的 时间 不 够 用 。

I don't have enough time.

够 can also be used as an adverb before some adjectives, meaning "enough" or "really". For example,

Jīntiān de tiānqì gòu lěng wǒmen kěyǐ chī huǒguō
今天 的 天气 够 冷， 我们 可以 吃 火锅。

Today's weather is cold enough for us to have hot pot.

Kāi chē gòu kuài, bàn gè xiǎoshí jiù kěyǐ dào Bīngmǎyǒng bówùguǎn

开车够快，半个小时就可以到兵马俑博物馆。

Driving is really fast, and it takes only half an hour to get to the Terracotta Warriors museum.

Complements expressing result

An adjective or a verb phrase is often used after a verb as its complement to indicate result. For example,

Subject	Verb	Complement
Wǒ 我	xiě 写	wán le 完了。
I finished writing.		
Tā de shǒujī 她的手机	zhǎo 找	bú dào le 不到了。
She couldn't find her mobile phone.		
Nǐ 你	kàn 看	dǒng le ma 懂了吗？
Did you understand that?		
Wǒ 我	zhǔnbèi 准备	hǎo le 好了。
I'm (fully) ready.		
Yīfu 衣服	xǐ 洗	gānjìng le 干净了。
The clothes have been cleaned.		
Nǐ 你	zuò 做	duì le 对了。
You did it right.		

Questions about size with (有) 多大 / 长 / 宽

(yǒu duō dà cháng kuān)

多 means "to what extent" when used in questions. It is often used to modify words expressing measurements such as 大, 长, 宽, 高, etc. The verb 有 is optionally used in the questions about sizes. In answers to questions about sizes, the word expressing measurement can be used as the predicate. 有 can also be used to introduce the size followed by the word expressing measurement.

Question

Subject	Predicate	
	Verb	Question word
Zhège tǐyùchǎng 这个体育场	yǒu (有)	duō dà 多大？
How big is the sports ground?		

Answers

Subject	Verb	Measurement	Size	Measurement
Zhège tǐyùchǎng 这个体育场		cháng 长	500 mǐ 米。	
Zhège tǐyùchǎng 这个体育场	yǒu (有)		500 mǐ 米	cháng 长。
This sports ground is 500m long.				
Zhège tǐyùchǎng 这个体育场		kuān 宽	400 mǐ 米。	
Zhège tǐyùchǎng 这个体育场	yǒu (有)		400 mǐ 米	kuān 宽。
This sports ground is 400m wide.				

Unit 6

Expressing passive voice using 被 (bèi)

被 is used to form passive voice sentences, emphasizing the object being acted upon and the changes that take place as a consequence of the action. The object being acted upon is used as the subject before 被. The doer of the action is used after 被, and can be omitted if it is not known or not necessary to be mentioned.

Subject	Adverbial		Verb	Complement
	bèi 被	Doer		
Wǒ de yīfu 我的衣服	bèi 被	rén (人)	ná 拿	zǒu le 走了。
My clothes were taken (by someone).				
Wǒ de wǎnfàn 我的晚饭	bèi 被	dìdi 弟弟	chī 吃	le 了。
My dinner was eaten by my little brother.				
Zhè běn shū 这本书	bèi 被	tā 他	mǎi 买	le 了。
This book was bought by him.				

Expressing a continuing action or state with 着 (zhe)

着 is used after a verb to indicate the continuation of an action or a state. The verb should be stative, expressing the status of something resulting from an action, such as 穿, 戴, 坐, 写, 放, 贴, 挂, etc.

For example,

Subject	Verb	zhe 着	Object
Yǒngmín 永民	dài 戴	zhe 着	tàiyángjìng 太阳镜。
Yeong-min is wearing sunglasses.			
Tā 她	chuān 穿	zhe 着	hóng qúnzi 红 裙子。
She is wearing a red skirt.			
Fángjiān li 房间 里	zuò 坐	zhe 着	yí wèi xiānsheng 一位 先生 。
There is a gentleman sitting in the room.			
Zhuōzi shang 桌子 上	fàng 放	zhe 着	yí gè diànhuà 一个 电话。
A telephone is on the table.			
Ménkǒu 门口	guà 挂	zhe 着	hóng dēnglong 红 灯笼 。
Red lanterns are hanging from the gate.			

是(shì)……的(de) constructions

是……的 is used to talk about a certain aspect of a past action or event. In this structure the focus is not on the action or event itself, but on one aspect of the action such as time, place, manner, purpose or target of the action or event.

是 is usually placed right after the subject and can be omitted in an affirmative or interrogative sentence, while 的 is put at the end of the sentence and cannot be omitted.

Subject	shì 是	Time/ Place/ Manner	Predicate	de 的
Nǐ 你	shì 是	zěnme 怎么	rènshi tā 认识 她	de 的？
How do you know her?				
Wǒ 我	shì 是	zài Běijīng 在 北京	rènshi tā 认识 她	de 的。
I met her in Beijing.				

Subject	shì 是	Time/ Place/ Manner	Predicate	de 的
Nǐ 你	shì (是)	shénme shíhou 什么 时候	qù Měiguó 去 美国	de 的？
When did you go to America?				
Wǒ 我	shì (是)	shàng gè yuè 上 个 月	qù 去	de 的。
I went last month.				

In addition, if the main verb is followed by an object, 的 can be put either before or after the object. For example,

Wǒ shì zuótiān qù de xuéxiào
我 是 昨天 去 的 学校 。

Wǒ shì zuótiān qù xuéxiào de
我 是 昨天 去 学校 的。

I went to the college yesterday.

Unit 7

Noun phrases with 的 (de)

的 is used after a noun, pronoun, verb or adjective to form a noun phrase. It is used to refer to someone or something that is already known in the context. Therefore the head noun is usually left out. 的 can also be used to indicate a certain type of people or things.

Referring to a known object/person	
adjective + 的 (de)	Gōngyuán li de huā kāi le, yǒu hóng de, yǒu huáng de 公园 里 的 花 开 了，有 红 的，有 黄 的。 The flowers in the park have bloomed. There are red and yellow ones.
pronoun + 的 (de)	Zhè bù shǒujī bú shì wǒ de, shì tā de 这 部 手机 不 是 我 的，是 他 的。 This mobile phone isn't mine, it's his.
noun + 的 (de)	Tāmen de yīfu dōu shì hēisè de 他们 的 衣服 都 是 黑色 的。 Their clothes are all black.
verb + 的 (de)	Tā shuō de bú duì 他 说 的 不 对。 What he said is not correct.

Indicating a certain category	
adjective de +的	Wǒ xǐhuan chī tián de 我喜欢吃甜的。 I like eating sweet things.
noun de +的	Xīn tóngxué shì gè nán de 新同学是个男的。 The new classmate is male.

Giving instructions using imperatives

Imperatives are commonly used to give instructions, orders or make requests. As the instruction or request is usually directed to the hearer, the subject is understood by both parties, and therefore often dropped. Other than that, an imperative is similar to an ordinary statement. The adverb 请 is often used at the beginning of an imperative to make it sound polite, and the particle 吧 is often added at the end of an imperative to soften the tone.

Adverbial	Verb	Object
Zài guō li 在锅里	jiā 加	yì wǎn jī tāng 一碗鸡汤。
Add a bowl of chicken broth to the pot.		
Qǐng gěi wǒ 请给我	ná 拿	yì bēi shuǐ 一杯水。
Please bring me a glass of water.		
	Chī 吃	fàn ba 饭吧！
Eat up!		

bǎ 把 sentences

The 把 construction includes the agent, the object acted on, the act itself and the result of the action. The object is usually a definite noun, known to both the speaker and hearer. The result of the action can be an adjective or noun expressing the changed state of the object, or a place or person that is involved in the action.

Subject	bǎ 把	Object	Verb	Complement
	Bǎ 把	ròu 肉	chǎo 炒	shú 熟。
Stir-fry the meat until cooked.				
	Bǎ 把	cōng 葱	qiē 切	chéng mò 成末。
Finely chop the spring onions.				
Wǒ 我	bǎ 把	Zhōngwén shū 中文书	fàng 放	zài jiā li le 在家里了。
I left the Chinese book at home.				

Unit 8

Duplication of verbs

Duplication of verbs is used to soften the tone of a sentence. By duplicating a verb, the speaker wants to sound either less decisive, or more polite. Duplication of verbs is often used when making suggestions or requests. 一 can be placed between the duplicated verbs to express a mild tone.

Subject	Verb	Object	Other
Wǒ 我	kànkan 看看	nǐ de shū 你的书，	kěyǐ ma 可以吗？
Is it OK for me to have a look at your book?			
Nǐ 你	chīchi 吃吃	wǒ zuò de jiǎozi 我做的饺子。	
Have a taste of the dumplings I made.			
Wǒmen 我们	dǎda 打打	wǎngqiú 网球，	zěnmeyàng 怎么样？
We'll play a bit of tennis, OK?			
Nǐ 你	shì yí shì 试一试	zhè tiáo kùzi 这条裤子。	
Try on these trousers.			

"The more ... the more ..." yuè 越……yuè 越……

越……越…… is used to link a verb or adjective with a verb phrase or adjective phrase, meaning the degree increases as something goes on or increases.

Subject	yuè 越	Verb/ Adjective	yuè 越	Verb phrase/ Adjective phrase
Wǒ 我	yuè 越	chī 吃	yuè 越	xiǎng chī 想 吃。
The more I eat, the more I want to eat.				
Tā 他	yuè 越	shuō 说	yuè 越	bù gāoxìng 不 高兴。
The more he talks the less happy he is.				
Xiǎomíng 小明	yuè 越	gāoxìng 高兴	yuè 越	bù xiǎng zǒu 不 想 走。
The happier Xiao Ming was, the less he wanted to leave.				
Wèntí 问题	yuè 越	shǎo 少	yuè 越	hǎo 好。
The fewer problems the better.				

Notional passive

Notional passive is used when the focus is on how the object is dealt with and the result of the action, without the need to mention the doer or agent of the action. In a notional passive sentence, the object being acted upon is used as the subject, followed by a verb and its complement. There is no 被 in a notional passive sentence. A notional passive sentence sounds more active than a passive voice sentence with 被, as the focus is on the result or changed state of the object acted upon. For example,

Biǎo tiánwán le
表 填完 了。

The form is filled in.

Zuòyè fàng zài jiā li le
作业 放 在 家 里 了。

The homework is at home.

Shǒutào zhǎo bú dào le
手套 找 不 到 了。

The gloves could not be found.

Unit 9

Expressing result of an action with dào 到

到 can be used after many different verbs to form a verb complement indicating the result of an action. Depending on the meaning of the verbs, the verb complement can be a place or an object following 到. For instance, when used after 回 or 来, the complement with 到 indicates a place.

Verb	Complement	
	dào 到	Place
huí 回	dào 到	sùshè 宿舍
return to the dormitory		
lái 来	dào 到	xuéxiào 学校
come to the college		
lái 来	dào 到	Běijīng 北京
come to Beijing		

When used after sensory verbs (看, 听, 想) or action verbs (找, 拿, 买), the complement with 到 indicates an object. 不 is used between the verb and 到 to express a negative result. For example,

Verb	Complement	
	dào 到	Object
kàn 看	dào 到	hěn duō rén 很 多 人
see many people		
zhǎo 找	bú dào （不）到	wǒ mèimei 我 妹妹
(can't) find my little sister		
ná 拿	bú dào （不）到	bàozhǐ 报纸
(can't) pick up a newspaper		
mǎi 买	dào 到	yí jiàn hěn hǎokàn de T xù 一 件 很 好看 的 T 恤
buy a nice-looking T-shirt		

Expressing percentages using bǎifēnzhī 百分之……

占……百分之…… is used to express the percentage of something in a group. 占 means "constitute", "make up" or "account for". An adjective phrase is used before 百分之 to state what the percentage is a proportion of. It can be left out if this is known in context.

For example,

Subject	Verb	Adjective phrase	Percentage
Shuìjiào shíjiān 睡觉 时间	zhàn 占	suǒyǒu shíjiān de (所有 时间的)	bǎifēnzhī 百分之 sānshí 三十。
The time spent sleeping is 30% (of the total time).			
Zuò dìtiě 坐 地铁 shàngbān de rén 上班 的人	zhàn 占	suǒyǒu shàngbān 所有 上班 rénshù de 人数 的)	bǎifēnzhī 百分之 wǔshí 五十。
People who go to work by subway constitute 50% (of all the commuters).			

chúle yǐwài hái
除了……以外，还……

除了 is a preposition used before a noun, a verb or an adjective. When it is used in a sentence with 还, 除了 means "as well as". The word placed after 除了 should express something that is of the same nature as what is stated in the main clause with 还. For example,

Chúle qúnzi yǐwài tā hái mǎile dàyī
除了 裙子 以外，她 还 买了 大衣。

Besides a skirt, she also bought a coat.

Chúle pǎobù yǐwài tā hái xǐhuan dǎ lánqiú
除了 跑步 以外，他 还 喜欢 打 篮球。

In addition to jogging, he also likes playing basketball.

However, if 除了 is used in a sentence without 还, it means "except" or "apart from". For example,

Chúle tā suǒyǒu rén dōu qù kàn diànyǐng le
除了 他，所有 人 都 去 看 电影 了。

Everyone went to see the film except him.

Chúle Xīngqīliù yǐwài wǒ měitiān dōu kěyǐ lái
除了星期六（以外），我 每天 都 可以 来。

I can come every day except Saturday.

Chúle shuǐzhǔyú wǒ xǐhuan suǒyǒu de cài
除了 水煮鱼，我 喜欢 所有 的 菜。

I like all the dishes except the spicy fish.

Unit 10

Serial verb constructions

In serial verb constructions, the predicate of a sentence can contain more than one verb phrase expressing consecutive actions. These verb phrases are related in manner or purpose, and their order cannot be changed. Usually the first verb phrase regards manner, while the last verb phrase concerns purpose. For example,

Subject	Predicate	
	Verb phrase 1	Verb phrase 2
Zhōngguórén 中国人	tiē chūnlián 贴 春联 (manner)	qìngzhù xīnnián de dàolái 庆祝 新年 的到来。
Chinese people stick up Spring Festival couplets to celebrate the arrival of the New Year.		
Wǒ 我	zuò huǒchē 坐 火车 (manner)	qù Běijīng 去 北京。
I took the train to Beijing.		
Wǒmen 我们	qù Wáng Yù jiā 去 王 玉 家	bàinián 拜年。(purpose)
We went to Wang Yu's home to pay a New Year visit.		
Wǒmen 我们	qù Sìchuān fànguǎn 去 四川 饭馆	chīfàn 吃饭。(purpose)
We went to a Sichuan restaurant to eat.		

Affirmative-negative questions

Affirmative-negative questions are used to ask whether something is positive or negative. The question word consists of a verb or an adjective and their negative form with 不 or 没, for example, 好不好/ 看没看. 不 is used to ask about a simple fact, while 没 is used to ask about whether something has happened or not, except when using 有没有 to ask about possession.

Affirmative-negative questions can be used after the subject as the predicate or part of the predicate, or at the end of a statement as a follow-up question. The answer to an affirmative-negative question is either positive or negative. There is no need to provide any new information to answer such questions.

Subject	Predicate	
	Adjective / Verb	Object
Tā 他	shì bú shì 是不是	Yáo Míng 姚明？
Is he Yao Ming?		
Nǐ 你	qù bú qù 去不去	Chéngdū 成都？
Are you going to Chengdu?		
Zhè tiáo qúnzi 这条裙子	hǎokàn bù hǎokàn 好看不好看？	
Does this skirt look nice?		
Nǐ 你	kàn méi kàn 看没看	diànshì 电视？
Did you watch television?		
Wáng Yù 王玉	lái méi lái 来没来？	
Did Wang Yu come?		

Statement	Tag question
Zuò dìtiě qù 坐地铁去，	hǎo bù hǎo 好不好？
Going by subway, is that OK?	
Xiàwǔ sān diǎn zhōng 下午三点钟，	kě bù kěyǐ 可不可以？
Three o'clock in the afternoon, is that possible?	
Zhè tiáo qúnzi hěn hǎokàn 这条裙子很好看，	shì bú shì 是不是？
This skirt is really pretty, isn't it?	

Expressing immediate actions with (就) 要……了 (jiù yào le)

(就) 要……了 is used to express that an action or event is about to happen in the near future. **就** is used before **要** to emphasize the immediacy in time. Adverbs expressing time are often used before **(就) 要** to indicate how soon the action or event is to take place. **就** is often left out in spoken Chinese and less formal situations.

Subject	Adverb	Predicate	
Wǒ 我		yào 要	huí guó le 回国了。
I'm going home (to my country) soon.			
Tā 她		jiù yào （就）要	xià chē le 下车了。
She's about to get off (the bus/train).			
Wǒmen 我们	mǎshàng 马上	jiù yào （就）要	dào Chéngdū le 到成都了。
We're about to arrive in Chengdu right now.			
Shǔjià 暑假	hěn kuài 很快	jiù yào （就）要	dào le 到了。
The summer holidays will begin very soon.			

Unit 11

The auxiliary word 地 (de)

地 is often used after an adjective to form an adverbial phrase, placed before a verb to describe the manner of an action. It is part of the adverbial phrase, and cannot be placed after the verb. For example,

Subject	Modal verb	Adverbial phrase		Verb
Tā 她		hěn kuài 很快	de 地	líkāi le 离开了。
She left very quickly.				
Wǒmen 我们	yīnggāi 应该	jiànkāng 健康	de 地	shēnghuó 生活。
We should live healthily.				
Nǐ 你	yào 要	rènzhēn 认真	de 地	fùxí 复习。
You need to revise diligently.				

多 and 少 (duō, shǎo)

多 and **少** are two adjectives, meaning "many, much, a lot of, more" and "little, few, less" respectively. They are often used before a verb, indicating a greater or smaller quantity. For example,

Nǐ yīnggāi duō kàn, shǎo shuō
你应该多看，少说。
Keep your mouth shut and your eyes open.

Zǎofàn yào chī hǎo wǔfàn yào chī bǎo wǎnfàn yào chī shǎo
早饭要吃好，午饭要吃饱，晚饭要吃少。
Have a good meal for breakfast, a heavy meal for lunch, and a light meal for supper.

Shǎo chī ròu duō chī shūcài
少吃肉，多吃蔬菜。
Eat less meat and more vegetables.

Expressing the duration of action

When expressing the duration of an action, the same verb is used after a verb phrase containing an object, followed by a noun phrase as the complement to express the length of time. 了 is put after the second verb to express something that has already happened. For example,

Subject	Adverbial	Verb phrase	Verb	le 了	Duration
Tā 他	měitiān 每天	kàn shū 看书	kàn 看		bàn gè 半个 xiǎoshí 小时。

He reads books for half an hour every day.

Subject	Adverbial	Verb phrase	Verb	le 了	Duration
Tā 她	xiàwǔ 下午	mǎi dōngxi 买东西	mǎi 买	le 了	liǎng gè 两个 xiǎoshí 小时。

She went shopping for two hours in the afternoon.

Subject	Adverbial	Verb phrase	Verb	le 了	Duration
Mǎkè 马克	zhōngwǔ 中午	xǐ yīfu 洗衣服	xǐ 洗	le 了	shíwǔ 十五 fēnzhōng 分钟。

Mark spent 15 minutes doing laundry at lunchtime.

Subject	Adverbial	Verb phrase	Verb	le 了	Duration
Yǒngmín 永民	zuótiān 昨天	zuò zuòyè 做作业	zuò 做	le 了	sān gè 三个 xiǎoshí 小时。

Yesterday Yeong-min did homework for three hours.

The noun phrase expressing the length of time can also be placed between the verb and the object to act as the complement to express duration of the action. If the action has already been taken, 了 must be used between the verb and the noun phrase. For example,

Subject	Adverbial	Verb	le 了	Complement	
				Noun phrase	Object
Mǎkè 马克	měitiān 每天	kàn 看		bàn gè xiǎoshí 半个小时	de (的) shū 书。

Mark reads book for half an hour every day.

Subject	Adverbial	Verb	le 了	Complement	
				Noun phrase	Object
Wáng Yù 王玉	xiàwǔ 下午	mǎi 买	le 了	liǎng gè xiǎoshí 两个小时	de (的) dōngxi 东西。

Wang Yu went shopping for two hours in the afternoon.

Subject	Adverbial	Verb	le 了	Complement	
				Noun phrase	Object
Tā 他	zhōngwǔ 中午	xǐ 洗	le 了	shíwǔ fēnzhōng 十五分钟	de (的) yīfu 衣服。

He spent 15 minutes doing laundry at lunchtime.

Subject	Adverbial	Verb	le 了	Complement	
				Noun phrase	Object
Tā 他	zuótiān 昨天	zuò 做	le 了	sān gè xiǎoshí 三个小时	de (的) zuòyè 作业。

Yesterday he did homework for three hours.

Unit 12

Wh-questions

The wh-questions in English are called special questions in Chinese. The position of most question words in Chinese is different from the position of wh-words in English. In English wh-words are usually placed at the beginning of questions, whereas in Chinese the question words are usually placed where the answers would be expected to appear.

Question Type			
What	Zhè 这	shì 是	shénme 什么?
	What is this?		
	Zhè 这	shì 是	zhàoxiàngjī 照相机。
	This is a camera.		

Question Type				
Who	Mǎkè 马克		shì 是	shéi 谁？
	Who is Mark?			
	Mǎkè 马克		shì 是	wǒ gēge 我 哥哥。
	Mark is my elder brother.			
	Shéi 谁		zhīdào 知道	zhè jiàn shì 这 件 事？
	Who knows about this?			
	Lǎoshī 老师		zhīdào 知道	zhè jiàn shì 这 件 事。
	The teacher knows about this.			
Where	Nǐ 你		shì 是	nǎlǐ rén 哪里 人？
	Where are you from?			
	Wǒ 我		shì 是	Shànghǎirén 上海人 。
	I am from Shanghai.			
	Nǎlǐ 哪里		yǒu 有	mài diànhuàkǎ 卖 电话卡 de 的？
	Where is there that sells phone cards?			
	Duìmiàn 对面		yǒu 有	mài diànhuàkǎ 卖 电话卡 de 的。
	Opposite is a place selling phone cards.			
When	Nǐ 你	shénme 什么 shíhou 时候	zuò 做	yùndòng 运动？
	When do you do exercise?			
	Wǒ 我	měitiān 每天 xiàwǔ 下午	zuò 做	yùndòng 运动 。
	I do exercise every afternoon.			

Question Type				
Why	Tā 她	wèishénme 为什么	yào 要 qǐngjià 请假？	
	Why does she want to take leave?			
	Tā 她	bìng le 病 了	yào 要 qǐngjià 请假。	
	She wants to take leave because of illness.			
How	Wǒmen 我们	zěnme 怎么	qù 去	gòuwù zhōngxīn 购物 中心？
	How do we get to the shopping centre?			
	Wǒmen 我们	zuò dìtiě 坐 地铁	qù 去	gòuwù zhōngxīn 购物 中心 。
	We get to the shopping centre by subway.			

Difference between 有 一点 (yǒu yìdiǎn) and 一点儿 (yìdiǎnr)

In Chinese, both 有一点 and 一点儿 mean "a little bit". However, these phrases are used in different contexts. 有一点 can only be used before an adjective, meaning "to a small degree", and often has a negative connotation. For example, 有一点慢, 有一点急, 有一点不舒服.

When 一点儿 is used before a noun, it means the amount is not much. When 一点儿 is used after an adjective, it indicates the need for more of something.

Before a noun	
yìdiǎnr qián 一点儿钱	a little money
yìdiǎnr niúròu 一点儿牛肉	a little beef
yìdiǎnr shuǐ 一点儿水	a little water
After an adjective	
guì yìdiǎnr 贵一点儿	a bit more expensive
dà yìdiǎnr 大一点儿	a bit bigger
fāngbiàn yìdiǎnr 方便 一点儿	slightly more convenient

一点儿 can also be used after an adjective in a comparative structure with 比, meaning slightly higher in degree. For example,

Tā bǐ wǒ shíjì yìdiǎnr
他比我实际一点儿。

He's a little more practical than me.

Xiǎo gǒu bǐ dà gǒu kě'ài yìdiǎnr
小狗比大狗可爱一点儿。

Small dogs are a bit cuter than big dogs.

Yǒngmín bǐ Mǎkè gāo yìdiǎnr
永民 比马克 高一点儿。

Yeong-min is slightly taller than Mark.

The auxiliary words 的 / 地 / 得 (de / de / de)

Although the auxiliary words 的, 地 and 得 are all pronounced "de" with a neutral tone, they are used to form different components of a sentence.

的 is used with an adjective phrase or verb phrase to modify a noun. 地 is used between an adverb or adjective and a verb describing the manner of an action. 得 is used between an adjective or verb and its complement expressing result or degree. For example,

Yí gè gāodà de nánrén zǒu guolai
一个高大的男人走过来。

A big guy walked over.

Tā hěn kuài de líkāi le
他很快地离开了。

He left very quickly.

Jiànkāng de shēnghuó hěn zhòngyào
健康 地 生活 很 重要 。

Living healthily is very important.

Tā gāoxìng de xiào qilai
她高兴得笑起来。

She was so happy she laughed.

Tā xiě zì xiě de hěn hǎo
他写字写得很好。

He writes very well.

Picture captions

Unit 1 p15 A stallholder paints a traditional opera mask at the Silk Market, Beijing / p18 Workers picking tea / p19 Temple of Heaven, Beijing / p20 *Baita* (White Dagoba), Beihai Park, Beijing / pp22-23 The Great Wall of China, Badaling, Beijing

Unit 2 p25 Snow-covered village in northeast China / p28 The Forbidden City, Beijing / p31 Zhujiajiao, a water village near Shanghai / pp32-33 Ice sculpture at the ice & snow festival, Harbin, Heilongjiang province

Unit 3 p35 Chinese New Year family dinner / p38 Child wearing traditional clothing with New Year lantern, Nanjing / pp42-43 Lion dance for the lantern festival in Pingliang, Gansu province

Unit 4 p45 Teenager riding a BMX bike in front of the Bell Tower, Xi'an / p48 Rickshaws in a Beijing hutong / p50 Buddhist temple on a plateau in western China / p52 Hu Jiazhi, a 112-year-old artist from Nanjing, makes a paper-cutting

Review 1 p58 Zen Buddhist temple

Unit 5 p59 Boy eating candied haw, a traditional winter snack / p62 The Drum Tower, Xi'an / p64 Lijiang, Yunnan province / pp66-67 Shaanxi cave dwelling

Unit 6 p69 Qin dynasty bronze chariot, Xi'an / pp70-71 Terracotta Warrior and horse, Xi'an / p72 Kneeling archer figure, Xi'an / p73 *Tangsancai* camel and musicians figurine / p75 Dragon boat race / pp76-77 Mingsha Dunes near Dunhuang, Gansu province

Unit 7 p79 *Shuizhuyu*, fish in hot chilli oil, a Sichuan dish / p87 Dimsum, Cantonese food that often goes with tea

Unit 8 p89 Mosuo girl weaving cloth in her shop, Lijiang, Yunnan province / p92 Jars of green leaf tea with traditional Chinese decoration / p93 Chinese doll in traditional Qing costume / pp94-95 Qing-era bridge, Geese Springs, Guangxi Zhuang autonomous region

Review 2 p102 Victoria Harbour, Hong Kong

Unit 9 p103 Jiuzhaigou Valley, Sichuan / p104 Five-Colour Pond, Jiuzhaigou Valley / p105 Wuyi Mountain scenic area, Fujian province / pp108-109 Jiuzhaigou Valley / pp110-111 Huashan, Shaanxi province

Unit 10 p113 Woman with traditional parasol / p116 Beijing opera masks / p118 Monguor woman in traditional clothing / p119 Twin pagodas, Guilin, Guangxi Zhuang autonomous region / p120 A famous painting of Zhou Fang from the Tang dynasty / p121 Girl in Beijing opera costume

Unit 11 p123 A traditional Chinese pharmacy gives out porridge in winter, Hangzhou, Zhejiang province / p128 Statue of a crane, symbol of longevity, the Forbidden City, Beijing / pp128-129 Buddhist monks practise kung fu, Chengdu / p130 Traditional Chinese pharmacy

Unit 12 p133 Tibetan dancer / p138 Traditional doorway design / p139 Beijing opera performer in Monkey King costume / p140 Statue of Confucius at a temple in Shanghai / p142 Old man in Baoxing County, Henan province

Review 3 p145 Cyclists on bicycle and *sanlunche* / p146 Lijiang, Yunnan province

Pair work activities p148 Chinese calligraphy equipment / p150 Chinese village / p151 Chinese farmer, Yangshuo county, Guangxi Zhuang autonomous region / p152 Chinese water town / p154 Painted clay figurine / p156 Hakka fortified house, Fujian province / p157 Summer Palace, Beijing / p158 Mogao Grottoes, Dunhuang, Gansu province / p159 South Gate of the ancient city wall, Xi'an

English translations

Unit 1

Vocabulary and listening

Steve: After class, let's go and eat together. There's a Shanghai restaurant near the east gate that's pretty good.

Amanda: I've been to that restaurant. The food there is very tasty! But I can't go today.

Steve: Why not?

Amanda: I'm going to go and play tennis.

Yeong-min: Really? I didn't know you could play tennis. Who are you playing with?

Amanda: With Wang Yu. She plays tennis very well. Can you play tennis?

Yeong-min: No, I can't. Steve, how about you?

Steve: I can't either. I think I should do more sport. When I lived in London, I went jogging every day before class, but I can't do that in China.

Yeong-min: Why can't you do it in China?

Steve: Because in China the time classes start is too early. Classes start at eight o'clock in the morning every day. I think getting out of bed to go to the classroom so early is difficult. Of course getting up so early to go jogging is impossible!

Amanda: I think eight o'clock is not that early. I get up at seven o'clock every day, eat breakfast, then go to class.

Steve: Yeong-min, shall you and I go and eat?

Yeong-min: Sorry, my Chinese homework isn't finished, and I need to hand it in to the teacher tomorrow. I also need to do revision to prepare for the test on Wednesday.

Amanda: It doesn't matter. We can eat together next time.

Reading and writing

12th January, Wednesday

Today was really busy! I got up at half past seven, and went straight out without eating breakfast. There were lots of people on the street, and I was late. I only arrived at the classroom at five past eight. The teacher had already started the lesson. I felt very embarrassed. During the lesson, the teacher had us read some stories in Chinese. A few of my classmates thought that reading stories is not useful. They like to read Chinese newspapers. But I thought these stories were very interesting. When I have time, I want to go to the library to borrow some Chinese storybooks.

After class, I went to the park and met my friend Li Ming. The weather today was very good. We took some pretty photographs in the park. I felt very happy.

In the evening at eight o'clock, I had dinner with Wang Yu and Yeong-min. We ate and talked, and everyone was happy. I didn't get back to the dormitory till eleven o'clock at night. I feel very tired. Once I've finished writing my diary I'll go to bed and sleep.

Unit 2

Vocabulary and listening

Amanda: Mark, why are you wearing so many clothes? The weather is very nice today. The temperature is 20 degrees.

Mark: The weather here is colder than in Brisbane. So of course I have to wear a bit more.

Yeong-min: So what clothes are you going to wear when we go travelling to Xi'an? I hear the winters in Xi'an are very cold. It is very windy, and could even snow.

Amanda: I love the snow!

Mark: Snow?! I could put on a few more jumpers, wear a scarf and gloves, and bring a coat too.

Yeong-min: How are you going to walk around if you wear so much? The Xi'an winter temperature is not too different to Seoul. I don't plan on bringing too many clothes.

Amanda: What's the weather in Chengdu like? Is it as cold as Xi'an?

Yeong-min: Chengdu isn't as cold as Xi'an. Chengdu is in the south. It's warmer there than the north.

Amanda: So I can wear my favourite T-shirt and shorts, and wear sunglasses!

Mark: I can wear surf shorts!

Yeong-min: No, no! Although Chengdu isn't as cold as Xi'an, the temperature in winter is still below ten degrees. You can't wear T-shirts and shorts. Of course, if you want to look cool, you can wear sunglasses.

Reading and writing

Weather Report

From next week onwards, cold air will affect most regions of the country. Subjected to the effects of the cold air, temperatures in the north will decrease 4–8°C. In many places the difference between daytime and nighttime temperatures will reach 10°C. The temperature difference in some places in the northwest and southwest will be 15°C or more.

Xi'an

Date	Monday 7 February	Tuesday 8 February	Wednesday 9 February
Weather	Cloudy, becoming sunny	Cloudy, becoming overcast	Snow
Temperature	-4°C/1°C	-5°C/2°C	-6°C/1°C

Chengdu

Date	Monday 7 February	Tuesday 8 February	Wednesday 9 February
Weather	Sunny	Cloudy, becoming overcast	Drizzle
Temperature	1°C/7°C	0°C/6°C	-2°C/6°C

Unit 3

Vocabulary and listening

Amanda: Wang Yu, happy New Year!

Wang Yu: Happy New Year! Come in, come in. Dad, Mum, my friends are here. Let me introduce you. These are my parents. These are my friends Amanda, Yeong-min and Steve.

Amanda & others: Uncle, Auntie, happy New Year!

WY's father: Happy New Year! Here are your red packets.

Amanda & others: Thanks, Uncle and Auntie.

WY's mother: Do sit down. Please have some sweets, and fruit. Would you like to drink tea, or fruit juice?

Amanda: I would like fruit juice.

Steve & YM: I'll have tea.

Yeong-min: Your family's place is very big, and pretty.

Wang Yu: Let me show you around my home. This is the living room, and beside it is the dining room.

Steve: How many bedrooms are there in your home?

Wang Yu: Three. This is my elder brother's room, and opposite it is the bathroom.

Amanda: Whose room is this?

Wang Yu: That's me and my elder sister's room. My mum and dad's room is opposite.

Yeong-min: What's that fragrant smell?

Wang Yu: My mum is making her speciality, sweet and sour fish. How about I take you to have a look at the kitchen?

Amanda & Steve: Great!

Reading and writing

It's New Year! by Steve

This year I spent Spring Festival in China! Spring Festival is also Chinese people's New Year, the festival when families get together. Many people put up spring couplets on the doorways of their homes, hang red lanterns, celebrating the coming of the new year.

On the night of New Year's Eve, I went to the college's New Year's Eve party. Many of my classmates did not go home. They were all staying in Beijing over the Spring Festival. We played games and sang songs. Everyone enjoyed themselves.

On the first day of the new year, many people get up very early and go to pay New Year visits at their friends' houses. At noon, Yeong-min, Amanda and I went to Wang Yu's home for a New Year visit. First we made *jiaozi*, then we ate. Wang Yu's mother prepared a lot of dishes. My favourite dish was the sweet and sour fish.

I think China's Spring Festival is both exciting and fun.

Unit 4

Vocabulary and listening

Yeong-min: Xi'an at last! After more than ten hours on a train. Oh yeah, how do we get to the Old City Hotel?

Mark: The Old City Hotel should be near the Bell Tower. Let's go outside and ask someone. … Excuse me, how do we get to the Bell Tower from here? How far is it?

Passerby: The Bell Tower is in the city centre. It's quite close by, about five kilometres. If you take a taxi you'll get there in ten minutes.

Mark: Where is the taxi rank?

Passerby: Go straight ahead for 50 metres, then turn right and you'll be able to see the taxi rank.

Amanda: Thank you. Do you know how to get from the city centre to the ancient city walls and the Terracotta Warriors?

Passerby: The ancient city walls are on the south side of the city centre, so you can get there on foot. The Terracotta Warriors are very far away, 30 kilometres east of Xi'an. You can go there by taxi or by bus.

Yeong-min: Does Xi'an have other interesting places?

Passerby: You ought to go to the Big Wild Goose Pagoda. It is to the south of Xi'an city.

Mark: Does the Big Wild Goose Pagoda look like a big wild goose? Haha…

Yeong-min: Mark, don't mess about.

Amanda: What about the Great Mosque?

Passerby: You should pay a visit there too. The Great Mosque is near the Bell Tower. It's very easy to find!

Amanda: I see. Thank you so much.

Passerby: Don't mention it. I wish you a happy time in Xi'an. Goodbye.

Reading and writing

Xi'an Travel Guide

How do I get to the Terracotta Warriors museum?

From the city centre, you can get to the Terracotta Warriors by taxi, as well as by bus or train.

Taxi/Driving a car

Taking a taxi or driving a car is quick and convenient. The taxi fare will be about ¥180. It only takes about 15 minutes from the city centre to the motorway. After 30 minutes on the motorway, you enter Lintong. After coming off the motorway, continue for about another 10 minutes and you will arrive at the Terracotta Warriors museum.

Bus

Going by bus is comparatively slow, taking about an hour and a quarter. There are buses to the Terracotta Warriors museum from the Xi'an railway station. Tickets are ¥7 each.

Train

Taking the train is not as convenient as going by taxi or bus. After getting the train from Xi'an to Lintong station, you will still need to catch a taxi before reaching the Terracotta Warriors museum. The fare is not too expensive—the train ticket costs ¥6, and the taxi fare is about ¥30. If there are traffic jams on the motorway, the train is quicker. But sometimes the train can be late.

Unit 5

Vocabulary and listening

Receptionist: Hello! Welcome to the Old City Hotel.

Mark: Hello. We'd like to check in.

Receptionist: Do you have a reservation?

Mark: Yes, my name is Mark Johnson.

Receptionist: Could I see your passports, please?

Amanda & YM: Here you are.

Receptionist: You have reserved a standard room and a single room, for a total of four days, is that right?

Mark: That's right.

Receptionist: Please fill in the registration card.

Mark: OK. … Finished, there you go.

Receptionist: Thank you. … Excuse me, is your mobile number 16628958963?

Mark: No, my mobile number is 16628958763. This is a seven, not a nine.

Receptionist: OK. Your room numbers are 826 and 832. These are the room cards.

Amanda: Excuse me, can we use the Internet in our rooms?

Receptionist: Yes, you can.

[In the room]

Receptionist: Hello? How may I help you?

Amanda: Hello! I'd like to get online, but I can't find the Internet connection.

Receptionist: The connection point is beneath your desk.

Amanda: Could you also give me another quilt? It's very cold here.

Receptionist: Opposite the bathroom in your room is a wardrobe. At the very top of the wardrobe is a quilt–you can take it down and use it.

Amanda: Thank you, goodbye.

Reading and writing

Love travel, love life

Old City Hotel

Star rating: ★★★

Area: Xi'an city centre

Address: 18 West Street, Xi'an City

Recommended Amanda Posted 7 Feb

This hotel is in the city centre. Transportation is very convenient. The rooms here are good. The bed sheets and towels are all very clean. The basic items in the room, such as toothpaste, toothbrushes, soap, combs and so on, are all provided free. The hotel laundry service is quick and good. I put a coat to wash in the afternoon, and by the evening it had already been cleaned. Some people think the rooms are too small, but I think the room size is just right, and very comfortable. Also, there was an Internet connection in my room. I could use my own computer to go online – it's very convenient.

Not recommended Wang Wei Posted 5 Feb

Transportation to and from this hotel is very convenient. The service is also very good, but the rooms are too small. The room I stayed in was 3 metres long and 2.5 metres wide, much smaller than rooms in other hotels. The bed in the room was also not big enough. The single bed is 1.8 metres long and 1.2 metres wide, not big enough for a tall person.

Unit 6

Vocabulary and listening

Ticket seller: Hello.

Mark: Hello. Three student tickets, please.

Ticket seller: Could you let me see your student IDs?

Mark: Here.

Ticket seller: Thank you. That's three tickets. It will be ¥135 in total. Your guide will wait for you at the entrance.

[Inside the museum]

Yeong-min: Excuse me, how were the Terracotta Warriors discovered?

Guide: A local farmer discovered the Terracotta Warriors in 1974 while he was digging a well. This Terracotta Warrior is 1.83m tall, about the same height as a real person.

Amanda: Were Chinese people of that time really 1.83m tall? Most people aren't that tall now.

Guide: It might be a little bit taller than the people of the time.

Yeong-min: The Terracotta Warrior looks like our Chinese teacher — Teacher Ding. Don't you think so?

Amanda: Yes! He looks really like Teacher Ding when we haven't handed in our homework, hahaha.

Guide: Shh... Please be quieter, you can't talk loudly here.

Mark: We should take a picture for Teacher Ding.

Yeong-min: Hold on, that sign says "no photography".

Mark: Sorry, I didn't see it.

Amanda: I want to go and see how tall that Terracotta Warrior is.

Mark: Don't go over there, this sign says "no entry".

Amanda: What? You're not allowed to do anything here...

Reading and writing

The Shaanxi History Museum

On our third day in Xi'an, we visited the Shaanxi History Museum. There are 370,000 artefacts in the museum. It's a great place to get to know Chinese history.

There are many artefacts from the Han Dynasty (206BC-220CE) in the museum. The largest ethnicity of the Chinese people, the Han, get their name from the Han Dynasty. What the Han people speak is called *Hanyu*, and the script they use is called *Hanzi*. Of course, nowadays most Chinese people can speak *Hanyu* and write *Hanzi*.

This is an item from the Tang Dynasty (618-907CE), called *Tang San Cai*. The Tang Dynasty was one of the most prosperous eras in Chinese history. From that time, people in the South called themselves "Tang people". Those Chinese who went overseas the earliest called themselves "Tang people", therefore the "Chinatown" areas are also called "Tang people's street".

Unit 7

Vocabulary and listening

[In a taxi]

Mark: Do you like Sichuan food?

Yeong-min: I like it. Sichuan food numbs your tongue and it's hot. It's very tasty.

Amanda: You're Korean, of course you like spicy food. I like Cantonese food. It's not salty or spicy. It has a comparatively light flavour.

Mark: Shanghai food is also very tasty. It's sweet and delicious.

Amanda: Don't you only love eating McDonald's and KFC?

Mark: Although I do love fast food, we're in Sichuan, so we ought to eat Sichuan food.

Yeong-min: We're nearly at the restaurant. Stop the car on the left, please.

[In the restaurant]

Waitress: How many people?

Yeong-min: Three.

Waitress: This way, please. May I ask what you would like to drink?

Mark: Please bring me a bottle of beer.

Amanda: I would like a glass of apple juice.

Yeong-min: I'll have a glass of water.

Waitress: Here's the menu.

Yeong-min: What are your specialities?

Waitress: Mapo tofu, Kung Pao chicken, and fish boiled in hot chili oil.

Yeong-min: We'll have those three dishes, then.

Waitress: Would you like any other dishes?

Amanda: Stir-fried egg, please — not spicy. Also, we'd like three bowls of plain rice. And please also bring us three pairs of chopsticks and three spoons.

Waitress: All right. Please wait a moment, your food will be ready soon.

Reading and writing

Learning How to Make Chinese Food — "Mapo Tofu"

[Ingredients]

300g tofu, 100g minced beef (minced pork or chicken are also OK)

a small amount of oil, two spoonfuls of spicy soybean paste, a small amount of Sichuan pepper powder, small amounts of spring onion, ginger and garlic, half a bowl of chicken broth

[Time]

10–15 minutes

[Cooking steps]

1 Cut the tofu into small pieces. Cut the spring onion, ginger and garlic into tiny pieces.

2 Put the oil into the pan, heat up. First add the ginger, then the meat. Stir-fry the meat until it is welldone, then put it into a bowl.

3 Put oil into the pan and heat it. First put in the spring onion, ginger, garlic and spicy soybean paste and stir-fry it until it gives off a fragrance. Then add the tofu and meat and stir-fry for two minutes. Add the chicken broth, and boil for five minutes. Finally, add the Sichuan pepper powder.

Unit 8

Vocabulary and listening

Stallholder: Hello! Come in and have a look.

Mark: Miss, how much is this panda?

Stallholder: Very cheap, seventy *yuan*.

Mark: That's too much. How about a bit cheaper?

Stallholder: OK, a little bit cheaper. How about fifty *yuan*?

Amanda: We're students, we don't have much money. Make it a bit cheaper still. Is thirty *yuan* OK?

Stallholder: You really can bargain. I'll sell it to you for thirty *yuan*.

Mark: Thanks. Yeong-min, do you think Wang Yu will like this panda?

Yeong-min: She'll definitely like it! But how are you going to bring it home? We already have too much luggage.

Amanda: There's the post too. There's a post office near the hotel. I still want to send my family some postcards.

Stallholder: Is this your first time in Chengdu? You speak Mandarin very well!

Mark: Your Mandarin is very good too! What souvenir do you think our Korean friend should buy?

Stallholder: How about this traditional Chinese jacket? The colour is very attractive, and it is very Chinese.

Yeong-min: Can I try it on?

Stallholder: No problem. This Tang jacket is pure silk. It's very comfortable to wear.

Amanda: Oh, very chic! Mark, Yeong-min, I'd like to take a look over that way. Let's meet back at the hotel in a while.

M&YM: OK, see you later!

[At the post office]

Mark: Excuse me, I'd like to send this parcel to Beijing.

Worker: You need to fill in this form. Can you read (understand) it?

Mark: No problem. … I've filled it in, here it is.

Worker: First let's check the weight. … 1.2 kilograms, for ordinary postage that's seven *yuan* and three *jiao*. For air mail it's twelve *yuan* eight *jiao*.

Mark: How long will ordinary mail take? How long is it for air mail?

Worker: Ordinary postage takes about two weeks, air mail will get there in five days.

Mark: I'll send it by air mail. Here's the money.

Worker: Thirteen *yuan*. Here's your change, two *jiao*.

Mark: Thank you, goodbye.

Reading and writing

Wang Yu:

Hello!

Mark, Yeong-min and I have already arrived in Chengdu. Chengdu has lots of interesting landmarks. We're all having a great time. Yesterday evening we went to eat at a restaurant near the city centre. The name of the restaurant was "Old Chengdu". We had heard that the Sichuan cuisine there is very authentic. We ordered mapo tofu, Kung Pao chicken, and fish boiled in hot chili oil. When we started eating I thought the flavour was very nice, but the more I ate the hotter it seemed. In the end I had to drink a big glass of water, and then I felt a bit better. But Mark and Yeong-min aren't at all afraid of spicy food. They ate up all the dishes very quickly.

This afternoon, we went shopping at a market. There are lots of things there, and they're very cheap. Yeong-min bought a Tang jacket. He looks very handsome in traditional Chinese clothes. I saw this tea set and this scarf, they're very pretty. I would like to buy one of them as a gift for your mum. Can you tell me if your mum would prefer the tea set or the scarf?

Best wishes!

Amanda

Unit 9

Vocabulary and listening

Mark: The weather's really nice today.

Yeong-min: The scenery here is amazing!

Amanda: Yes. This lake is especially pretty.

Yeong-min: Look, the water was blue just now, and now it's changed to green.

Mark: The guide book said this lake is called "Five-Colour Pond", so there ought to be five colours. I can only see two now, green and blue. The bookshop should give me a refund!

Amanda: Haha, very funny. The water over there in the lake has a lot of colours, do you see?

Mark: I see them! Blue sky, white clouds, the multi-coloured water and green mountains, so beautiful.

Amanda: It's like a picture.

Mark: I really like this kind of natural scenery. The mountains here are particularly pretty, completely different from the mountains in Australia.

Yeong-min: They're not like the mountains in Korea either. They're very distinctive. I've never seen scenery like this before.

Amanda: I like it here too. The air is good, and it's peaceful. Do you hear that? The birds are singing.

Mark: Haha, yes. You can't hear that in the city.

Yeong-min: Look, here are the photos that I have taken. What do you think?

Amanda: Great. Take a photo of us, please.

Yeong-min: No problem. One, two, three—smile!

Reading and writing

Sichuan Travel Guide

Wolong Reserves

The Wolong Reserves are situated to the north-west of Chengdu, approximately 130km from Chengdu. In the reserves are more than 100 giant pandas, 10% of the total number in the whole country, and so it's also known as "panda country".

Aside from giant pandas, the reserves also have many other animals and plants that are protected by the state.

Transport: tourist bus (Chengdu—Wolong) 3 hours

Jiuzhaigou

Jiuzhaigou is over 400km from Chengdu. The snow-capped mountains, waterfalls, lakes and forests here are extremely beautiful. It is called "paradise on earth".

There are over 100 lakes, large and small, in Jiuzhaigou. Among them is Five-Colour Pond, it is so clear that you can see the bottom of the water. With the blue sky, white clouds and trees reflected in the water, it is colourful and entrancing. Jiuzhaigou also has many waterfalls. The biggest of these waterfalls is 200m wide and over 40m high.

Transport: aeroplane (Chengdu—Jiuhuang airport) 45 minutes

tourist bus (Chengdu—Jiuzhaigou) 10 hours

Unit 10

Vocabulary and listening

Amanda: I'm back! What are you two doing?

Yeong-min: We're watching TV. What souvenirs did you buy?

Amanda: I bought some silk scarves and postcards for my family. Oh, and I met two new friends.

Mark: Really?

Amanda: I'm going to go and meet them at a café in a while. Are you coming?

Yeong-min: I don't really feel like going. I'm very comfortable sitting here watching TV.

Amanda: My new friends are both girls.

Yeong-min: Is this café nearby?

Amanda: Ah, now you're interested! The café is behind the hotel, very close by. It takes about five minutes to walk there.

Mark: What are your new friends like?

Amanda: One is called Lisa, she's a German overseas student. She has long blonde hair, blue eyes and medium height. She's very slim. The other is called Sun Yuxiang, she's from Shanghai. Her hair is shorter, and she's not really tall or short. She's a bit more plump than Lisa.

Mark: Sounds interesting, but you have not mentioned the most important thing.

Amanda: What's the most important thing?

Yeong-min: Mark most wants to know if they are pretty, and whether they have boyfriends!

Amanda: I'm going to go. If you want to know, just come with me.

Reading and writing

Amanda:

I'm glad to know you have arrived in Chengdu and that you're having a great time. I'd like to see what Yeong-min looks like in traditional Chinese clothes. Very handsome, I'm sure. The two things you've chosen are both very pretty. I think my mum may like the tea set more.

Also, thanks for helping me out by taking the football shirt for my cousin. Tomorrow evening he'll go to the hotel you're staying in to collect the shirt. My cousin is called Wang Ming. He's 17 years old, very tall, fairly skinny, with short hair, and he wears glasses. His mobile number is 16521659870. If you have any questions, you can call me.

Wishing you a pleasant trip!

Wang Yu

Xiao Ming:

Long time no see! Are you doing well lately? Your birthday is coming. I got a friend to bring back a football shirt for you from Britain. It's your favourite team's. The shirt has two colours, blue and white, and I thought you should wear a medium size. I hope you like it.

My friend Amanda has gone on holiday to Chengdu, so I got her to bring the shirt for you. Amanda is Brazilian. She isn't very tall. She has an average build, black skin, and long hair. She's staying at Chengdu Hotel. You can go and find her at the hotel tomorrow evening. Her phone number is 16912764805.

Happy birthday!

Wang Yu

Unit 11

Vocabulary and listening

Doctor:	Please sit down! What is your name?
Mark:	My name is Mark.
Doctor:	Whereabouts do you feel unwell?
Mark:	I have a bit of a headache, a fever, and I have diarrhoea.
Doctor:	How long has this been going on?
Mark:	Two days.
Doctor:	Have you been away recently?
Mark:	Yes. I went travelling to Chengdu with two friends and only just got back.
Doctor:	First let's do some examination. Open wide, let me see your throat.
Mark:	Aaaaaaaah.
Doctor:	Now I'll have a listen to your lungs.
Mark:	Doctor, what disease have I caught?
Doctor:	It's not anything serious, just an ordinary cold. You're feeling ill because you haven't had enough rest, and you've caught a cold.
Mark:	So how should it be treated? Do I need an injection?
Doctor:	There's no need for an injection. I'll give you a prescription. Get a good rest, don't eat anything too spicy, and you'll be back to normal in no time.
Mark:	Thank you, Doctor.

[At the dispensary]

Nurse:	Mark, here's your medicine. This is medicine for your cold and to bring down the fever. Take it three times a day, two tablets each time. You can take it either before or after meals. Please note, after taking the medicine you may feel drowsy.
Mark:	Thank you. Goodbye.

Reading and writing

Tips for a Healthy Life

A healthy body is very important for everyone. Do you know how to live healthily? These lifestyle tips may help you!

Is what you eat healthy?

You should eat more vegetables and fruit, and less of foods that have lots of oil or salt.

Do you have breakfast, lunch and dinner at fixed times and with fixed amounts?

You should have your meals at fixed times. Eat well at breakfast, eat till you're full at lunch, and eat less at dinner.

Do you drink enough water every day?

You should drink plenty of water, at least eight glasses per day.

Do you exercise often?

You should do plenty of exercise. Half an hour every day is best. Don't spend all day watching television and playing online games at home.

Do you get enough sleep every day?

Sleep early and rise early. You should sleep at least eight hours a day. Don't go to bed very late.

Unit 12

Vocabulary and listening

Amanda: Who else is coming today, Wang Yu?

Wang Yu: There's still a good friend of mine to come. You can get to know her a bit. I think you'll really like her.

Mark: Great! What's her name?

Wang Yu: Her name's Kate. She's a Canadian. She just started working in Beijing last week.

Amanda: How do you know each other?

Wang Yu: When Kate came to Beijing last year to learn Chinese, I was her teacher.

Mark: What's she like?

Wang Yu: She has a medium figure, big blue eyes, curly blonde hair, and she's the same height as me.

Amanda: She's a beautiful girl! We should introduce her to Steve and Yeong-min. By the way, what's her personality like?

Wang Yu: She's a lot like you — very optimistic, very self-confident. Although she's a little quick-tempered, she cares a lot for her friends. Kate likes making friends, and she likes singing and dancing. She can sing pop songs and folk songs. In particular, she sings the Chinese folk song "The Half-Moon Rises" very well.

Mark: Let me guess, is she an Aries?

Wang Yu: How do you know?

Mark: I'm interested in star signs. Her personality is a lot like an Aries.

Wang Yu: You can ask her when she gets here. I hope you guessed right.

Amanda: Steve is a Leo. I heard that Leo and Aries go well together.

Wang Yu: Then we'll definitely have to introduce Kate and Steve to each other. Oh, do you know about the Chinese zodiac? Many people believe that the Chinese zodiac is also connected to people's characteristics.

Kate: Sorry I'm late!

Reading and writing

Who am I?

1 My favourite colour is

a red or yellow.

b brown or grey.

c blue or green.

2 When I go shopping, I will

a go straight to buy what I want.

b ask friends' opinions.

c go to lots of different shops, comparing items and prices.

3 When I'm on summer vacation, I will

a do part-time work to earn money.

b go travelling, mountain climbing or diving with my friends.

c stay at home, reading books or listening to music.

4 When I'm ill, I will

a go to see the doctor right away.

b phone my mum and ask her what to do.

c go online to find information, and try new medicine.

5 The pet I would most like to have is

a a cat.

b a dog.

c several fish.

10–16

You are practical and careful. You always think before you act.

18–22

You like making friends. You care a lot about your friends, but you're not very independent.

24–30

You are very independent, self-confident and optimistic. You like an exciting life.

Vocabulary list

	WORD	PINYIN	PART OF SPEECH	MEANING	UNIT
A	阿姨	āyí	*n.*	aunt	3
	啊	ā	*interj.*	ah	11
	矮	ǎi	*adj.*	short (height)	10
	爱	ài	*v.*	love, like	7
	安静	ānjìng	*adj.*	silent	6
	按时	ànshí	*adv.*	on time	11
B	巴西	Bāxī	*n.*	Brazil	10
	把	bǎ	*prep.*	(used to put the object of a verb before it)	7
	白酒	báijiǔ	*n.*	rice wine	7
	白天	báitiān	*n.*	daytime	2
	白羊座	Báiyángzuò	*n.*	Aries	12
	百分之	bǎifēnzhī	*n.*	percent	9
	拜年	bàinián	*v.*	pay a New Year visit	3
	办理	bànlǐ	*v.*	handle, process	5
	帮助	bāngzhù	*v./n.*	help	5
	包	bāo	*v.*	wrap, make	3
	包裹	bāoguǒ	*n.*	parcel, package	8
	饱	bǎo	*adj.*	full, replete	11
	保护	bǎohù	*v./n.*	protect; protection	9
	保护区	bǎohùqū	*n.*	nature reserve	9
	报纸	bàozhǐ	*n.*	newspaper	1
	杯	bēi	*n.*	cup, glass	7
	悲观	bēiguān	*adj.*	pessimistic	12
	被	bèi	*auxiliary word*	(for passive voice)	6
	被子	bèizi	*n.*	quilt	5
	本	běn	*measure word*	(used for books)	1
	本地	běndì	*n.*	local area, place	11
	鼻塞	bísè	*n.*	stuffy nose	11
	鼻子	bízi	*n.*	nose	10

* The words in colour are not target words for the units.

	WORD	PINYIN	PART OF SPEECH	MEANING	UNIT
	比	bǐ	*v.*	compare, contrast	2
	比较	bǐjiào	*adv.*	comparatively, in comparison	4
	变成	biànchéng	*v.*	change into	9
	标准	biāozhǔn	*n.*	standard	5
	表(格)	biǎo gé	*n.*	form, table	8
	表弟	biǎodì	*n.*	cousin (younger male)	10
	宾馆	bīnguǎn	*n.*	hotel	4
	博物馆	bówùguǎn	*n.*	museum	4
	不得不	bùdébù		have no choice, have to	8
	不过	búguò	*conj.*	however, but	8
	不好意思	bù hǎoyìsi		embarrassed	1
	不客气	bú kèqi		You're welcome.	4
	不同	bùtóng	*adj.*	different	12
	部分	bùfen	*n.*	part	2
C	猜	cāi	*v.*	guess	12
	才	cái	*adv.*	not until	1
	彩	cǎi	*n.*	colour	9
	菜单	càidān	*n.*	menu	7
	参加	cānjiā	*v.*	take part in, participate	3
	差别	chābié	*n.*	difference	2
	茶	chá	*n.*	tea	3
	茶具	chájù	*n.*	tea set	8
	差不多	chàbuduō	*adj.*	almost; nearly the same	2
	长	cháng	*adj./n.*	long; length	5
	常识	chángshí	*n.*	general knowledge, common sense	11
	朝代	cháodài	*n.*	dynasty	6
	炒	chǎo	*v.*	stir-fry	7
	吵架	chǎojià	*v.*	argue	1

WORD	PINYIN	PART OF SPEECH	MEANING	UNIT
车	chē	n.	carriage of a train	4
车费	chēfèi	n.	(bus/train/taxi) fare	4
称	chēng	v.	call; weigh	8
成	chéng	v.	become, turn/ change into	7
诚实	chéngshí	adj.	honest	12
橙子	chéngzi	n.	orange	3
池	chí	n.	pond, pool	9
迟到	chídào	v.	be late	1
宠物	chǒngwù	n.	pet	12
出	chū	v.	go/come out	5
除了……以外	chúle... yǐwài	prep.	except for, besides	9
除夕	chúxī	n.	New Year's Eve	3
穿	chuān	v.	wear (clothes)	2
床	chuáng	measure word / n.	bed	1
床单	chuángdān	n.	bed sheet	5
春节	Chūnjié	n.	Spring Festival, Chinese New Year	3
春联	chūnlián	n.	spring couplets	3
春天	chūntiān	n.	spring	2
次	cì	n.	service number of a train	4
刺激	cìjī	v.	exciting	12
葱	cōng	n.	spring onion	7
聪明	cōngming	adj.	clever	12
错	cuò	adj.	wrong	9
D 达到	dádào	v.	reach, get up to	2
打工	dǎgōng	v.	work, labour	12
打井	dǎ jǐng	v.	dig a well	6
打喷嚏	dǎ pēntì	v.	sneeze	11
打针	dǎzhēn	v.	have/give an injection	11
大	dà	adj.	big, large	2

WORD	PINYIN	PART OF SPEECH	MEANING	UNIT
大方	dàfang	adj.	generous	12
大年初一	dànián chūyī		first day of lunar New Year	3
大约	dàyuē	adv.	approximately	4
带	dài	v.	bring, take	2
戴	dài	v.	wear (clothing accessories like hat, scarf, etc.)	2
单人	dānrén	n.	single (person)	5
当地	dāngdì	n.	local	6
当时	dāngshí	n.	at that time	6
当日	dàngrì	n.	on the date stated	4
导游	dǎoyóu	n.	tour guide	6
岛	dǎo	n.	island	9
到达	dàodá	v.	arrive	4
倒映	dàoyìng	v.	reflect, mirror	9
得病	débìng	v.	acquire/get disease	11
得名	démíng	v.	get one's name	6
德国	Déguó	n.	Germany	10
地	de	particle	(used to indicate an adverbial phrase)	11
得	de	auxiliary word	(to indicate result, degree or condition)	1
灯笼	dēnglong	n.	lantern	3
登记	dēngjì	v.	register	5
等	děng	v.	wait (for)	6
底	dǐ	n.	bottom	9
地道	dìdao	adj.	typical, authentic	8
地区	dìqū	n.	area	2
点	diǎn	v.	order	8
电脑	diànnǎo	n.	computer	5
电视	diànshì	n.	TV	10
定量	dìngliàng	v.	with fixed quantity	11

WORD	PINYIN	PART OF SPEECH	MEANING	UNIT
定时	dìngshí	v.	at a fixed time	11
冬天	dōngtiān	n.	winter	2
懂	dǒng	v.	understand	8
豆瓣酱	dòubànjiàng	n.	spicy soybean paste	7
独立	dúlì	adj.	independent	12
读	dú	v.	read	1
堵车	dǔchē	v.	traffic jam	4
肚子痛	dùzi tòng	v.	stomach ache	11
度	dù	n.	degree	2
短	duǎn	adj.	short (length)	10
短裤	duǎnkù	n.	shorts	2
对了	duì le		by the way, that's right	10
对面	duìmiàn	n.	opposite	3
多云	duōyún	n.	cloudy	2
E 而且	érqiě	conj.	and, but also	10
耳朵	ěrduo	n.	ear	10
F 发烧	fāshāo	v.	fever; have a fever	11
发现	fāxiàn	v.	discover	6
饭厅	fàntīng	n.	dining room	3
放	fàng	v.	put, place	7
放学	fàngxué	v.	school is over	1
非常	fēicháng	adv.	very, extremely	9
肥皂	féizào	n.	soap	5
肺	fèi	n.	lung	11
风	fēng	n.	wind	2
风景	fēngjǐng	n.	scenery	9
风衣	fēngyī	n.	windcheater	2
服务员	fúwùyuán	n.	attendant, waiter, waitress	5
服用	fúyòng	v.	take (medicine)	11
复习	fùxí	v.	revise, review	1
G 干净	gānjìng	adj.	clean	5
感觉	gǎnjué	v./n.	feel; feelings	8

WORD	PINYIN	PART OF SPEECH	MEANING	UNIT
感冒	gǎnmào	n./v.	cold	11
刚才	gāngcái	n.	just now, a moment ago	9
高速公路	gāosù gōnglù	n.	motorway, freeway	4
告示牌	gàoshìpái	n.	sign, noticeboard	6
告诉	gàosu	v.	tell	8
歌曲	gēqǔ	n.	song	12
个子	gèzi	n.	height, stature	5
更	gèng	adv.	more, even more	10
公斤	gōngjīn	measure word	kilogram	8
公里	gōnglǐ	n.	kilometre	4
狗	gǒu	n.	dog	12
够	gòu	v.	adequate, enough	5
古	gǔ	adj.	old, ancient	4
固执	gùzhi	adj.	stubborn	12
故事	gùshi	n.	story	1
挂	guà	v.	hang up	3
拐	guǎi	v.	turn	4
关系	guānxi	n.	relationship, connection	12
关心	guānxīn	v.	care about; care	12
光	guāng	adj.	used up, all gone	8
光临	guānglín	v.	come, be present	5
锅	guō	n.	wok, pan	7
果汁	guǒzhī	n.	fruit juice	3
H 还	hái	adv.	still, yet; also	1
海浪	hǎilàng	n.	wave	9
海滩	hǎitān	n.	beach	9
海外	hǎiwài	n.	overseas	6
韩国	Hánguó	n.	Republic of Korea	7
汉语	Hànyǔ	n.	Chinese language	6
汉族	Hànzú	n.	Han ethnicity	6

	WORD	PINYIN	PART OF SPEECH	MEANING	UNIT
	好笑	hǎoxiào	*adj.*	funny	9
	喝	hē	*v.*	drink	3
	河流	héliú	*n.*	river	9
	褐色	hèsè	*n.*	brown	12
	红包	hóngbāo	*n.*	red packet (for gifts of money)	3
	红茶	hóngchá	*n.*	black tea	7
	红酒	hóngjiǔ	*n.*	red wine	7
	喉咙	hóulóng	*n.*	throat	11
	胡子	húzi	*n.*	moustache	10
	湖(泊)	hú pō	*n.*	lake	9
	互联网	hùliánwǎng	*n.*	the Internet	5
	护士	hùshi	*n.*	nurse	11
	护照	hùzhào	*n.*	passport	5
	花椒粉	huājiāofěn	*n.*	pepper powder	7
	欢迎	huānyíng	*v.*	welcome	5
	灰色	huīsè	*n.*	grey	12
J	机场	jīchǎng	*n.*	airport	9
	鸡	jī	*n.*	chicken	7
	鸡蛋	jīdàn	*n.*	(chicken) egg	7
	急	jí	*adj.*	irritable; fast, quick	12
	记事本	jìshìběn	*n.*	notebook	8
	纪念品	jìniànpǐn	*n.*	souvenir	8
	加	jiā	*v.*	add	7
	加大号	jiādàhào	*n.*	extra large size	10
	加热	jiārè	*v.*	heat up	7
	家	jiā	*measure word*	(used for families or companies)	8
	夹克	jiákè	*n.*	jacket	2
	间	jiān	*measure word / n.*	(used for rooms); room	3
	检查	jiǎnchá	*v.*	check up, examine	11
	健康	jiànkāng	*adj.*	healthy; health	11
	将	jiāng	*adv.*	(for future tense, written)	2
	姜	jiāng	*n.*	ginger	7
	讲价	jiǎngjià	*v.*	bargain	8
	交	jiāo	*v.*	hand in, submit	1
	饺子	jiǎozi	*n.*	dumplings	3
	教室	jiàoshì	*n.*	classroom	1
	接口	jiēkǒu	*n.*	connection, interface	5
	街	jiē	*n.*	street	5
	节日	jiérì	*n.*	festival	3
	介绍	jièshào	*v.*	introduce	3
	借	jiè	*v.*	borrow; lend	1
	金色	jīnsè	*n.*	golden, blond(e)	10
	进	jìn	*v.*	come in, enter	3
	进入	jìnrù	*v.*	enter	4
	禁止	jìnzhǐ	*v.*	forbid	6
	经常	jīngcháng	*adv.*	often	11
	久	jiǔ	*adj.*	long (time)	10
	就	jiù	*adv./conj.*	exactly; as soon as	1
	卷发	juǎnfà	*n.*	curly hair	12
K	咖啡	kāfēi	*n.*	coffee	10
	开	kāi	*v.*	drive (a car); open; prescribe	4
	开玩笑	kāi wánxiào		make a joke	4
	开心	kāixīn	*adj.*	happy	1
	考虑	kǎolǜ	*v.*	consider	12
	考试	kǎoshì	*n.*	exam, test	1
	咳嗽	késou	*v.*	cough	11
	可乐	kělè	*n.*	cola	7
	可能	kěnéng	*adj.*	possible	1
	克	kè	*measure word*	gram	7
	客房部	kèfángbù	*n.*	housekeeping	5
	客厅	kètīng	*n.*	living room	3
	肯德基	Kěndéjī	*n.*	KFC	7
	空气	kōngqì	*n.*	air	2

WORD	PINYIN	PART OF SPEECH	MEANING	UNIT
空邮	kōngyóu	v.	air mail	8
哭	kū	v.	cry	1
块	kuài	n.	piece	7
快	kuài	adj.	fast	4
快乐	kuàilè	adj.	happy	10
筷子	kuàizi	n.	chopsticks	7
宽	kuān	adj./n.	wide; width	5
L 拉肚子	lādùzi	v.	suffer from diarrhoea	11
辣	là	adj.	spicy, hot	7
老	lǎo	adj.	old	8
乐观	lèguān	adj.	optimistic	12
累	lèi	adj.	tired	1
冷	lěng	adj.	cold	2
离开	líkāi	v.	leave	4
梨	lí	n.	pear	3
里	lǐ	n.	in, inside	5
俩	liǎ	num.	two (coll.)	10
脸	liǎn	n.	face	10
凉爽	liángshuǎng	adj.	cool	2
了解	liǎojiě	v.	get to know, understand	6
零下	língxià	n.	below zero	2
领带	lǐngdài	n.	tie	8
另	lìng	pron.	other, another	10
另外	lìngwài	conj.	in addition, besides	5
流鼻涕	liú bítì	v.	runny nose	11
留学生	liúxuéshēng	n.	overseas student	10
流行	liúxíng	adj.	popular	12
旅游	lǚyóu	v.	tour; tourism	9
M 麻	má	adj.	numb, numbing	7
麻烦	máfan	v.	bother, trouble	7
马上	mǎshàng	adv.	immediately, at once	12
麦当劳	Màidāngláo	n.	McDonald's	7
卖	mài	v.	sell	8
慢	màn	adj.	slow	4
忙	máng	adj.	busy	1
猫	māo	n.	cat	12
毛	máo	measure word	Chinese currency unit; *jiao* (coll.)	8
毛笔	máobǐ	n.	writing brush	8
毛巾	máojīn	n.	towel	5
毛衣	máoyī	n.	sweater, jumper	2
帽子	màozi	n.	hat	2
没错	méicuò		right	9
没关系	méiguānxi		it doesn't matter	1
眉毛	méimao	n.	eyebrow	10
美	měi	adj.	beautiful	9
美极了	měi jí le		amazing	9
米饭	mǐfàn	n.	rice	7
免费	miǎnfèi	adj.	free of charge	5
苗条	miáotiao	adj.	slim, slender	10
民歌	míngē	n.	folk song	12
民族	mínzú	n.	ethnic group	6
明信片	míngxìnpiàn	n.	postcard	8
墨镜	mòjìng	n.	sunglasses	2
N 拿	ná	v.	take	5
拿手菜	náshǒucài	n.	signature dish	3
耐心	nàixīn	adj.	patient	12
难	nán	adj.	difficult	1
能	néng	modal v.	can	1
鸟	niǎo	n.	bird	9
您	nín	pron.	you (respectful form)	4
牛奶	niúnǎi	n.	milk	7
牛肉末	niúròumò	n.	minced beef	7
牛仔裤	niúzǎikù	n.	jeans	2
农民	nóngmín	n.	farmer; rural people	6

	WORD	PINYIN	PART OF SPEECH	MEANING	UNIT
	女孩	nǚhái	*n.*	girl	10
	暖和	nuǎnhuo	*adj.*	warm	2
O	呕吐	ǒutù	*v.*	vomit	11
P	怕	pà	*v.*	be afraid, fear	8
	旁边	pángbiān	*n.*	next to, beside	3
	胖	pàng	*adj.*	plump, fat	10
	配	pèi	*v.*	match	12
	皮带	pídài	*n.*	belt	8
	皮肤	pífū	*n.*	skin	10
	皮鞋	píxié	*n.*	leather shoes	8
	脾气	píqi	*n.*	temper, disposition	12
	片	piàn	*measure word*	tablet	11
	票	piào	*n.*	ticket	4
	平邮	píngyóu	*v.*	ordinary postage, surface mail	8
	苹果	píngguǒ	*n.*	apple	7
	瓶	píng	*n.*	bottle	7
	葡萄	pútao	*n.*	grape	3
	普通	pǔtōng	*adj.*	ordinary, common	11
	普通话	Pǔtōnghuà	*n.*	Mandarin Chinese	8
	瀑布	pùbù	*n.*	waterfall	9
Q	其中	qízhōng	*n.*	among	8
	起	qǐ	*v.*	since, starting from	2
	起床	qǐchuáng	*v.*	get up	1
	气温	qìwēn	*n.*	air temperature	2
	汽水	qìshuǐ	*n.*	soft drink	7
	前	qián	*n.*	before	1
	前台	qiántái	*n.*	front desk/ reception	5
	钱包	qiánbāo	*n.*	wallet	8
	强盛	qiángshèng	*adj.*	powerful, prosperous	6
	墙	qiáng	*n.*	wall	4

	WORD	PINYIN	PART OF SPEECH	MEANING	UNIT
	切	qiē	*v.*	cut	7
	清澈	qīngchè	*adj.*	clear	9
	清淡	qīngdàn	*adj.*	lightly flavoured	7
	晴	qíng	*adj.*	sunny	2
	庆祝	qìngzhù	*v.*	celebrate	3
	秋天	qiūtiān	*n.*	autumn	2
	球鞋	qiúxié	*n.*	sports shoes	10
	球衣	qiúyī	*n.*	jersey, kit for ball games	10
	去年	qùnián	*n.*	last year	12
R	让	ràng	*v.*	let, allow	1
	热	rè	*adj.*	hot	2
	热闹	rènao	*adj.*	bustling and exciting	3
	人间	rénjiān	*n.*	(human) world, the earth	9
	认真	rènzhēn	*adj.*	careful; serious	12
	日记	rìjì	*n.*	diary	1
	日用品	rìyòngpǐn	*n.*	daily necessities	5
	容易	róngyì	*adj.*	easy	4
	如果	rúguǒ	*conj.*	if	2
	入口处	rùkǒuchù	*n.*	entrance	6
	入内	rùnèi	*v.*	enter	6
	入住	rùzhù	*v.*	check in	5
S	嗓子疼	sǎngzi téng	*v.*	sore throat	11
	森林	sēnlín	*n.*	forest	9
	沙发	shāfā	*n.*	sofa	5
	山	shān	*n.*	mountain, hill	9
	山水	shānshuǐ	*n.*	scenery	9
	伤心	shāngxīn	*adj.*	sad	1
	商店	shāngdiàn	*n.*	shop	12
	上	shàng	*n./v.*	above, on top of; begin to do	2
	上/下车	shàng xià chē	*v.*	get on/off (a vehicle)	4
	上床	shàngchuáng	*v.*	get in bed, go to bed	1

WORD	PINYIN	PART OF SPEECH	MEANING	UNIT
上课	shàngkè	*v.*	have class	1
上网	shàngwǎng	*v.*	go online	5
稍	shāo	*adv.*	a little, slightly	7
勺子	sháozi	*n.*	spoon	7
少量	shǎoliàng	*adj.*	small quantity	7
身材	shēncái	*n.*	figure, stature	10
身体	shēntǐ	*n.*	body	11
生病	shēngbìng	*v.*	get sick	11
生活	shēnghuó	*v./n.*	live; life	11
生气	shēngqì	*adj.*	angry	1
声	shēng	*n.*	voice, sound	6
失物招领	shīwù zhāolǐng		lost and found	6
狮子	shīzi	*n.*	lion	12
石头	shítou	*n.*	stone	9
实际	shíjì	*adj.*	practical	12
手表	shǒubiǎo	*n.*	watch	8
手套	shǒutào	*n.*	gloves	2
受	shòu	*v.*	suffer, receive, be subjected to	2
售票员	shòupiàoyuán	*n.*	ticket seller	6
瘦	shòu	*adj.*	thin, skinny	10
叔叔	shūshu	*n.*	uncle	3
梳子	shūzi	*n.*	comb	5
舒服	shūfu	*adj.*	comfortable	5
蔬菜	shūcài	*n.*	vegetable	11
熟	shú	*adj.*	well done	7
属相	shǔxiang	*n.*	Chinese zodiac	12
树木	shùmù	*n.*	trees	9
数	shù	*n.*	number, figure	6
水	shuǐ	*n.*	water	7
水果	shuǐguǒ	*n.*	fruit	3
睡觉	shuìjiào	*v.*	sleep	1
说话	shuōhuà	*v.*	speak	1

WORD	PINYIN	PART OF SPEECH	MEANING	UNIT
丝巾	sījīn	*n.*	silk scarf	10
送	sòng	*v.*	give (as a gift); send	6
送餐服务	sòngcān fúwù	*n.*	room service	5
酸	suān	*adj.*	sour	7
蒜	suàn	*n.*	garlic	7
虽然	suīrán	*conj.*	although	2
所以	suǒyǐ	*conj.*	therefore, so	6
所有	suǒyǒu	*adj.*	all	8
T 太阳	tàiyáng	*n.*	sun	2
汤	tāng	*n.*	soup	7
唐装	tángzhuāng	*n.*	traditional Chinese clothes	8
糖	táng	*n.*	sugar, sweets	3
糖醋鱼	tángcùyú	*n.*	sweet and sour fish	3
套	tào	*n.*	set	8
特别	tèbié	*adv.*	especially, particularly	9
剃须刀	tìxūdāo	*n.*	razor	5
天气	tiānqì	*n.*	weather	1
甜	tián	*adj.*	sweet	7
填	tián	*v.*	fill in	5
挑选	tiāoxuǎn	*v.*	choose	10
贴	tiē	*v.*	paste, put up	3
听说	tīngshuō	*v.*	it is said that, I hear that	2
停	tíng	*v.*	stop	7
同学	tóngxué	*n.*	classmate	1
头发	tóufa	*n.*	hair	10
头痛	tóutòng	*v.*	headache	11
头晕	tóuyūn	*v.*	dizzy	11
图画	túhuà	*n.*	picture	9
图书馆	túshūguǎn	*n.*	library	1
团圆	tuányuán	*v.*	get together	3

	WORD	PINYIN	PART OF SPEECH	MEANING	UNIT
	退钱	tuìqián	v.	refund	9
	退烧	tuìshāo	v.	bring down a fever	11
W	袜子	wàzi	n.	socks	10
	外面	wàimiàn	n.	outside	4
	完	wán	v.	complete	1
	完全	wánquán	adv./adj.	completely; entire	9
	玩	wán	v.	play	3
	玩具	wánjù	n.	toy	8
	晚	wǎn	adv.	late	11
	晚点	wǎndiǎn	adj.	delayed	4
	碗	wǎn	n.	bowl	7
	万	wàn	num.	ten thousand	6
	围巾	wéijīn	n.	scarf	2
	喂	wéi	interj.	hello, hey	5
	卫生间	wèishēngjiān	n.	washroom, toilet	3
	为什么	wèishénme	adv.	why	1
	位	wèi	measure word	(for a person, respectful)	7
	位于	wèiyú	v.	be located in	9
	味道	wèidào	n.	taste, feel	8
	文物	wénwù	n.	cultural relic, artefact	6
	文字	wénzì	n.	writing, script	6
	问题	wèntí	n.	question, problem	10
	卧室	wòshì	n.	bedroom	3
X	西瓜	xīguā	n.	watermelon	3
	吸烟	xīyān	v.	smoke tobacco	6
	洗	xǐ	v.	wash	5
	洗衣	xǐyī	v.	wash clothes	5
	下次	xiàcì	n.	next time	1
	下降	xiàjiàng	v.	decrease	2
	下面	xiàmian	n.	under, beneath	5
	下雪	xiàxuě	v.	snow	2

	WORD	PINYIN	PART OF SPEECH	MEANING	UNIT
	夏天	xiàtiān	n.	summer	2
	先	xiān	adv.	first	3
	仙境	xiānjìng	n.	paradise	9
	咸	xián	adj.	salty	7
	乡	xiāng	n.	hometown, countryside	9
	相信	xiāngxìn	v.	believe	12
	香	xiāng	adj.	fragrant (smell or taste)	3
	香蕉	xiāngjiāo	n.	banana	3
	向	xiàng	prep.	to	4
	像	xiàng	v.	look like	4
	小	xiǎo	adj.	small	2
	小心	xiǎoxīn	adj.	careful	12
	笑	xiào	v.	smile, laugh	9
	星座	xīngzuò	n.	constellation, star sign	12
	行	xíng	v.	OK, right	2
	行动	xíngdòng	v./n.	act; action	12
	行李	xíngli	n.	luggage	8
	兴趣	xìngqù	n.	interest	10
	性格	xìnggé	n.	character	12
	羞怯	xiūqiè	adj.	shy	12
	休息	xiūxi	v.	rest	11
	嘘	xū	interj.	shh	6
	悬崖	xuányá	n.	cliff	9
Y	牙膏	yágāo	n.	toothpaste	5
	牙刷	yáshuā	n.	toothbrush	5
	研究	yánjiū	v.	research, study	12
	盐	yán	n.	salt	11
	眼睛	yǎnjing	n.	eye	10
	养	yǎng	v.	raise, feed	12
	样子	yàngzi	n.	appearance, look	8
	药	yào	n.	medicine	11
	夜间	yèjiān	n.	nighttime	2

WORD	PINYIN	PART OF SPEECH	MEANING	UNIT
一边	yìbiān	adv.	while, at the same time	1
一定	yídìng	adv.	definitely, for sure	8
一共	yígòng	adv.	altogether, in total	5
一会儿	yíhuìr	n.	a little while	8
一样	yíyàng	adj.	same	2
衣柜	yīguì	n.	wardrobe	5
已经	yǐjīng	adv.	already	1
以上	yǐshàng	n.	above	2
椅子	yǐzi	n.	chair	5
意见	yìjiàn	n.	advice	12
因为	yīnwèi	conj.	because	1
阴	yīn	adj.	overcast	2
引起睡意	yǐnqǐ shuìyì	v.	cause drowsiness	11
饮酒	yǐnjiǔ	v.	drink alcohol	6
饮食	yǐnshí	n./v.	food and drink; eat and drink	6
影响	yǐngxiǎng	v./n.	influence; affect	2
硬座	yìngzuò	n.	hard seat	4
勇敢	yǒnggǎn	adj.	brave	12
用	yòng	n./v.	use	1
邮寄	yóujì	v.	post, send by post	8
油	yóu	n.	oil	7
游戏	yóuxì	n.	game	3
有趣	yǒuqù	adj.	interesting	1
有时(候)	yǒushí hou	adv.	sometimes	4
有效	yǒuxiào	v.	valid	4
又	yòu	adv.	again; also	3
右	yòu	n.	right side, right	4
于	yú	prep.	at, in	6
愉快	yúkuài	adj.	happy, pleasant	10
羽绒服	yǔróngfú	n.	down jacket	2

WORD	PINYIN	PART OF SPEECH	MEANING	UNIT
雨	yǔ	n.	rain	2
雨鞋	yǔxié	n.	rain boots	2
雨伞	yǔsǎn	n.	umbrella	2
预报	yùbào	n./v.	forecast	2
预订	yùdìng	v.	reserve	5
元	yuán	n.	*yuan*, Chinese currency unit	4
原料	yuánliào	n.	ingredients	7
月亮	yuèliang	n.	moon	12
越	yuè	adv.	more	8
Z				
再	zài	adv.	then; again	2
再见	zàijiàn	v.	goodbye	4
咱们	zánmen	pron.	we, us	4
早	zǎo	adj.	early	1
占	zhàn	v.	occupy, make up	9
张	zhāng	measure word/v.	(for thin, flat things); open	4
长	zhǎng	v.	grow, develop	10
着凉	zháoliáng	v.	catch a cold	11
找	zhǎo	v.	look for, find	4
照相	zhàoxiàng	v.	take a photo	9
这么	zhème	pron.	so, such	1
着	zhe	auxiliary word	(used to indicate continuation of action or state)	6
真丝	zhēnsī	n.	real silk, 100% silk	8
整天	zhěngtiān	n.	whole day, all day	11
正好	zhènghǎo	adj.	just right	5
正在	zhèngzài	adv.	in the process of	3
证	zhèng	n.	certificate	6
挣钱	zhèngqián	v.	make money	12
之一	zhīyī	n.	one of	6
直接	zhíjiē	adj.	direct	12
植物	zhíwù	n.	plant	9
治	zhì	v.	treat (disease)	11

WORD	PINYIN	PART OF SPEECH	MEANING	UNIT
中等	zhōngděng	*adj.*	medium	10
中号	zhōnghào		medium size	10
终于	zhōngyú	*adv.*	be at last, finally	4
种	zhǒng	*measure word*	kind, type	9
重量	zhòngliàng	*n.*	weight	8
重要	zhòngyào	*adj.*	important	10
猪肉	zhūròu	*n.*	pork	7
煮	zhǔ	*v.*	boil	7
注意	zhùyì	*v.*	note, pay attention to	11
祝	zhù	*v.*	wish	4
祝好！	Zhù hǎo		Best wishes.	8
转	zhuǎn	*v.*	change	2
准备	zhǔnbèi	*v.*	prepare (for)	1
桌子	zhuōzi	*n.*	desk, table	5
资料	zīliào	*n.*	information, data	12

WORD	PINYIN	PART OF SPEECH	MEANING	UNIT
自己	zìjǐ	*pron.*	oneself	5
自然	zìrán	*n.*	nature	9
自信	zìxìn	*adj.*	self-confident	12
总机	zǒngjī	*n.*	operator	5
总是	zǒngshì	*adv.*	always	12
总数	zǒngshù	*n.*	total number	9
走路	zǒulù	*v.*	walk	4
嘴	zuǐ	*n.*	mouth	11
最后	zuìhòu	*n.*	finally	7
最近	zuìjìn	*n.*	recently	10
昨天	zuótiān	*n.*	yesterday	8
左	zuǒ	*n.*	left side, left	7
作业	zuòyè	*n.*	homework	1
做法	zuòfǎ	*n.*	method, cooking steps	7